English
for
Specific Purposes

Editorial Advisors
Prof. C.R. Visweswara Rao
Vice-Chancellor
Vikrama Simhapuri University
Nellore

Prof. Pingali Sailaja
Director, Centre for English Language Studies
University of Hyderabad
Hyderabad

Editors.
Dr. N. Usha
Associate Professor & Head
Department of English
Krishna University
Machilipatnam

Dr. J. Mythili
Assistant Professor
Department of English
Krishna University
Machilipatnam

English for Specific Purposes

Teaching and Learning Strategies

PROCEEDINGS OF THE NATIONAL CONFERENCE ON ENGLISH FOR SPECIFIC PURPOSES (NCESP-2011)

Edited by

N. USHA
J. MYTHILI

Prestige
an international publishing house

Published by
Prestige Books International
New Delhi 110 060
Ph. 9818755529
email: prestigebooks@gmail.com
website: asiabookclub.com

Associate Office
Concord, NSW 2137
Australia

ISBN: 81-7851-092-8

Printed at Chaman Offset Press, New Delhi 110 002

Contents

Foreword

It gives me great pleasure to note the successful conduct of APSCHE-sponsored National Conference on 'English for Specific Purposes' by the Department of English, Krishna University, in Vijayawada on 4 and 5 February, 2011. Our great country, India was under British rule for about 250 years and consequently influenced by its systems in all areas of education and administration. As a part of it, the adoption of English language is prominently visible in all educational institutions. English Language, by virtue of its flexibility and accommodation of number of words in its lap from many foreign languages like German, Spanish, Latin etc., has acquired a stature of international language. Its usage and need increased by leaps and bounds and touched almost every area of education and the personal lives of every Indian. Adding glamour to the glory, Liberalization, Privatization and Globalization have forced this beautiful language to reach the zenith of pre-eminence. Needs of Localization further strengthened its indispensability.

English has become a link-language for globe trotters and corporate-houses, besides the governments. We have arrived at a point where it is becoming impossible to grow without its knowledge. The importance and dominance of English is increasing day by day, at par with its enrichment in the vocabulary. It is a fact that every language that exists in the world possesses its own beauty and rhythm. They are popular only in some frontiers and boundaries of knowledge. They are respected well and studied by the natives thoroughly. But the necessity of learning English has become a part of our own survival and existence. It is not an exaggeration if I say that many Indian students are more inclined to learn English language than their mother-tongue. The availability of larger number of technical and technological terms made it the most suitable and convenient medium to communicate freely and spread knowledge touching all areas viz. Physical Sciences, Biological Sciences, Social Sciences, Engineering, Medicine and Management Sciences and what not, in every area and in every country. This kind of increasingly prompting situation has allowed the English language to attain a polymorphic status.

This way the gamut of English Language has proved to be effective and efficacious. I wish to emphasize that these reasons lying within ambit of it, have, in recent times, become a subject of serious study. It is in this context that this National Conference on 'English for Specific Purposes' was planned by the Department of English of Krishna University. One may state modestly that Krishna University is an infant, having been established in 2008. I can say with all confidence that this infant succeeded in doing an adult's job more adeptly by holding a National Conference of this magnitude, with the co-operation of the Government Agencies, the Faculty and the Administration of Krishna University. Krishna University always tries to fulfill its academic obligations as its first priority. It never wants to retain its treasure trove of knowledge generated from time to time to itself, but is anxious to spread it among all the stake-holders, as its social obligation. It believes that gaining comes by offering. It empties its vessels of knowledge for the benefit of the society, the student-community and the faculty. Krishna University knows that 'precept' is better than 'concept' and example is better than precept. This prime principle has driven it to conduct more number of National Seminars in other fields also viz. Biotechnology, Journalism and Telugu Language. I am glad to say that proposals for some more National and International Seminars are forthcoming.

As long as the search for quality and excellence does not find a finish line, Krishna University will not long for rest. It hopes to acquire further academic excellence, surpassing its own previous records.

I am also happy to note that this National Conference on English for Specific Purposes received an overwhelming response, beyond the imagination of the University. The participants from within the country and abroad contributed their mite in a meaningful way. The Organizers of the Conference received as many as

162 papers for presentation and 74 papers for publication. They were all subjected to "quality-sorting," a novel method adopted for assessment of the quality-standards of the content of each paper and the intent of the presenter/writer. This method enabled the Organizers to weed out the papers of inferior quality and standard. The Seminar Organizers were surprised to note the preciseness and quality in some of the Papers presented at the Conference. I feel glad that this National Conference, aimed at different groups of people, achieved its goal more than expected level and brought laurels to this infant University, signifying that nothing is impossible provided there is will. Simultaneously, the National Seminars conducted by Krishna University increased its burden of further refining its quality element and ignited a spirit of advanced research among the faculty of the University. As brevity is the soul of an expression, I would like to believe that the National Seminar on English for Specific Purposes by Krishna University appears to have changed some of the Anglophiles into Anglophones.

Touching the home-front, I become indebted if I do not mention the untiring efforts of highly-learned scholars like Prof. C. Subba Rao, former chairman of APSCHE for inaugurating this conference, Prof. C.R. Visweswara Rao, Vice-Chancellor, Vikrama Simhapuri University, Nellore and Prof. Pingali Sailaja, Centre of English Language Studies, University of Hyderabad, in giving their best as Members of the Editorial Board. They are assiduously followed by our Krishna University youngsters Dr. N. Usha and Dr. J. Mythili. They have toiled much and tilled the articles in order to give an appreciable shape to the book. The culmination of the indefatigable efforts of the Organizing Committee could be seen in the outcome of the proceedings of the National Seminar in a readable and interesting way. The quality that has been incorporated in the publication of this book reflects the onerous task handled by this team. I am also equally happy to note that Prestige Books, New Delhi, came forward to publish the proceedings on the desired lines. I should not end up without placing on record the sincere and ever-attending nature of our young Registrar, Prof. D. Suryachandra Rao, in securing funds for conducting the conference and bringing out the proceedings in an attractive way and also for the publication of this work within the stipulated time.

Lastly, I desire and wish from the depth of my heart, that the articles published in this book and the series of books published by Krishna University in different subjects would inspire and arouse passion for excellence among the students, scholars, teachers, and readers from different walks of life. I hope I am not too presumptuous if I expect that our efforts would be received well and appreciated by all those who saw, participated, heard, and read the publications of Krishna University.

Prof. M.K. Durga Prasad
Vice-Chancellor
Krishna University
Machilipatnam

Acknowledgements

The papers in this volume were originally presented at the APSCHE- sponsored National Conference on "English for Specific purposes," organized by the Department of English, Krishna University, in Vijayawada on 4 and 5 February 2011. We thank Andhra Pradesh State Council of Higher Education for the financial support, both for organizing the conference and for publishing the proceedings of the conference in the form of this book.

This conference has taken concrete form with the excellent support of our respected Vice-Chancellor Prof. M.K. Durga Prasad. We are thankful for his encouragement and guidance at every stage of the Conference and this book. We thank our Registrar Prof. D. Surya Chandra Rao, for his constant support and co-operation in bringing out this book. Thanks are also due to our guests Prof. C. Subba Rao, Prof. Pingali Sailaja, Prof. V.V.N Rajendra Prasad, Prof. S.P. Dhanavel, Mr. V.V Raja Rao and Mr. K. Srimali for their immediate response and commitment.

We are grateful to several academics and institutions like State Bank of India, Bazaar Branch, Machilipatnam; P.G Department of English, P.B. Siddhartha College of Arts and Science, Vijayawada; K.B.N College, Vijayawada; Prabhas College, Vijayawada; S.D.M.S Mahila Kalasala, Vijayawada; Sri Vidya Degree College, Gudivada; Gautam Degree College, Vijayawada; Oxford University Press India; for their generous assistance.

We thank all the participants including 162 paper-presenters whose critical perspectives and scholarly discussions helped to make our first National Conference in English an unqualified success. We also thank all the sponsors who, with their timely help made it possible.

We owe a deep sense of gratitude to our colleagues in the department of English, particularly Dr. M. Koteswara Rao, Mr. A.

Kiran Kumar and Ms. G. Sushmita for their unfailing support. Our planning and teamwork elicited a good response and admiration from all the participants. Finally we thank Prestige Books for bringing out this volume expeditiously and elegantly.

Editors

Introduction

Today the most influential and popular language on the planet spoken by 508 million speakers across the continents, and the official language of many countries, is English. Once dubbed as colonial language, English is the key to science and technology, commerce and higher education in contemporary India. So advanced research methods of English language teaching (ELT) and learner-centred approach should be encouraged at the tertiary level in the Indian universities instead of worn-out methods.

English for Specific Purposes (ESP), an approach to language learning has transformed the content of English resource books from "General English" to English for Business Communication, Science and Technology, Engineering, law, journalism, etc., diversifying into varied fields of activity. Developments in Linguistics, educational psychology and globalization have contributed to the growth of ESP. It is not just about technical terms and grammatical structures for science and technology or business. Combining pedagogy with technology, ESP offers a balanced approach for enabling adult language learners to acquire mastery in the communicative forms of language required for their professional needs. It can also help equip students with the tools necessary to continue their linguistic development outside the classroom.

Harding views that the ESP teacher has 'five key roles': as language consultant, course designer and materials provider, researcher, collaborator with subject teachers and finally evaluator. Today teachers need to start ESP course design process with target situation analysis, a rigorous analysis of linguistic features of the situation, and design learning-centred and context-specific English courses with vocabulary learning strategies for diversified group of learners. Hutchinson and Waters use Kipling's analogy of six honest serving men "Why, what, when, who, where and how" to outline the basic questions in a needs analysis of ESP. Authentic materials, organization charts, language descriptions, and learning theories are useful in ESP teaching. The whole world of multimedia is open to teachers to present language through Internet (World Wide Web, Google search, and online dictionaries), communication tools (email, blogs, wikis, podcasting, social networking groups, face book, webinars) and software applications (multimedia software and Interactive White Board).

The focus of the National Conference on "English for Specific Purposes" was to understand, explore and apply classroom action and research into teaching of English for Specific Purposes. This was a platform for university and college teachers to understand, recognize and train themselves in applied ESP. Prof. C. Subba Rao, former chairman of APSCHE, inaugurated the National Conference on 4 February 2011 and asserted the importance of teaching English for specific purposes at different academic levels, challenges and prospects for teaching English in today's educational system. Prof. Pingali Sailaja, Director, Centre for English Language Studies, University of Hyderabad, delivered the keynote address entitled "English for Specific Purposes: Issues concerning Language, the Learner and the Teacher." She gave a power-point presentation on the history of ESP and the place of ESP in the learner's mind, the role of learner-proficiency, what is expected of the teacher, and whether ESP fits into a communicative approach. Prof. M.K. Durga Prasad, Vice-Chancellor of Krishna University, presided over the inaugural programme. He highlighted the importance of English communication skills for students and said that such conferences would be highly effective to gain insight in teaching and learning English for specific purposes. A souvenir with 146 abstracts was released on the occasion by Prof. V.V.N Rajendra Prasad of Sri Krishnadevaraya University. He spoke on "Communicative Competence and English Language Teaching."

The valuable component of the Conference was the presentation of 162 academic papers by English professors and teachers in the course of two days. Around 350 professors, lecturers and research scholars from various universities and colleges across India, Australia and Oman participated in the conference.

Mr. K. Srimali, Chief of Bureau, *The Hindu*, spoke on "English for Journalism" from a practical point of view, citing examples from English used in newspapers. In his Valedictory address entitled "English for All Purposes," Prof. S.P. Dhanavel of Anna University reiterated the fact that all human languages are primarily a means of communication. He said that, with the industry expectations bordering on very basic ordinary communication, those who learn English at the university and college level should be able to communicate for all purposes. He cited examples of the jargon used in engineering and technology and from everyday use. Mr. V.V Raja Rao, Regional Manager, *The Hindu*, delivered his speech on "English for Mass Communication." The academic papers discussed the origin and growth of ESP, needs analysis in ESP, course design, teacher and learner-generated materials, assessment, English for various disciplines and its future. The conference provided valuable inputs to equip teachers with new knowledge and brought together professionals from other states of India and international scholars from Australia and Oman. The Oxford University Press Resources Exhibition, showing the latest published materials and computer software was especially lauded by the participants during the conference.

The papers that make up this book examine numerous approaches to ESP. Sasidhar Bandu's paper relates Computer-aided language learning approach to ESP while Deepak Kumar, Hanuman and Madhavi discuss various aspects of ESP today.

Jyothi Hymavathi Devi stresses on the specialized language for Medical purposes. Kiran Kumar, Radhika, Padmaja, Sarmistha Roy and others discuss English for Engineering Purposes. Globalization and global trends in ESP are highlighted by Suvarna Lakshmi and Narasimha Rao. Sharada, Lakshmi, Padmaja and Sravani highlight the usage of English for Business Communication. Susheela's paper is concerned with Scientific Lexis in everyday's usage. Surprisingly, a few teachers also touched upon new approaches like Sreenatha Chary's paper deals with differences in teaching ESP in Telugu culture and Sivasai's paper on Mysticism and language. Language for Tourism is another important area discussed by Pranuthi and Vishnu Vandana Devi. Each of the twenty-eight papers in the volume raise questions different from each other and deal with the action plan from different perspectives. I hope this book will make ESP a practical learning experience for budding professionals and inspire the present generation of teachers to explore new strategies for effective teaching because a good education is where a student learns to adapt to the changing scenario.

N. Usha
Conference Secretary
NCESP

English for Specific Purposes: Issues Concerning Language, the Learner, and the Teacher

PINGALI SAILAJA

1.1. ESP: History and Terminology

ESP is considered to be a sub-division of ELT, requiring its own distinct methodology, materials and research. Most importantly, it should be informed by insights from other disciplines in its practice. The field developed from the 1960s, and world events shaped its development in different directions.

The explosive growth in science and technology may be said to have provided the greatest impetus to the development of ESP. In the early 1960s, ESP stood for English for Special Purposes, which in turn became 'English for Specific Purposes'. Since the primary focus in the early days of ESP was on science and technology, EST was almost synonymous with ESP. As understanding progressed, a broad division into English for Academic Purposes (EAP) and English for Occupational Purposes (EOP) evolved, which is still current. Since then, each discipline has found a need for its own English, and hence we have English for medicine, engineering, business and so on, all constituting the sub-branches of ESP. Hutchinson and Waters' (1987) tree on the next page is a useful representation of the relationship of the various aspects of teaching English.

1.2 Linguistics and Language Teaching

Language teaching has been generally related to linguistic theories—the structural approach to linguistics had a major role to play in the development of the audio-lingual method. A divide between linguistics and language teaching set in with the Chomskyan revolution. Transformational grammar was considered

TREE OF ELT

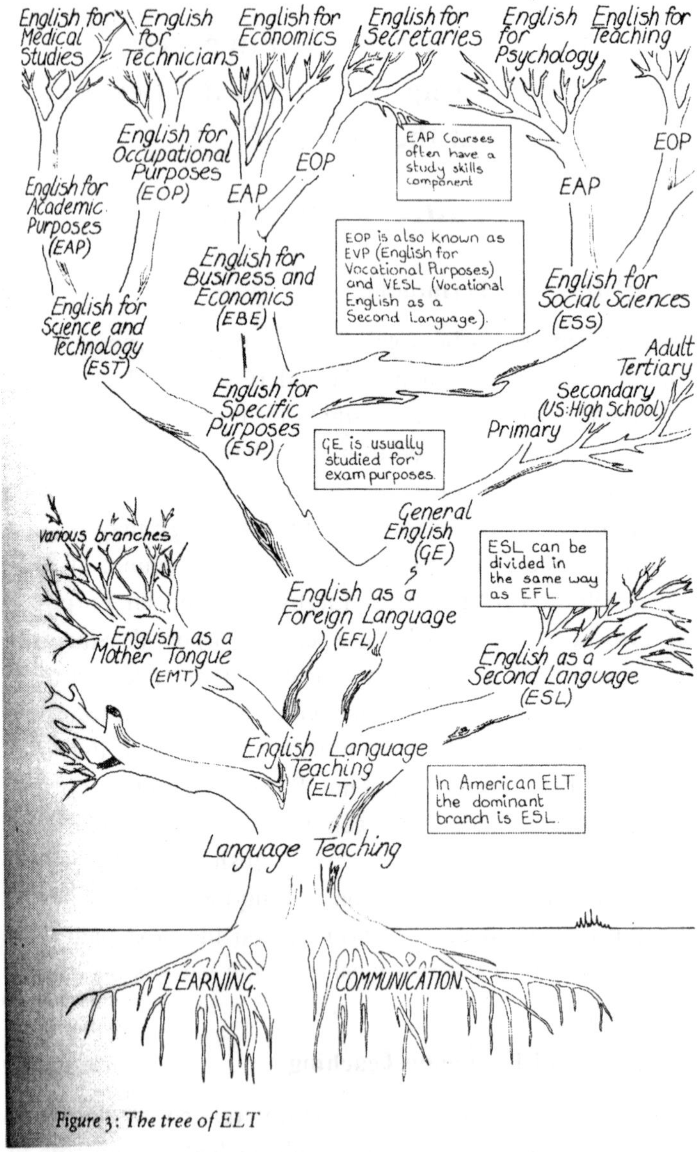

Figure 3: The tree of ELT

Hutchinson and Waters 1987:17

to be too complex and unusable in language teaching theories. The extension from Chomsky's competence and performance, to communicative competence, of Dell Hymes, more or less completed the divide between linguistics and language teaching. Any attempts to claim that communicative competence was also linguistics were not accepted by hard-core linguists.

Linguistic theories have dealt with language differently. ESP however developed partly due to studies in language variation. Variation studies deal with the differences in language according to situation and context. Consequently, *language* became central to ESP, with focus on register. In course of time, discourse and then skills and strategies began to be dealt with in ESP courses.

Irrespective of whether it is stated overtly or not, any language teaching situation or theory encompasses within it a view of language. In what follows, I will comment briefly on the view of language as may be deduced from texts and general perceptions.

1.3 Learner Proficiency

Let us approach this issue of teaching ESP from a different point of view. All language courses are generally oriented towards the non-proficient user of the language. Have English languages courses for the proficient user, especially ESP courses, ever been contemplated? It is also usually observed that proficient users of English in India scoff at English classes. For them, it is the 'light' period. How many engineers, doctors, linguists in this country have undergone a course in ESP? One would imagine—a very minuscule minority. What makes them exempt from these courses? If several of our doctors, engineers, nurses, scientists are managing (and reference here is not to those whose English we find wanting), why was such a course not necessary for them? The reason for this is that language, when learnt in its entirety (to the extent that language can be learnt in entirety), makes a course in ESP superfluous. By this, I am not arguing that there isn't a discourse specific to each discipline or profession or that people don't need help in writing; they do. But I am arguing that those kinds of help are different from the help that a course in ESP would give.

Take the following example from one of the documents placed on the website of a leading software company:

> Enterprise architecture (EA) is increasingly being acknowledged as the way to maximizing existing IT investment while planning for future growth. As a discipline, enterprise architecture is tasked to ensure Business-IT alignment through architectural oversight and guidance. It provides enterprises with a 4-dimensional model (Business, Information, Application and Technical architecture) to analyze and determine the right set of IT-related decisions to enable and support business strategies.
>
> Service-Oriented Architecture (SOA) is essentially about bridging the gap between the business and IT through well-defined, business-aligned services, developed by subscribing to established design principles, frameworks, patterns, and methods.

The objectives of EA and SOA are quite similar. However, EA is a framework that covers all dimensions of IT architecture for the enterprise, while SOA provides an architectural strategy that uses the concept of "Service" as the underlining business-IT alignment entity.

Even proficient users of English, outside the field will find this text baffling, even if they know the meaning of some of the words. While the overall structure and sentences may seem correct, even well-written, the content would be completely lost to one not trained in the specific area. To illustrate this point further, examine the following extract: "Most of the business intelligence system interventions are aimed reducing time spent on above said upstream activities that are of no/ low value addition." Any English teacher or proficient user of English will straightaway point out the grammatical error that has crept in here. These users will automatically supply the missing word and carry on with the reading. If the rest of the writing is "good," they will also put it down to a typographical error rather than a mistake.

What is striking here is that all or many readers will point out one error in the writing. Now, if users of English are able to supply the missing word, it indicates that what is required is not only English but business language, in order to comprehend.

Below are the first two stanzas from a poem in Lewis Carroll's *Through the Looking Glass*:

> 'Twas brillig, and the slithy toves
> Did gyre and gimble in the wabe:

All misy were the borogoves,
And the mome raths outgrabe.
"Beware the Jabberwock, my son!
The jaws that bite, the claws that catch!
Beware the Jubjub bird, and shun
The frumious Bandersnatch! (Carroll 1993: 126)

In terms of comprehensibility, this is like the technical writing we saw earlier. The first two stanzas are explained by Humpty Dumpty:

"Brillig" means four o'clock in the afternoon—the time when you begin broiling things for dinner.'

'That'll do very well,' said Alice: 'and "slithy"?'

'Well, "slithy" means "lithe and slimy." "Lithe" is the same as "active." You see it's like a portmanteau—there are two meanings packed up into one word.'

'I see it now,' Alice remarked thoughtfully: 'and what are "toves"?'

'Well, "toves" are something like badgers—they're something like lizards—and they're something like corkscrews.'

'They must be very curious looking creatures.'

'They are that,' said Humpty Dumpty: 'also they make their nests under sun-dials—also they live on cheese.'

'And what's the "gyre" and to "gimble"?'

'To "gyre" is to go round and round like a gyroscope. To "gimble" is to make holes like a gimlet.'

'And "the wabe" is the grass-plot round a sun-dial, I suppose?' said Alice, surprised at her own ingenuity.

'Of course it is. It's called "wabe," you know, because it goes a long way before it, and a long way behind it—'

'And a long way beyond it on each side,' Alice added.

'Exactly so. Well, then, "mimsy" is "flimsy and miserable" (there's another portmanteau for you). And a "borogove" is a thin shabby-looking bird with its feathers sticking out all round—something like a live mop.'

'And then "mome raths"?' said Alice. 'I'm afraid I'm giving you a great deal of trouble.'

'Well, a "rath" is a sort of green pig: but "mome" I'm not certain about. I think it's short for "from home"—meaning that they'd lost their way, you know.'

> 'And what does "outgrabe" mean?'
>
> 'Well, "outgribing" is something between bellowing and whistling, with a kind of sneeze in the middle: however, you'll hear it done, maybe—down in the wood yonder—and when you've once heard it you'll be quite content. Who's been repeating all that hard stuff to you?' (Carroll 1993: 175-76)

Once the meanings of individual words are explained, the whole makes sense. Is business English or any other type of English any different from this?

If we analyse the language here, there is nothing that a user of English will not be familiar with. The structures are more or less what one would use in other contexts, and these are structures that are useful for many different kinds of writing. Yet, the text is almost incomprehensible. If General English (I use this for want of a better term) is taken care of properly, these aspects of a particular genre are best dealt with by the subject expert.

Aspects of language that are relevant in a course in ESP are noted in Dudley Evans and St. John (1998). These are verbs and tense, voice, modals, articles, nominalization and logical connectors. Other features of discourse etc are also described in their work. Even making allowances for these specific structures, I am placing a premium on vocabulary as has been done traditionally in ESP works. The reasons for this are as follows: Linguistically speaking, there is a difference between words and sentences. While words have to be independently learnt sentences do not.

Notice that in all of this, language is viewed as an object. That is, language is dissected into certain features that are learnt or learnable. So, there is vocabulary (a particular register), grammar, structures, rhetorical devices and/or discourse features.

1.4 Some Texts

A significant aspect of ESP is needs analysis. Ideally, the context of use should be studied well before a course is prepared. Secondly, ESP is primarily text-based. However, not all texts are based on needs analysis.

There are several textbooks published recently in the area of English for Specific Purposes. McDonough (2010) providing a survey of texts published between 2007 and 2009 states that there were around 45 students' books and including teachers' books, the total was 59. The publishers were CUP, OUP and Pearson Longman.

I will now examine a text *Cambridge English for Engineering* written by Mark Ibbotson, an engineer. This work is not necessarily representative of all the texts that have been produced but gives the English teachers a glimpse of what is expected of them. The stated objectives of the text are:

> to improve your professional communication skills. . . .
>
> The course covers high-priority language that is useful in any branch of engineering . . . focusing on skills such as drawings, describing technical problems and discussing dimensions and precision. (Ibbotson 2008: 3)

Notice that the skills listed are *not* language skills. However, the author does add that the units contain:

- realistic listening activities so you can learn the language in technical discussions
- situation-based speaking activities so that you can practise the language you've learned
- relevant vocabulary presented and practised in professional contexts
- engaging topics and articles to make your learning interesting and motivating. (Ibbotson 2008: 3)

The text of the first audio unit is given in the appendix. It may be noted, incidentally, that the audio texts across the units are not necessarily by native speakers. Different accents from different parts of the world, presumably with the intention of representing non-native speakers, are used. This is not an issue I am delving into here.

The exercises that are based on a text such as this one are as follows:

> The pre-listening tasks include such questions as
>
> 1a. In pairs, think about two or three products you use regularly and discuss the following questions.
>
> What are the main functions of the products? (What do they do?)
>
> What are their different applications? (What are they used for?)

These are almost general questions that one may use in modern classrooms, because almost everybody has some product/gadget or other and the English teacher can generate a discussion in the classroom. But now let us look at question 1b:

> 1b. what do you know about Global Positioning System (GPS) devices? In pairs, describe their main function, and give some examples of different applications of GPS devices.

The English teacher would be at a total loss here with regard to the content of the matter. It would be like the above situation wherein a mechanical correction of the grammar may be possible, but an intelligent participation is impossible.

The post-listening tasks are mostly content-oriented and have the old problem of our textbooks dealing ultimately with content and not with language skills. One example is:

> Complete the following notes:
> The primary application of GPS (1) ______________ Associated applications Tracking systems for (2) __________ Tracking systems for (3) ____________ More creative features (4) ________________ alarms (5) ________________ buttons Not technical innovations (6) ________________ the technology

Many of the exercises are of this nature. There are 17 exercises for unit (1) and there is the usual focus on vocabulary in the texts and a few set phrases that are used in contexts such as these. All the different kinds of vocabulary—technical, sub-technical and general vocabulary, are covered. In other units, some other aspects of grammar are covered such as prepositions, correct use of verbs, etc.

Dudley Evans and St. John make a distinction between carrier language and real language. This means that the content (carrier) is simply the context for language (real) learning. But this, I believe, is not unproblematic. While there is an attempt to impart *English,* much of the work is content-oriented, so much so that whether the student learns any English or not, the English teacher must learn engineering. Ideally, these tasks should be done in the subject classrooms. It was possible for an engineer (with English teaching experience) to write a book such as this. An English teacher can only do it in collaboration with a qualified engineer.

No matter what the role of the English teacher: teacher, researcher, collaborator, etc., she *must* know the subject. There is no pretence here that the two—engineering and English—are being taught simultaneously.

Another interesting aspect of this text is that the units may be studied in any order. This implies that there is no gradation or sequencing of language tasks or activities in terms of difficulty. This too is a comment on the author's perception of language. In the acquisition of a language as a natural process, a child is not necessarily exposed to simpler forms first and then to complex forms. While concessions are made, a child is likely to hear very complex language around her as spoken by adults.

1. 5 ESP

Dudley Evans and St. John give an overview of the definitions of ESP as stated in the literature. I find Strevens' characterization most useful in defining ESP, who makes a distinction between absolute characteristics and variable characteristics. The absolute ones are:

- designed to meet specified needs of the learner;
- related in content (that is in its themes and topics) to particular disciplines, occupations and activities;
- centred on language appropriate to those activities in syntax, lexis, discourse, semantics and so on, and analysis of the discourse;
- in contrast with 'General English'. (From Dudley Evans and St John 1998: 3)

The variable characteristics are:

- may be restricted as to the learning skills to be learned (for example reading only)
- may not be taught according to any pre-ordained methodology.

Dudley Evans and St. John (1998) give a variation of this as their definition of what constitutes ESP in which the "in contrast with General English" is removed. It is very crucial in the above definition that ESP is placed in contrast with general English.

It is important to go back to the tree now. By focusing only on ESP, we notice that the top branches are the primary goal, without any foundation. How effective and lasting would such a course be? If ESP is a sub-branch of ELT, it cannot be separated from ELT. Some of these aspects are acknowledged by the authors. They do maintain that there is commonality of language and learning for many and also say that it is not just vocabulary that is relevant to ESP. But I believe that this aspect that a sound grounding in the language is required has not been given the consideration it deserves.

Next, and importantly, the tree suggests that only EFL and ESL students require ESP. There are very significant implications for this. It implies that once a learner *knows* a language, then other 'specializations' are automatically learnt. In turn, this means that if learners have native-like competence in a language, in other words, if the foundation is good, then higher branches may not be necessary.

1.6 The Relevance of ESP

Does this mean that ESP has no relevance or significance? Communicative approach to language learning has been found to be psychologically sound. It is believed that ESP is communicative for certain reasons.

The most important aspect of ESP is the use of authentic material. The importance of the use of authentic materials has been highlighted in language learning theories. Authenticity of materials makes a lot for motivation. When functional English classes are taken (or Functional Hindi, etc.,) the immediate need and use of the language become apparent. It should be remembered here that students very often know what they need from a language. (Usually they will give a list of what they want, though.) Direct relevance makes students want to participate in activities. In this, the approach becomes very communicative. The activities for speaking in Ibbotson's work are definitely communicative in nature. (Incidentally, the book is also supposed to be a self-study book, which is perhaps a violation of the notion 'communicative'.)

However, great caution needs to be exercised in using such materials. For one thing, often, the student knows more about the subject than the English textbook gives and knows more about the subject than the teacher herself. In this situation, the teacher can feel tremendously inadequate. And, not all students want their subject to be studied in every class.

Here, language is not viewed in totality but in bits and pieces. The student has instrumental motivation and believes that there are capsules that are available that will make him proficient in the use of the language. And that language can be dissected.

Practical needs also seem to call for ESP. Generally, an English course in the Indian context lasts about 10 months. Unless intensive and focused work happens, the student has no chance of learning anything of the language.

It seems to me to make sense that ESP should be taught after a considerable exposure to the language. And it should be taught to proficient or semi-proficient users of a language as well. If we turn our attention to the extract from the software company website for a while, we will notice that the complex structures presented there are not likely to be produced by learners within a space of ten months.

I turn my attention specifically to the Indian context now. In the academic setting, we have a need to write. In India, most learners are second language learners and they come with differing proficiency to the classroom. It is believed therefore that learning rather than acquisition takes place. However, some amount of acquisition is also a part of the Indian English-learning situation.

The focus on writing is great in the Indian academic setting and students are seldom, if ever, prepared for spoken communication skills. Academic writing is of different kinds and essays and reports that we may expect from students have features that are common across disciplines. At the college level in the US, all students are expected to take a course in writing, irrespective of whether they are native speakers of English or not. Writing is considered to be a skill that needs to be learnt. If we consider the following features to be relevant in a piece of writing: an argument, presentation style, logic and rhetorical devices and coherence, with appropriate use of cohesive devices, I think the needs would be met.

At the spoken level, in academics, there is very little scope for language use. But there are some contexts of oral communication. In some institutions, seminar presentations are essential and these can be taught in a manner similar to the features of writing. These are skills that can be carried forward into specific professions.

With regard to occupational use of English, we must keep in mind that as long as any feature is *imparted* formally, it is done in an academic setting. Unless we can give hands-on training, it is not possible to teach EOP. There are situations like internships and house residency. In such situations, the English teacher is usually nowhere on the scene. Crucially, McDonough sees a divide between EAP and EOP, and a divide between research in ESP and the *use* of ESP. Most research in ESP as seen in journals is based on academic contexts.

To conclude, I believe that there is a case for ESP, but with conditions. The content of any course, in our complex and specialized world is something to be drawn-up and monitored by people who understand both the language and the business area. Further, needs analysis is required at a micro level which should focus on two aspects: (1) the level required to be attained by the learners to understand and study their subjects and perform well in class; and (2) the amount of learning the learners require individually from where they are, since our classrooms invariably consist of students with differing proficiency levels. Mass-produced textbooks such as the ones brought out by OUP and CUP are likely to be unusable in specific contexts. They may actually sell well, but this is primarily due to the lack of other materials. Thus ESP comes with conditions.

Bibliography

Carroll, Lewis. 1993. *The Complete Stories of Lewis Carroll.* London: Magpie Books.

Dudley Evans, Tony and Maggie Jo St John (1998). *Developments in English for Specific Purposes: A Multi-Disciplinary Approach.* Cambridge: CUP.

Hutchinson, Tom and Alan Waters (1987). *English for Specific Purposes: A Learning-Centred Approach.* Cambridge: CUP.

Ibbotson, Mark (2008). *Cambridge English for Engineering.* Cambridge: CUP.

McDonough, Jo (2010). "English for Specific Purposes: A survey review of current materials," *ELT Journal* 64/4, pp. 462-477.

Appendix: Audioscript 1.1

Paula: Obviously navigation is the primary application of most GPS devices.

Jose: Sure.

Paula: Then you've got associated applications, uses that are related to navigating, such as tracking systems you can use for monitoring delivery vehicles and finding stolen cars, that kind of thing.

Jose: Mm.

Paula: And then there are more creative features. A good example would be on a boat GPS, you get drift alarms. So if the anchor starts to drag and the boat starts moving, there's a setting on the GPS that allows it to detect the movement, and an alarm sounds to warn you, and prevents the boat from drifting unnoticed.

Jose: I see.

Paula: Or another example on boat systems is man overboard buttons. So if you are sailing along and someone falls into the sea, you hit a button which logs the position and ensures that you don't lose track of where you were, which then enables you to turn round and come back to the same point and find the person.

Jose: Right.

Paula: So, these are the kinds of applications we want to develop, more specialized, and more creative.

Jose: So, effectively, you're not talking about technical innovations. What you are really looking for is innovative ways of actually using the technology.

Paula: Precisely. Because these days, from the end-user's point of view, accuracy is no longer the main selling point. Most devices are accurate enough. The key is to make them more useful. So in terms of development. That's the kind of . . . (Ibbotson 2008 p. 86)

English for All Purposes

S. P. DHANAVEL

Introduction

English is being taught all over the world for a variety of purposes. The primary purpose is to enable communication among people of different languages. However, in course of time, the concept of English for Specific Purposes (ESP) became popular. As a result, courses have been designed with a view to catering to specific needs of engineers, lawyers, medical professionals, etc. The ground reality now is stark. It demands basic and common communication skills from all people. Hence it is necessary to rethink about ESP seriously and come out with alternative paradigms of syllabus design and implementation of the same in the classrooms.

Varieties of English

There are varieties of English based on regional uses. For example, British English is somewhat different from American English; all other varieties like Australian, Canadian, and Indian Englishes have some peculiarities. In the case of Indian English, the local language too affects the nature and style of English. Generally, these varieties are mutually intelligible. However, certain specific words, their use and pronunciation may cause difficulty in communication.

For example, an Oriya speaker may tend to pronounce the word 'image' in a totally unintelligible way for a Malayalam speaker. Similarly, the word 'simple' is not simple for a Malayalam speaker but for a Hindi-speaking person it is very difficult to understand. Similarly, a well-educated British person may not be able to understand the English of an Afro-American in New York. These are varieties to be reckoned with in any English Language Teaching (ELT) program.

English for Specific Purposes

Variety of English depending upon the region or mother tongue is understandable and it can be easily tackled. It is not a big issue at all in ELT programs. At the beginning, English was taught to all students almost alike. When different purposes were identified based on register, the specific use of language in a particular branch of study or field of work, primarily due to certain vocabulary or certain use of language, the ELT scenario became different. Material production and marketing activities turned out be much more vigorous than the teaching and learning of English. In particular, business is abundant in Business English and English for Science and Technology. But then there has been some uncomfortable feeling among the educators that students do not really acquire the skills expected of them after the course is completed. Occupational English, Business English, Academic English, Engineering English, Scientific English, Technical English, etc., have been doing the rounds in educational institutions. These are, however, unable to fulfill the market and industrial expectations, which are close to the expectations of the learners themselves.

Initially, when the number of students learning English was less, the situation appeared to be favourable for English for Specific Purpose. When the number became quite huge, particularly after globalization, ESP does not seem to work. Even business English has not been able to succeed satisfactorily as it was thought to be. It is clear now that specific purpose syllabus is only one dimension of the issue of developing communicative competence in a particular field. It is not enough if the English educators identify the purpose of learning English. It is the learners who have to feel the need and fill the need. The approach to ELT then should be to create awareness and also a scenario, of course, with a textbook, a classroom, multimedia tools, etc., for learners of English.

English for Science and Technology

One of the most popular varieties of English program is English for Science and Technology. It became operational in India with the support of the British Council. Some technical universities like Anna University in Chennai and Indian School of Mines in Dhanbad, participated in the academic adventure. The ESP course at Anna University was introduced in 1989 with the academic guidance of the British Council experts from Thames Valley University, the UK. In contrast to literature and value-based English, real and technical English was brought in. Selections from poetry and prose were removed. Questions like annotations, short answers, and essays were done away with. Instead, objective type and application- oriented questions were tried out. A major shift from teacher to student, from content to skill, from grammar to communication, from translation to creation, from knowledge to use became visible. A new textbook in two volumes- English for Engineers and Technologists- was published in 1990 and used in the classes. It has reading passages from real, authentic, science and technology related topics, including many branches of Engineering—Civil, Mechanical, Electrical, Computer, and Printing. It is a skill-based book. It offers scope for training students in the four language skills of listening, speaking, reading, and writing. In course of time, however, the ESP course became oriented towards conducting examination, which focused on writing and neglected listening, speaking and reading.

Features of ESP Courses

ESP courses relating to science and technology have certain features in common. These are rhetorical functions, lexical items and grammatical relations. The main rhetorical functions are Description, Definition, Classification, Comparison, Cause and Effect, Verbal-Visual Transformation, Instruction, Checklist, Recommendation, etc. The lexical items include the technical vocabulary. For example, beam, governor, impulse, etc., have typical technical meanings which ordinary people may have difficulty in understanding. Some other vocabulary items include compound nouns, compound and comparative adjectives, purpose and numerical expressions, etc. Some grammatical relations like passive voice, modals, simple present and simple past tense are given additional focus in ESP courses. It does not mean that in other areas such features are not required. Somehow, an aura of unique identity was given to ESP courses with such tags.

Basic Communication Skills

All people require communication skills and these are very basic requirements for human survival. The four basic language skills of Listening, Speaking, Reading, and Writing, have been part of most ELT programs, including ESP. However, teaching and learning them have not been very successful. One of the reasons for this unexpected and undesirable outcome is that the skill of thinking has not been thought of as a communication skill. If thinking is given utmost importance and treated as the most basic skill, then ELT would be on its way to incredible success. The fact is that listening, speaking, reading and writing are skills that cannot be carried out without thinking. The famous expression of 'clarity of thought' stands testimony to the importance of thinking in communication.

English for Life

The need of the hour then is to develop the basic communication skills in students, irrespective of their stream of study. All of them need almost similar kinds of skills. The contexts may vary a little. Then, it is necessary to promote the concept of English for life not for study of a particular discipline and carrying out jobs in a specific area. It is also equally important to understand that communication is a matter of language alone. Mental and emotional maturity is very much necessary to participate in the communication process successfully. To develop the basic communication skills in English for life, focusing on emotional quotient, it is essential to go back to literature. In the old curriculum, English literature was prominent. Now there are many options from literatures in English from all over the world. Literature in English translation is another source to be exploited for understanding the multicultural society, which is the order of the day.

English for All Purposes

In order to teach English for life then, it is necessary to teach English for all purposes, not specific purposes. Hence, no purpose of communication can be omitted from the teaching of English. Some purposes may be more or less dominant in teaching English. Individual preferences of teachers and textbook writers may colour the purpose. However, it is the students who alone should decide for which purpose they use English in their life. Students may use English for a variety of purposes like Creative/ Critical/ Professional/ Personal/ Social/ Therapeutic/ purely informational, etc. If students are prevented from using English in a variety of ways, they become handicapped. Therefore, the best English that can be given to students at all levels is multi-purpose English, which can best be taught through suitable forms of literature: poetry, prose, drama, short fiction, and fiction. Of course, non-fictional forms should be included to offer more variety to learning and teaching of English in India.

Conclusion

Today, ELT has reached a stage where students learning English have to decide the kind of English they have to learn. Success in life is a major parametre for students to measure their proficiency in life. ESP seems to have hindered rather than facilitated learning of English, as seen in the case of India, especially Anna University, Chennai. The employers would like to have graduates who would be able to use simple English effectively for everyday functions in their workplaces. ESP has not been able to cater to this need. Hence, it is necessary to go beyond ESP to Multipurpose English. Each teacher or student may go one's own way individually to achieve this. It would be useful for all students and teachers to have a common way forward. The ELT community is bound to give it in the years to come.

Bibliography

Department of Humanities and Social Sciences. (2006). *English for Engineers and Technologists.* Combined Edition. Chennai: Orient BlackSwan.

Department of Humanities and Social Sciences. (2002). *English for Engineers and Technologists: A Skills Approach.* 2 Volumes. 2nd edition. Chennai: Orient BlackSwan

Dhanavel, S.P. (2009). *English and Communication Skills for Students of Science and Engineering.* Chennai: Orient BlackSwan.

_____. (2010). *English and Soft Skills*. Hyderabad: Orient BlackSwan.

Hutchinson, Tom. and Alan Waters. (1987). *English for Specific Purposes.* Cambridge: Cambridge University Press.

Sharma, R.S. (1991). "The Teaching of Technical English in the Indian Context." *Applied Linguistics: Stylistics and Language Teaching.* New Delhi: Atlantic.

Trimble, Louis. 1985. *English for Science and Technology: A Discourse Approach.* Cambridge: Cambridge University Press.

CALL Courseware Evaluation Criteria: A Reference to ESP

SASIDHAR BANDU

Introduction

As computer technology becomes more integrated into the language curriculum, language teachers are increasingly being called upon to make courseware acquisition decisions. However, not all teachers have the knowledge or experience to make decisions of this kind. Obviously, making courseware recommendations presupposes informed decisions based on adequate knowledge of courseware resources and their evaluation. Yet many language teachers are at a loss about how to make recommendations, as can be judged by the regular appearance on the various listservs of requests for courseware suggestions from colleagues. While such advice may be helpful, in the end courseware selection must be made relative to local curricular circumstances. This paper provides some insights into making such decisions by outlining essential procedures of courseware evaluation.

Courseware Evaluation

Courseware evaluation is more challenging—and time - consuming—than textbook selection. In addition to content area and methodological expertise, it also requires a certain level of technological competence. Also, unlike a book, good courseware is not linear in nature; the richer and more interactive a program is, the harder it is to get an overall view of it. Users need to "play" with it, explore it in some depth, before they can make any informed judgments about it. This is why comprehensive courseware reviews are so important to the process of courseware selection. Above all, published courseware reviews allow readers to get, in the hour or so it might take them to thoroughly digest their contents, an overview of the program from a perspective that usually takes a reviewer several weeks to attain. However, no matter how comprehensive a review is, actual courseware selection can only be made on the basis of teachers' own local assessment, relative to their own particular curricular needs. Obviously, in the absence of published reviews, there is no alternative to local courseware assessment.

The basic tenet of courseware selection is that pedagogy must drive technology and not vice versa. This principle means identifying curricular needs first, then looking for courseware that meets these needs.

Courseware selection really needs to be a multistep process involving not just a single assessor, but as many people as possible who will potentially be using the courseware, including students themselves, who are the ultimate end-users of the product. It is amazing the amount of courseware that sits unused on computers because of erroneous assumptions made by evaluators about what students might think of the programmes' usefulness.

While no one would deny the importance of defining curricular needs before looking for appropriate courseware, in actual practice courseware selection is not an entirely sequential process. One reason is that, as with textbooks and ancillary pedagogical materials (audio/video), available courseware rarely fits exactly into a specific curricular mould. Some degree of adaptation is almost always needed (to the curriculum and/or the courseware). A second reason not to be too restrictive in courseware selection is that new programmes are constantly appearing which may inspire pedagogical innovations not originally considered when determining your curricular needs. All of which is to say that pedagogy must come first, but that teachers also need to be flexible and prepared to adapt their curriculum to take advantage of what new courseware has to offer.

By far the easiest approach to courseware selection, and one which certainly should be considered in the first instance when substantial curriculum review and revision are involved, is to adopt an integrated courseware/textbook package. The great attraction of bundled courseware is precisely the promise that all the hard work has already been done. The content is age and language-learning level appropriate, the methodology is sound, and total curricular integration is assured. That, at least, is what the book publishers want us to believe. Whether it is true in fact, each of us will need to determine for ourselves, hopefully with the aid of published reviews.

This issue brings us to the critical part of this paper: what should one look for in evaluating language learning courseware? The simplest approach to courseware evaluation is to work from a checklist, of which several exist. Checklists are appealing because they only require ticking off features present or absent in the courseware. (A more sophisticated variant of this approach uses Likert-type scales [e.g., rating something on a scale from 1 to 5].)

There is, however, a major problem with checklists, and that is their very simplicity. A program can get good marks in many categories and still, intuitively, users may not be very impressed with it. One of the main reasons for this situation is that checklist items typically have the same relative weight, whereas in any particular situation some features of the courseware may be more important than others. Likewise, there is enormous variety in available courseware (some intended for stand-alone usage, others for exploitation over the web; some are tutorial in nature, others collaborative, still others facilitative, etc.), so it can be very difficult to know how predetermined checklist categories should apply.

A viable alternative to courseware evaluation checklists, which look for specific features, consists of looking at critical systematic properties. Unlike a checklist approach, this approach is an intrinsically discursive process. Although more demanding, it does produce much more meaningful results. Before any courseware program can be recommended for purchase, it must meet the first two of the following requirements and some combination of the last three:

1. Pedagogical validity: It must conform to sound instructional methodology.
2. Curriculum adaptability: It must fit, or be adaptable to, curricular objectives.

3. Efficiency: It must make something teachers are already doing easier to accomplish.
4. Effectiveness: It must produce better results.
5. Pedagogical innovation: It must allow teachers to do something new and different.

The fundamental question here is not whether a courseware program meets these conditions, but the extent to which and how it meets them. Determining the answer to this question involves a close analysis of key program parameters. In order to make this undertaking feasible for classroom teachers, the parameters under consideration need to be generalized so as to keep their number within practical limits. Based on the work of Hubbard (1987, 1988), who has written extensively on the topic of language courseware evaluation, the following four generic parameters are proposed as a basic guide to courseware evaluation:

1. Technical Features
2. Activities (Procedure)
3. Teacher Fit (Approach)
4. Learner Fit (Design)

Technological Features

The technological features of a courseware program are by far the easiest to assess. These features include the following:

1. simplicity of installation (adequacy of instructions, trouble free, easy to uninstall),
2. speed of program operation (where are the delays: at start up, loading videos, web page loading?),
3. reliability of operation (crashes and stalls),
4. platform compatibility (PC/Macintosh, operating system, Web browser versions),
5. screen management (aesthetics, navigational transparency),
6. user interface (ease of use, operational consistency, online help), and
7. exploitation of computer potential (effective use of sound, video, speech recognition, speech synthesis, intelligent response handling, student record keeping, adaptability based on user profiles, links to www).

Activities (Procedure)

As with technological features, program activities are relatively straightforward to deal with. It is essentially a matter of determining what students actually do when they use a program and how well these activities are designed. Judgments here must always be made relative to activity type. Some teachers may be personally opposed, for example, to the use of grammar exercises, but, in evaluating such exercises, they cannot criticize them for not being collaborative in nature. One has to judge the quality of exercises relative to their instructional purpose. (The appropriateness of activities is a separate issue, determined by the teacher's particular curricular objectives, and will be dealt with under Teacher Fit below). Broadly speaking, activities can be classified into three major types:

1. instructional (tutorials, drills, text reconstruction),
2. collaborative (games, simulations, discussion forums, peer group writing), and
3. facilitative (dictionary, database, verb conjugator, spell/grammar checker, authoring system).

Obvious activity features to consider are:

1. linguistic focus (discourse, syntax, lexis, morphology, spelling, pronunciation),
2. language skills (reading, listening, writing, speaking),
3. sociolinguistic focus (information gathering/authentic tasks), and
4. supplementary/complementary/central relationship to the curriculum.

Teacher Fit (Approach)

An assessment of teacher fit primarily involves looking at the theoretical underpinnings of student activities; judging how well they conform to accepted theories of cognitive development, second language acquisition, and classroom methodology; and determining how closely they accord with the teacher's curricular objectives. (This is where the teacher can legitimately reject the structuralist activities of a courseware for not fitting collaborative objectives.) Linguistic accuracy (e.g., grammaticality, authenticity, typos, etc.) and the appropriateness of socio-cultural representations (e.g., stereotypes or gender bias) also contribute to how well a program meets pedagogical objectives.

Teacher fit is the most critical parameter of courseware evaluation, for it determines the pedagogical soundness and appropriateness of the program. No matter how technically brilliant a program may be or how rich the activities it provides, if it does not advance the teacher's curricular objectives, there is no point in acquiring it. Not surprisingly, the assessment of teacher fit is the most difficult courseware parameter to determine, partly because courseware developers do not always explicitly state the theoretical/ methodological assumptions underlying their program, thereby obliging the assessor to extract them by implication. On the other side of the coin, courseware producers are very much aware of what methodological approaches are in favour (e.g., communicative, learner-centred, constructivist, and experiential) and label their products accordingly, whatever the truth of the matter may be. Also, it has to be recognized that some language teachers themselves may lack the formal training (e.g., in cognitive psychology, applied linguistics, or language teaching methodology) needed to make informed decisions about theoretical considerations.

Learner Fit (Design)

In considering learner fit, teachers are in essence defining the potential user of the courseware program. In doing so, they are also determining the extent to which the program is appropriate for, or can be adapted to, the needs of their students. Properties affecting learner fit include:

1. linguistic level (grammar, vocabulary, register),
2. response handling (error correction, feedback),
3. adaptation to individual learner differences (age, interests),
4. learning styles (recognition, recall, comprehension, experiential learning),
5. learning strategies (field-dependent/field-independent learning, deductive/inductive reasoning, visual-graphic/visual-textual learning, individual/group work),

6. learner control (sequencing, content, operating parameters), and
7. design flexibility/modifiability by instructor.

Conclusion

Courseware selection is a demanding task, requiring a good knowledge of where to find courseware resources and informative courseware reviews. Above all, it requires the ability to consistently evaluate courseware relative to local curricular goals.

As has been indicated, courseware evaluation is necessarily a multistep process involving as much grassroots level input as possible, including the trial of programs with students. Beyond the immediate need of acquiring resources for a computer lab, the involvement of foreign language teaching staff in the courseware selection process also plays an important role in the development of faculty instructional technology skills. Learning to critically evaluate foreign language courseware, knowing what constitutes good courseware, is an essential first step in learning how to create one's own courseware applications.

Bibliography

Burston, J. (2003). "*Software Selection: A Primer on Sources and Evaluation* "CALICO Journal, 21 (1), 29-40.

Hubbard, P.L. (1987). "*Language teaching approaches, the evaluation of CALL software and design implications.*" W. Flint Smith, ed., *Modern Media in Foreign Language Education: Theory and Implementation* (227-254).Lincolnwood, IL: National Textbook Company.

Hubbard, P. L. (1988). *An integrated framework for CALL courseware evaluation.* CALICO Journal, 6 (2), 51-72.

Language Learning: A Blended Approach

A.R.N. HANUMAN

Blended learning can be generally understood as the way teachers and students combine or 'blend' multiple teaching methods and learning styles together. For example, the combination of classroom study, guided individual study, and computer-based study, is a type of blended learning. There are numerous possible components and methods that can be used to make a blend. It was first used in the corporate world to refer to a course designed to allow workers to both continue in the workplace and study. Rather than taking time out on a residential seminar, training was delivered through self-study manuals, videos, and the web.

The goal of blended learning is to provide the most efficient and effective instruction experience by combining delivery modalities. The purpose of education is to prepare a student to realize his/ her potential and allow them enough space to translate it to a constructive end much to the benefit of society. The system is churning out professionals but not individuals, so the need of the hour is a balanced approach which includes an integration of various methods of learning. With the increasing use of a variety of approaches for learning in the information age, learners' preferences are changing from wanting to be taught mostly in lectures or direct training sessions to increase flexibility. No one single learning delivery method is capable of supporting the kind of flexibility that learners need. Therefore, a mix of traditional and new learning approaches and technology should be appropriately utilized for a flexible learning.

A blended learning approach combines face to face classroom methods with computer-mediated activities to form an integrated instructional approach. In the past, digital materials have served in a supplementary role, helping to support face to face instruction. For example, a blended approach to a traditional, face to face course might mean that the class meets once per week instead of the usual three-session format. Learning activities that otherwise would have taken place during classroom time can be moved online. As of now, there is no consensus on a single agreed-upon definition for blended learning. In addition, the terms "blended," "hybrid," and "mixed-mode" are used interchangeably in current research literature. The goal of a blended approach is to join the best aspects of both face to face and online instruction. Classroom time can be used to engage students in advanced interactive experiences. Meanwhile, the online portion of the course can provide students with multimedia-rich content at any time of day, anywhere the student has internet access. This allows for an increase in scheduling flexibility for students. Blended learning is on the rise in higher education.

Blended learning increases the options for greater quality and quantity of human interaction in a learning environment. Blended learning offers learners the opportunity "to be both together and apart." A community of learners can interact at any time and anywhere because of the benefits that computer-mediated educational tools provide. Blended learning provides a 'good' mix of technologies and interactions, resulting in a socially supported, constructive, learning experience. The instructor can combine two or more methods of teaching. A typical example of blended learning methodology would be a combination of technology-based materials and face-to-face sessions to present content. An instructor can begin a course with a well-structured introductory lesson in the classroom, and then proceed with follow-up materials online. Blended learning can also be applied to the integration of e-learning with a Learning Management System using computers in a physical classroom, along with face-to-face instruction. Guidance is suggested early in the process, to be used more sparingly as learners gain expertise.

With today's prevalence of high technology in many countries, blended learning often refers specifically to the provision or use of resources which combine E-learning or M-learning with other educational resources, also called hybrid courses. Some would claim that key blended-learning arrangements can also involve e-mentoring or e-tutoring. These arrangements tend to combine an electronic learning component with some form of human interaction, although the involvement of an e-mentor or e-tutor does not necessarily need to be in the context of e-learning. E-mentoring or e-tutoring can also be provided as part of a "stand alone" ("un-blended") e-tutoring or e-mentoring arrangement.

How to Blend?

There are no rules in place to prescribe what the ideal blend might be. The term "blended" encompasses a broad continuum, and can include any integration of face to face and online instructional content. The blend of face to face and online materials will vary depending on the content, the needs of the students, and the preferences of the instructor. The first generation of e-learning or Web-based learning programs focused on presenting physical classroom-based instructional content over the Internet. Furthermore, first-generation e-learning programs tended to be a repetition or compilation of online versions of classroom-based courses. The experience gained from the first-generation of e-learning, often riddled with long sequences of 'page-turner' content and point and-click quizzes, is giving rise to the realization that a single mode of instructional delivery may not provide sufficient choices, engagement, social contact, relevance, and context needed to facilitate successful learning and performance.

The original use of the phrase "blended learnıng" was often associated with simply linking traditional classroom training to e-learning activities, such as asynchronous work. However, the term has evolved to encompass a much richer set of learning strategies or "dimensions." Today a blended learning program may combine one or more of the following dimensions, although many of these have over-lapping attributes. At the simplest level, a blended learning experience combines offline and online forms of learning where the online learning usually means "over the Internet or Intranet" and offline learning happens in a more traditional classroom setting. We assume that even the offline learning offerings are managed through an online learning system. An example of this type of blending may include a learning program that provides study materials and research resources over the Web, while providing instructor-led, classroom training sessions as the main medium of instruction.

Learning approaches and choices.

Synchronous physical formats	Instructor-led Classrooms & Lectures Hands-on Labs & Workshops Field Trips
Synchronous online formats (live e-learning)	Online Meetings Virtual Classrooms Web Seminars and Broadcasts Coaching Instant Messaging Conference Calls
Self-paced, asynchronous formats	Documents & Web Pages Web/Computer Based Training Modules Assessments/Tests & Surveys Simulations Job Aids & Electronic Performance Support Systems (EPSS) Recorded Live Events Online Learning Communities and Discussion Forums Distributed and Mobile Learning

The Benefits of Blending

Blended learning is not new. However, in the past, blended learning comprised physical classroom formats, such as lectures, labs, books, or handouts. Today, organizations have a myriad of learning approaches and choices. Some of these are shown in the above Table. The concept of blended learning is rooted in the idea that learning is not just a one-time event—learning is a continuous process. Blending provides various benefits over using any single learning delivery medium alone.

Extending the Reach

A single delivery mode inevitably limits the reach of a learning program or critical knowledge transfer in some form or fashion. For example, a physical classroom-training program limits the access to only those who can participate at a fixed time and location, whereas a virtual classroom event is inclusive of remote audiences and, when followed up with recorded knowledge objects (ability to playback a recorded live event), can extend the reach to those who could not attend at a specific time.

Optimizing Development Cost and Time

Combining different delivery modes has the potential to balance out and optimize the learning program development and deployment costs and time. A totally online, self-paced, media-rich, Web-based training content may be too expensive to produce (requiring multiple resources and skills), but combining virtual collaborative and coaching sessions with simpler self-paced materials, such as generic off-the-shelf WBT, documents, case studies, recorded e-learning events, text assignments, and PowerPoint presentations (requiring quicker turn-around time and lower skill to produce) may be just as effective or even more effective.

Evidence that Blending Works

We are so early into the evolution of blended learning that little formal research exists on how to construct the most effective blended program designs. However, research from institutions such as Stanford University and the University of Tennessee have given us valuable insight into some of the mechanisms by which blended learning is better than both traditional methods and individual forms of e-learning technology alone. This research gives us confidence that blending not only offers us the ability to be more efficient in delivering learning, but more effective.

Stanford University has over 10 years of experience with self-paced enrichment programs for gifted youth. Their problem was that only slightly more than half of their highly motivated students would complete the programs. They diagnosed the problem as a mismatch between the student's desired learning style—

interactive, social, mentored learning—with the delivery technology. Their introduction of live e-learning into their program raised the completion rate up to 94% by addressing these needs. The improvement was attributed to the ability of a scheduled live event to motivate learners to complete self-paced materials on time; the availability of interaction with instructors and peers; and higher quality mentoring experiences. The Stanford research strongly suggests that linking self-paced material to live e-learning delivery could have a profound effect on overall usage and completion rates—enabling organizations to radically increase the return from their existing investments in self-paced content.

A variety of factors are required to be addressed to create a meaningful learning environment. Many of these factors are interrelated and interdependent. A systemic understanding of these factors can enable designers to create meaningful distributed learning environments. These factors comprise the Octagonal Framework. The framework has eight dimensions: institutional, pedagogical, technological, interface design, evaluation, management, resource support, and ethical. Each dimension in the framework represents a category of issues that need to be addressed. These issues help organize thinking, and ensure that the resulting learning program creates a meaningful learning experience.

Institutional

The Institutional dimension addresses issues concerning organizational, administrative, academic affairs, and student services. Personnel involved in the planning of a learning program could ask questions related to the preparedness of the organization, availability of content and infrastructure, and learners' needs. Can the organization manage offering each trainee the learning delivery mode independently as well as in a blended program? Has the needs analysis been performed in order to understand all learners' needs?

Pedagogical

The Pedagogical dimension is concerned with the combination of content that has to be delivered (content analysis), the learner needs (audience analysis), and learning objectives (goal analysis). The pedagogical dimension also encompasses the design and strategy aspect of e-learning. This dimension addresses a scenario where all learning goals in a given program are listed and then the most appropriate delivery method is chosen. For example, if a learner is expected to demonstrate a product (in sales training), then using product simulation as part of the blend is appropriate. If a learner is expected to come up with a new price model for a product, then using a discussion as one of the elements in the blend would be an appropriate choice.

Technological

Once we have identified the delivery methods that are going to be a part of the blend, the Technology issues need to be addressed. Issues include creating a learning environment and the tools to deliver the learning program. This dimension addresses the need for the most suitable learning management system (LMS) that would manage multiple delivery types and a learning content management system (LCMS) that catalogues the actual content (online content modules) for the learning program. Technical requirements, such as the server that supports the learning program, access to the server, bandwidth and accessibility, security, and other hardware, software, and infrastructure issues are addressed.

Interface Design

The Interface Design dimension addresses factors related to the user interface of each element in the blended learning program. One needs to ensure that the user interface supports all the elements of the blend. The interface has to be sophisticated enough to integrate the different elements of the blend. This will enable the learner to use each delivery type and switch between the different types. The usability of the user interface will need to be analyzed. Issues like content structure, navigation, graphics, and help also can be addressed in this dimension. For example, in a higher education course, students may study online and then attend a lecture with the professor. The blended learning course should allow students to assimilate both the online learning and the lecture equally well.

Evaluation

The Evaluation dimension is concerned with the usability of a blended learning program. The program should have the capability to evaluate how effective a learning program has been as well as evaluating the performance of each learner. In a blended learning program, the appropriate evaluation method should be used for each delivery type.

Management

The Management dimension deals with issues related to the management of a blended learning program, such as infrastructure and logistics to manage multiple delivery types. Delivering a blended learning program is more work than delivering the entire course in one delivery type. The management dimension also addresses issues like registration and notification, and scheduling of the different elements of the blend.

Resource Support

The Resource Support dimension deals with making different types of resources (offline and online) available for learners as well as organizing them. Resource support could also be a counsellor/ tutor always available in person, via e-mail, or on a chat system.

Ethical

The Ethical dimension identifies the ethical issues that need to be addressed when developing a blended learning program. Issues such as equal opportunity, cultural diversity, and nationality should be addressed.

Conclusion

While learning technologies and delivery media continue to evolve and progress, one thing is certain: Organizations (corporate, government, and academic) favour blended learning models over single delivery mode programs. Although blended learning courses are associated with improved student learning outcomes and cost savings, realizing these learning designs across the institution come with significant challenges. An institution must create the necessary policy, planning, resources, scheduling, and support systems to ensure that blended learning initiatives are successful. A policy framework should be developed, which explicitly states how blended learning supports the vision, values, and principles of the institution. Related to this document should be a set of strategic and operational plans. Blended Learning is likely to remain an important concept in language teaching since its overall focus is concerned with the search for 'best practice', i.e. the attempt to identify the optimum mix of course delivery in order to provide the most effective language learning experience.

Works Cited

Alderson, C.J (n.d.) *Innovations in language testing: Can the microcomputer help?* Lancaster: University of Lancaster.

Almeida d'Eca, T. (2007). First steps in experimenting with computers. In E. Hanson-Smith & S Rilling, ed., *Learning languages through technology* pp. 159-74. Alexandria, VA: TESOL.

Anderson, D. (2002). Interfacing e-mail tutoring: Shaping an emergent literate practice. *Computers and Composition,* 19, 71-87.

Ashworth, D. (1996). Hypermedia and CALL In M. C. Pennington, ed., *The Power of CALL*, pp. 79-96. Houston, TX: Athelstan.

Burger, K. (1985). Computer assisted instruction: Learning style and academic achievement. *Journal of Computer-Based Instruction,* 12, 21-22.

Burston, J. (2003). Proving IT works. *CALICO Journal, 20,* 219-26.

Cummins, J. (2000). Academic language learning, transformative pedagogy, and information technology: Towards a critical balance. *TESOL Quarterly, 34,* 537-48.

Curado Fuentes, A. (2001). Lexical behaviour in academic and technical corpora: Implications for ESP development. *Language Learning and Technology,* 5, 106-29.

Figura, K. and Jarvis, H. (2007). Computer-based materials: A study of learner autonomy and strategies. *System*, 35.

Flowerdew, J. (1996). Concordancing in language learning In M. C. Pennington, ed., *The Power of CALL* pp. 97-114. Houston, TX: Athelstan.

Hanson-Smith, E., ed. (2001). *Technology-enhanced learning environments.* Alexandra, VA: TESOL.

Hanson-Smith, E. & Rilling, S, ed. (2007). *Learning Languages through Technology* Alexadra, VA: TESOL.

Jarvis, H. (1997). The role of IT in English for Academic Purposes: A survey of provision on pre-sessional courses at British universities. *ReCALL, 9*, 43-51.

Jarvis, H. (2001). Internet usage on English for Academic Purposes courses. *ReCALL, 13*, 129-42.

Smith, G.D. & E. Baber, (2005). *Teaching English with information technology.* Chichester: Keyways Publishing.

Smith, F. (1984). *The promise and threat of microcomputers in language education.* Reading: University of Reading.

Teeler, D. & Gray, P. (2000). *How to use the Internet in ELT.* London: Longman.

Language *Matters*: Teaching ESP in Telugu Culture

V. SREENATHA CHARY

Introduction

English language is part of the Germanic branch of the Indo-European language family, along with, among others, Danish, Dutch, and German. Once confined to Britain, it is now used throughout the world. Its use and distribution can be discussed in various ways, including geographical distribution, status as an official or other language, and status as majority language or mother tongue (first language), alternative language, medium of education, second language, or foreign language. Telugu or Telegu is a Dravidian language of south India with some 80 million speakers. It is one of the major languages of India and the official language of the state of Andhra Pradesh. Written in a script based on southern Brahmi, it has a literary tradition that dates from the 11th century, though inscriptions dating from the 7th century point to an earlier development of the language. 'Telugu, unlike Tamil, is tolerant of borrowings from Sanskrit, and like Tamil has diglossic variation between a High {grânthika) and Low (vyâvahàrika) variety, with the modern standard based on the High variety[1]'.

Meaning of 'Mother Tongue'

A person's native language is called his/her mother tongue. 'Mother Tongue' [2] is a general term for the language of the childhood home, learned 'at one's mother's knee', often used synonymously with native language. Although the implication is usually clear, there is no necessary connection between a child's use of language and the language of its mother: some children learn the language of a nurse or ayah first; a mother may talk to her child in a language not originally her own; the mother may be dead. The term is often used to mean a national language, such as French, whether or not it is the first or referred language of all members of the nation.

Basic Differences between English and Telugu Languages

1. In English language there are Auxiliary Verbs or Helping Verbs. Such verbs are not there in the Dravidian languages such as Telugu or Tamil. All these years, for example, Telugu speakers or Tamil speakers are adjusted to use such languages, in which there are no Auxiliary Verbs, naturally think that their target language such as English too is just like their mother tongue and do not tend to use any Auxiliary Verbs while using English. The result is using sentences such as—I done the work (instead of 'I have done the work'), She given me a book (instead of 'She has given me a book'), or They eaten their lunch (instead of 'They have eaten their lunch'). This is all due to the influence of mother tongue.
2. In English language there are Articles (i.e. A, An & The) whereas in Telugu or Tamil there are no Articles. All these years, for example, Telugu speakers or Tamil speakers are adjusted to use such languages, in which there are no Articles, naturally think that their target language such as English too is just like their mother tongues and do not use any Articles while using English. The result is using sentences such as—This is pen (instead of 'This is a pen'), He is inspector (instead of 'He is an inspector'). This is all due to the influence of mother tongue.
3. In English language there are Prepositions whereas in languages like Telugu there are no prepositions but postpositions. All these years, for example, Telugu speakers are adjusted to use such a language, in which there are no prepositions, naturally think that their target language such as English too is exactly like their mother tongue and do not use any prepositions while using English. The result is using sentences such as—The book is the table on (instead of 'The book is on the table'), She is resting the bed in (instead of 'She is resting in the bed'). This is all due to the influence of mother tongue.

4. English language uses strict Word Order or Syntax. Though there is a clearly defined word order even in Telugu or Tamil, the meaning of the sentence is not distracted even if the word order is changed in Telugu or Tamil. This is not the case with any sentence in English language. In English, a sentence like 'Ravi killed a snake' has a pattern of syntax in which the Subject, the Verb and the Object have come in an order. We cannot make this sentence as 'A snake killed Ravi' unless the situation is so. In Telugu or Tamil, it is not like this.

Conclusion

In India, 'an estimated 30 million people (i.e. 4% of the population) regularly use English, making India the third largest English-speaking country in the world.'[1] If the Telugu medium students are taught clearly about the major differences between English and Telugu languages, they will try to learn English as it should be learnt. This way the learners can consciously avoid the mother tongue influence while learning English language.

References

1. Tom McArthur, ed. 1992. *The Oxford Companion to the English Language.* Oxford, New York: Oxford University Press, p.1030.
2. Ibid. p.671
3. Ibid. p.504

Bibliography

Block, David, ed.2002. *Globalization and Language Teaching.* Routledge-London: David Block and Deborah Cameron Publisher.

Crystal, David. 2002. *The Cambridge Encyclopedia of the English Language.* Cambridge, New York: Cambridge University Press.

English for Business Management

A. MADHAVI LATHA

Communication is the key for success in Business Management. It is often referred as Business Communication and it can be defined as the process of exchanging ideas between two parties in order to advance a commercial enterprise. Every conversation is worth a million dollars in this highly competitive environment. Therefore, maintaining consistency and clarity in the message that has to be conveyed to hundreds of employees all over the organization can be quite challenging. It is known to everyone that necessity is the mother of invention and it became evident from this particular situation wherein people invented a method of communication to maintain clarity and consistency in the message delivery, which is "Business English."

Many developing countries such as India have adopted this new language and eventually it has become an indispensable must. To encourage this situation, what needs to be taught is the communicative effectiveness of Business English and how it is different from speaking general English. Especially in countries with English as second language, teaching Business English is not an easy feat because of the diversified culture and languages. In order to overcome this situation it is very important for teachers to constantly come up with innovative methods to make students more comfortable in understanding and communicating in a language which is not their cup of tea.

Importance of Business English

According to Planken (2010), language plays a central role and is referred to as "the changing landscape of business communication" as increasing globalization and the evolution of media technologies transform the business arena. It proves that increasing globalization has triggered the importance of communicating in Business English. Since English is the global language in which everybody can communicate and understand each other, it has been selected as a common medium of communication and it has been refined since ages in such a way that talking in clichés has become more common for clarity purposes. This access to a language facility that has been shared has become indispensable and has been dominating since the past few decades as the language of international business.

The following conversation can be a perfect example of communicating in business terminology:

> *Tim, Harvey and John Scavo are working as sales representatives for a well known company. They both are having a conversation regarding the products and their sales. It is as follows:*
>
> Tim: Hello John! How are you doing today?
>
> John: I am spectacular Tim. How about yourself?
>
> Tim: Not too bad. I was wondering about the sales report. Is there any problem?
>
> John: Well yes. The sales order was incomplete as we ordered 500 units but when checked the consignment, it was obvious that we had not received them all.
>
> Tim: How many are we short?
>
> John: Well, they came in boxes of 40 and we had 32 and so we are short of 8 boxes.
>
> Tim: Then I believe that you can get it done by Monday. Let me know if you need any assistance.
>
> John: I sure will and thank you. Have a great day Tim.
>
> Tim: Thank you and you too enjoy your day.

This conversation can help everyone to understand how Tim and John perfectly organized the conversation and spoke very politely and communicated the message that needs to be delivered.

According to Susanne Ehrenreich (2010), English has become undoubtedly the dominant language in international business. Hence it is really important to understand that emerging business executives need to know the business terminology and communicate with other executives in the work environment.

Differences and commonalities between Business English and General English

Before understanding how to communicate using Business English it would be quite optimistic to focus on what are the differences and the similarities between English for Business and General English.

Business English	General English
Business correspondence	General Correspondence
Specialized business vocabulary	Use of common terms and phrases
Techniques for negotiation and presentation	No specific techniques necessary to communicate and negotiate
Goal-oriented conversations	General conversations

Commonalities are

- Grammar
- Vocabulary
- Small conversations
- Clarity of the message that has to be conveyed

After understanding this, it would be much easier to distinguish and learn it in a more precise manner.

Contextual features of Business English

Kankaanranta and Planken (2010), have identified three important contextual features of Business English. They are as follows:

1. The shared business domain

Every business organization has got its method of internal communication. Business domain is a part of it which can be explicitly explained as largely implicit knowledge which is shared within the business discourse community (Planken, 2010). It can be said that business domain is strictly task-oriented and more purposeful. Since it is not taught in daily classes it can be learnt only through real life practice. The business knowledge that stays as secret for outsiders, will always be a catalyst to aspire business professionals. In order to share this characteristic knowledge of an organization, every business executive must take an initiative to understand and tailor their approaches for further advancement.

2. The shared special field of expertise

This feature is related to the work culture that has been shared and the shared context in which the vocabulary is used. In an organization business executives tend to share their professional area of expertise that involves special concepts and terminology. By communicating effectively with other executives and sharing their expertise leads to amplification of the implicit knowledge that is related to the internal process in an organization.

3. The length of relationship with the communication partner

According to Kankaanranta and Planken, the better you know the other party, the better you know how to communicate with them and what kind of communication you can expect from them. These conversations usually trigger professional expertise, English proficiency and finally lead to amplified knowledge to both the parties that are involved in the conversation. One can acknowledge that it is an idiosyncratic combination and it will take some time to get used to them and put them in to practise. This can be made easier by using simplified and specific terminology and eventually one can adopt this hybrid language.

4. Important modules of Business English

As known to everyone, there are four important modules in Business English that needs to be focussed and obtain perfection. According to White and Joann, current workplace needs employees who can integrate reading, writing, listening and speaking into complex problem solving and critical thinking skills. They are as follows:

- Listening: Listening plays its crucial role in obtaining the desired outcome in a conversation. Whether it is selling a product, customer service or participating in a team meeting, listening to the other member and tailoring the approach accordingly will give better results. According to Boyd (2004), there is a real connection between quality listening and success in the workplace. Since effective listening requires attention and focus, it is important to prepare for listening before starting the conversation. Encouraging the other person to talk by probing can also help in focusing on the conversation. As mentioned by Boyd, the effective way of listening is to empathize with the other person by having a mental composure. Listening is a key managerial skill and plays a vital role in success.

- Reading: Reading is another module which gives more perspective about business communication. As mentioned earlier, clarity is needed in all the modules and reading plays a very important role in it as it gives the reader the detailed explanation. While reading a business letter or a memo, the reader must focus on the context of the reading which means the message that has been conveyed in the reading.
- Speaking: Out of all the four modules, speaking has its own space and importance in terms of Business English. For a business person to reach the heights, speaking makes all the difference. Business English speaking skills are utilized in job interviews, professional meetings, conferences and making presentations. As mentioned by Bailey (1993), proper organization is the first step to a successful business conversation. While participating in such conversations one should be prepared and organize the content and the method in which they are going to communicate to others. Apart from that, they should also be prepared to face the objections and clarify others' concerns.

Business English can be used while talking to coworkers, talking to the boss or to the subordinates. Having control over the content that has to be delivered is the key to a successful conversation at workplace. Speaking and listening go hand in hand with each other as they both are complementary. Public speaking is a common ritual to increase the brand identity and also the revenues (Butterman 2008). Hence while having such important conversations one should watch their body language as well.

Having knowledge of Business vocabulary helps a lot in business communication. Here are some examples:

Word *Part of speech*	Meaning	Example Sentence
accomplish	succeed in doing	We have a lot to accomplish

verb		today, so let's begin.
Address *verb*	deal with; speak on	I hope we do not have to address this matter again in the future.
Adjourn *verb*	close a meeting	If there are no further comments, we will adjourn the meeting here.
AGM *noun(abbr.)*	Annual General Meeting	We always vote for a new chairperson at the AGM.
AOB *noun(abbr.)*	Any Other Business (unspecified item on agenda)	The last item on the agenda is AOB.
apologies *noun*	item on agenda announcing people who are absent; apologies for absence	Everyone is present today, so we can skip the apologies.
consensus *noun*	general agreement	If we cannot come to a consensus by the end of the meeting we will put it to a vote.
designate *verb*	assign	If no one volunteers to take the minutes I will be forced to designate someone.
Motion *noun*	a suggestion put to a vote	The motion to extend store hours has been passed.
proxy vote *noun*	a vote cast by one person for or	There must have been one proxy vote because I count

	in place of another	twelve ballots but only eleven attendees.
show of hands *noun*	raised hands to express an opinion in a vote	From the show of hands it appears that everyone is in favour of taking a short break.
wrap up *verb*	finish	Let's wrap up here so that we can get back to our desks

- Writing: Increasing usage of information technology has amplified the importance of writing the message and communicating it with other employees in an organization. Employers emphasize that proficiency in business writing is a critical skill that they seek in job applicants (Betts and Carthy 2004). As discussed earlier, globalization is also another valid reason for this. According to Beagrie (2004), we are in the age of email and text messaging which emphasizes speed and brevity, especially in workplace communications. Because of this, the importance of well-crafted sentences is frequently underestimated. But writing a well-crafted letter or business proposal or a memo is very essential as it makes a lot of difference and makes a good impression on the reader and finally helps to obtain the desired outcome. How to succeed in this module? Top quality writing may not come naturally but one can master its basic principles (Beagrie). First of all, one should acknowledge that every business conversation is different and hence has a different aim. It is important to identify the aim of the conversation, target audience and what is the expected or desired outcome. Then, how to present the message i.e., media of communication should be determined. Secondly, knowing the audience and their level of knowledge is essential as it helps to understand how much technical language should be used in writing the proposal or the letter. Finally combining the relevant facts and opinions together in a very professional and convincing manner is the key to fulfill the purpose of writing a proposal. Here are some examples with specific English: Taking the Minutes before a meeting the minute-taker should review the following:

- The minutes from previous meeting
- All of the names of the attendees (if possible)
- The items on the agenda

It also helps to create an outline before going to the meeting. An outline should include the following:

- A title for the meeting
- The location of the meeting
- A blank spot to write the time the meeting started and ended
- The name of the chairperson
- A list of attendees that can be checked off (or a blank list for attendees to sign)
- A blank spot for any attendees who arrive late or leave early

Expressions for Business Letters

Dispatch Note

We are pleased to inform you that your goods were sent today.

We hereby inform you that your goods will be delivered tomorrow.

We hope that the goods will arrive in perfect condition.

We look forward to doing business with you again.

Acknowledgement of Receipt

We have received your delivery.

Your delivery arrived in perfect condition on . . .

Thank you very much for executing our order professionally.

Request

We got your address from . . .

Your advertisement has come to our attention.

We were told that you produce . . .

We intend to buy . . ./ We are considering the purchase of . . .

Offer

We are pleased to hear that you are interested in our products.

We hereby send you our offer.

Enclosed please find our offer.

Enclosed you will find our offer.

Order

Enclosed please find our order./ Our order is enclosed.

We would like to place the following order:

We herewith order the following items:

Invoice

Please find enclosed invoice no. . . . for . . .

Thank you for your order.

We look forward to doing business with you again.

Reminder

According to our records, we have not yet received a remittance for above invoice.

May we remind you that your payment is overdue for three months.

This is to remind you that above invoice is still unpaid.

Departments of a company

accounting department/ accounts department

EDP team (EDP = electronic data processing)

purchasing department

export department/ export team/ export sales department

administrative accounting

research and development team

References

Barnard, P.D. (1993). A Practical Guide for Business Speaking. *Security Management* .

Beagrie, S. (2004). How to produce powerful business writing. *Personnel Today*, 21.

Boyd, S. (2004). The Human Side of Business: Effective Listening. *Agency Sales*, 35-37.

Butterman, E. (2008). Speaking of Success. *Black Enterprise*, 44.

Planken, B. (2010, May). The changing landscape: Developments and direction in research.

Plenary paper presented at the 10th ABC Europe Conference, Antwerp, Belgium.

Global Competencies and Changing Trends in ELT

G. SUVARNA LAKSHMI

Education all over the world is more globalized and interconnected than it has ever been before as the need of the product (be it person or object) as global and general rather than individual and specific. The emerging global economy is both competitive and interdependent. It reflects the availability of modern communications and production technologies in most parts of the world. English has been recognized to be the language that is to be used for the success in the scientific environment. It supplements or co-exists with languages by allowing strangers to communicate across linguistic boundaries. It became the tool that opens windows to the world, expands our minds to the latest technologies and unlocks doors to opportunities. This is not a sudden ascent of English to this position, but a gradual change. It is being used for more distinct and varied purposes than before. The ways of speaking and writing are greatly influenced by technological and scientific developments, economies and management, literature and entertainment genres.

Changing Trends in English Language Teaching

A review of history of English language teaching brings to light that English was being taught-learnt in several parts of the world to facilitate British to colonize the countries. The need for teaching-learning English was to understand and respond to or implement the given commands by the colonized countries. This extended to appreciation of the literary genius of the language as part of language learning. Thus literature was established as materials for teaching-learning purposes and this tradition fortunately or unfortunately still continues though not in a major way. The methods of teaching and the purposes of learning the language have been changing from period to period according to the needs of the day. It started with grammar translation method to ICT (Information and Communication Technology).

English for Academic and Specific Purposes came into existence; Registers and patterns of communication for each specialized subjects mushroomed: Technical English, Business English, English for Medical Purposes, English for Media and Communication, Legal English, English for Travel and Tourism, Scientific English, and so on. Different Englishes came into existence, i.e., American, British, Australian, Canadian, Indian, Chinese speakers of English speak English differently and emerged as different dialects. Hence, it can be said that English also has changed as need - based learning.

In the present educational scenario, the courses offered in English are mostly need-based and tailor-made. English in India is not just a language to be learnt but the base for whole learning process at all levels starting from schools to universities. As all other professional courses are adapted to the present day's industrial needs, so is English language. Learning English through subjects and vice-versa is the present trend. Additional material to teach-learn English is not required as the need to learn English is functional. Spoken language occupies prime position compared to the written one.

Competencies Required

In addition to the above mentioned changes, the competencies which are expected from global professionals, particularly of technical and business fields have changed the established boundaries of English teaching-learning processes. These are in addition to the competition in amount of knowledge acquired and other competencies each professional field demands. Global competencies require global mind set which includes competitiveness, adaptability, multicultural team management, managing uncertainty and chaos (Rhinesmith, 1993). Added to this are other skills-global vision, cultural diversity and empathy, cross-cultural communication, interpersonal expertise, global negotiation skills, ethics and integrity and protocol power (Engholm & Rowland 1996).

An investigation of global needs gave a list of competencies which comprises cross-cultural savvy and sensitivity, personal maturity, openness, flexibility and international exposure (Claus 1999). This list is never ending as the change is constant and so are the needs. However, this list can be put under broad headings as follows:

1. Communication skills which include a range of skills: interview skills, presentations, negotiations, telephonic conversations, interpersonal skills, awareness of acceptable body language, effective business written communication and social skills are part of language skills classes now.
2. Critical thinking skills include a wide range of cognitive abilities: problem solving, analyzing, decision making, questioning, critiquing, interpreting, assessing, changing attitudes, enhancing the aptitude levels. Creativity, judgmental abilities, reasoning and logic are supported by the formerly mentioned skills.
3. Ethics are generally culture based and professionals are supposed to have knowledge of various cultures and the ethics that are adopted which help them in adaptation to the place and situation.
4. Cross-cultural savvy: A better understanding of the interdependency of language and culture is paramount to the development of appropriate professional relationships to meet the needs of an increasingly changing world. Cultural sensitivity towards the local and global cultures makes professionals more successful as *Glocalization* is the order of the day.
5. Group dynamics helps an individual be part of a team, work together for better results under time constraints. It is the ability to collectively work with a group of individuals whose existence as a collection is rewarding to the individuals along with the group.
6. Handling stress, time and chaos are the highest demands of the technologically developing world. Now the world is a place where time and amount of work to be complete are dis-

proportional, where failures are unpredictable, planned disasters like bomb blasts and natural calamities occur but still the business is not to incur any loss and where personal and professional lives are at loggerheads. This situation calls for lot of self-integrity, ability to foresee and be mentally prepared for the worst of the situations living in the best of it.

7. Emotional Intelligence (EI/EQ) is required to maintain effective personal and professional relations, have awareness, control and management of one's own emotions, and those of other people. A person's preparedness to expose or hide his/her feelings, vulnerabilities, thoughts, etc., is a feature of EI.
8. Interview Skills: The success of a professional (as an interviewer and interviewee) of any field is dependent on this skill as it is the key to get a job for employees. It is also very important for the employers to select the right person for the right job which is a prerequisite for the success of a business.

The above are just a few majors ones to mention and there are a hoard of other skills which each of the professions call for specifically and commonly. For example, quickness and patience, two contradictory qualities are needed for a doctor. The success of a doctor in his profession is mainly to know when to act quickly and when to be patient. Hence it can be said that English language teaching for specific purposes, particularly in India, has broadened its spectrum as it covers ALL THE PROFESSIONAL aspects required by the industry in a student, a prospective professional!

Challenges in ESP Contexts for English Language Teachers

With the above classification, we understand that just teaching how to use a verb in its right form is not enough to a professional as the demand is not just to speak but much more to hear or see. In other words, just the hard skills of language do not suffice to the needs. All the stated skills can be put under one single umbrella term, Soft Skills. The list of skills which fall under the term, soft skills, is unending and growing. There are about sixty skills that are mentioned under this heading by American companies that expect their (prospective) employees to possess (URL). Hence, the boundaries of teaching English to pass an exam or use it for a specific purpose are amplified to the extent of impressing people and gaining attention to sell self in an interview or product in a business interaction. The teaching of exhibition of appropriate attitudes and skills where and when needed is also part of the language classrooms.

The materials needed are not just literary texts but any informative text that can enrich the student professionals' understanding of the world. Restriction based on prescriptions (syllabus) is an obsolete practice. As the focus of language teaching has broadened from the teaching of discrete grammatical structures to the fostering of the above mentioned sets of skills, the role of teachers has changed to trainers, facilitators and mentors for the whole process of emerging professionals. They are expected to provide scaffolding for the enhancement of aptitude levels, change in attitude and provide training for the skills needed for the day, make the professionals ambitious goal setters, go-getters and finally be successful in whichever field they settle in. The state-of-the-art of an English language classroom earlier was just a chalk, board and teacher. But now, a multi-media laboratory which helps the students to be autonomous in learning, a video recorder and player to make the students aware of their oral verbal and non-verbal communication have turned to be mandatory.

The above discussion would be incomplete if the psychological aspect of the skills, Emotional Intelligence, is not dealt with. Emotional intelligence (Goleman, 1995, 2001) includes the capacity to accurately perceive emotions, use emotions to facilitate thinking, understand emotional meanings and manage emotions of self and others. Emotional intelligence is tested in professionals through psychometric tests in written form or stress interviews in oral form. This has brought in a major change in the training trends today. Emotional self is perceived to be formed because of personal experiences and mind-set and so cannot be changed through training. But as the present need is demanding, bringing in changes in the aptitude levels of a professional and the management of emotions also became part of the curriculum of language classrooms.

The greatest challenge now is time. Unlike before, each language skill or aspect cannot be taught independently because of two reasons: time constraints to do so as per the academic schedule and demands on part of the students; students cannot be dependent on the teachers forever to put all the independently learnt skills to use in an appropriate context.

Some Techniques to Handle Professional English Classes

The target students for any professional course are young adults. The teachers are expected to act as facilitators and pave way for 'experiential learning'. Learner autonomy has to emerge as one of the results of teaching-learning process in professional courses. Thus the old techniques for handling language classes are out of place. New and innovative techniques are to be adopted as per the need of the professional courses the students take up. The teacher has to be skillful enough to shift the responsibility of learning from the teacher to the learners and facilitate the process.

Integrated Skills Approach: This approach, teaching all the language skills weaved in one activity, is an accepted panacea for the problems faced by teachers to cope with the time-and need-based courses. The strain for the students to focus on each of the skills and then integrate when and where needed would be reduced, hence turning into student support approach.

Learner centred classroom: To create an effective learning situation in the classroom, Combs (1976) says that the classroom environment has to be changed. The learning environment should facilitate the exploration of meaning independent of the teacher. Teachers must help learners come out of all inhibitions to feel safe and accepted. They should be motivated enough to seek new knowledge and understanding. The classroom activities must be designed to involve the students and facilitate interaction, and socialization, along with a business-like approach to complete the task. Learners must be given frequent opportunities to confront new information and experiences in search of new interpretations. However, these opportunities need to be provided in ways that allow students to learn by doing than being passive receivers. Students must be given new challenges that permit them to use their past experience rather than depend on the teacher. The methods used to support personal discovery must be highly customized and adapted to the learner's style and pace for learning.

Activity based teaching: Teachers have to be creative in generating appropriate activities as per the skills the students are to learn in the course. Activities engage the students physically and mentally which is a source of motivation for them. The environment in the class has to be democratic. The activities can be role plays, projects, tasks, or writing of reports, each having its own objectives to be achieved by the end of the task.

Role-plays: The importance of role plays cannot be underestimated in this type of teaching. When students take part in a role play, they get into the psyche of the role and this influences their thinking. They learn to "think on their feet," ask relevant questions, take decisions, resolve conflicts, organize their thoughts, listen attentively and above all communicate effectively

Working on Tasks: As task-based learning requires the learners to take active role in learning, learning to learn on their own and/or taking the responsibility of learning are different tasks which the learners are generally not used to in the traditional teaching-learning processes. The tasks are to be designed to develop many complex cognitive and language skills simultaneously. For example an important but controversial video clipping (a visual stimulus), a speech (an audio file) or a plain reading text for the class can engage the students in many ways:

- Try and understand the content of the text (language, vocabulary, pronunciation and meaning as a whole)
- Think creatively to generate various meanings that can be from the provided text
- Identification and generating various solutions (brainstorming) and if the problem is very big, then breaking down the problem and finding the right solution (problem solving skills)
- Practicality of the solutions generated, choose the right and appropriate solution.

Group and Team Projects:

There's nothing like a group/team project to get students talking and they work well if:

- the topic is centred on the learners' interests;

- there is no time-consuming research;
- students can present their work orally to the rest of the class.

Students can work in small groups towards compiling top five examples. If the class is a Business English class, then the following can be given:

- Our top five business houses
- Our top five entrepreneurs—students can be encouraged to say why they like them, give a description of their personality and their work.
- Our top five advertisements (magazine or TV) with a final round up showing the ads and describing why they are effective.
- Our top five TV business programs

The main advantages are

- It gives students controlled opportunities to express themselves.
- It can be tailored to their curriculum or their own specializations.
- The final oral presentation stage gives excellent practice in extended speaking which is useful for higher levels. It can also be appropriate to the oral component of students' exams and gives them extra practice in talking about topics close to their hearts.
- It encourages group work.

Written Communication: One of the most important writing skills students are likely to need is writing effective business emails. The correct tone, structures and layout are all components students need to learn. Why not set a writing task and let students email you? You can reply with your comments. This is more realistic than students simply writing or typing out an email. By allowing them to do research on a particular topic, they can prepare either individually, in pairs or in small groups for a presentation or a piece of writing. Presentation skills are extremely useful, as is the ability to write concise reports. Therefore you are allowing students to practise vocabulary related to their field in addition to giving them the chance to do relevant research.

Conclusion

To conclude, the trends in the constantly changing world have drastically changed the status of English classroom physically and intellectually. Now the English classroom has a teacher (who monitors the language learning process), facilitator (who facilitates autonomy in acquiring skills), mentor (who directs and counsels the students for better aptitude levels, acceptable attitudes and appreciated emotional intelligence), a multi-faceted person involved in teaching language and training students to be acceptable professionals equipped with the competencies demanded by the globalized world. You don't need long arms to embrace the world, you need good English (with all skills mentioned above).

Bibliography:

Claus, L (1999). "Globalization and HR Professional Competencies." Paper delivered to the 22nd Annual Conference of the Institute for International Human Resources, Orlando FL

Combs, A.W. (1976). "Fostering maximum development of the individual." In W. Van Til & K.J. Rehage, ed. *Issues in Secondary Education.* (NSSE Yearbook, 1976). Chicago: National Society for the Study of Education.

Engholm, C. and D. Rowland (1996). *International Excellence: Seven breakthrough Strategies for Personal and Professional Success.* New York: Kodansha International

Goleman, D (1995). *Emotional Intelligence: Why it matters more than IQ.* New York: Bantam Books

Goleman, D.R.E. Boyatzis and AMcKee (2002): *Primal Leadership: Realizing the Power of Emotional Intelligence.* Boston: Harvard Business School press

Rhinesmith, S.H. (1993). *A Manager's Guide to Globalization: Six Keys to Success in a Changing World.* Alexandria, VA: Business One Irwin.

Thirumalai, M.S. (2002). *An Introduction to TESOL. Language in India*: 2 (2). URL: www.languageinindia.com

URL: www.workforce.com

URL: http://www.onestopenglish.com/News/Magazine/Archive/esl_teach_businessenglish.htm

English for Business Management in the Present Scenario

R. PADMAJA

Research has shown that for the most part, employees are very good at what they do. That's why they are hired, trained, retrained, and promoted. They are all subject matter experts. But problems occur when they attempt to communicate their subject to others. They have had extensive training and experience in performing their jobs, but very little training in effectively presenting their ideas to others. Learning to speak English will allow us to communicate with a massive number of people around the globe so it is known as an international language.

Importance of English in Business Management: Learning the English language is important in today's world. English is one of the most widely spoken languages in the world. In addition over one billion people currently learn English. It is an official language in over 50 countries around the world. In fact, it is estimated that one in four people learn English as a foreign language. The total number of people who can speak English, including those who speak it as a second language, is well over a billion. English is the global language of communication and businesses today. Also in today's international market, learning English as a foreign language or second language has almost become a necessity as English is the language of communication in International Business and International Politics. Most academic publications across a range of fields are in English. Internet and media has been dominated by the English language. As the main language of most of the world's largest companies and producers, English has emerged as an international language of commerce. Those who can speak not only their own tongue but also English have a distinct advantage both at home and abroad as the businesses operate more and more globally. The benefits of effective communication in Business English will be more effective presentations, more effective meetings and seminars (both one-to-one and one-to-group), elimination of confusion, increased productivity, increased morale and tremendous savings of time and money. Training and development with result-oriented programmes full of real-life practice sessions, allowing participants to take the maximum benefit in minimum time.

Usage of English Language in Business Management: English is used in Business Management in various areas and it is used in the fields of Business Communication, Management, Finance, Banking, Marketing and Sales. English for Business Communication is in the areas of background of business, customer care, public relations, business correspondence and communication, contracts, agreements, Business proposals, quotations, meetings, conferences, preparing, analyzing reports, interviews, negotiations and telephoning skills. English for Management is in the areas of the role of the manager, company organization, control, management strategy, decision-making, employment documentation, industrial relations like consultation and mediation, interviewing, selection, recruitment, staff training, appraisal, targets, budgets, human resources and inter-departmental communication. English for Finance and Banking is in the areas of company structure, financial organization, budgeting and financial planning, banking and bank services, currencies, foreign exchange, accountancy, financial transactions, investment appraisal, taxation, insurance, financial documentation, correspondence, examination practice for the International Certificate in Financial English (ICFE). English for Marketing and Sales is in the areas of marketing strategies, sales promotion, advertising, product awareness, marketing and sales presentations, meetings, conferences and negotiations, contracts and agreements, market research, surveys and statistics, forecasts and projections, effective oral and written communication.

Problems while Communicating in English: Language that describes what we want to say in our terms may present barriers to others who are not familiar with our expressions, buzz-words and jargon. The same word can have different meaning for different people due to background and cultural differences. Even when speaking the same language like English, sometimes we cannot accurately get the meaning from others. The problem does not lie with the fact that a word can mean differently to different people, the problem is we always assume other people interpret the word with the same meaning as we do. This is especially true of communication between men and women. The problems in having Effective English Communication Skills are Ability to frame grammatically correct sentences, Lack of Vocabulary, Fluency problems, Pronunciation problems, Fear of Speaking to Groups of People, Ineffective Presentation Skills, foreign accent communication barrier etc. All these problems are because of the following reasons. Our first language or native language is the language we are born into. This is the language our parents or family speak. This language is acquired through life experiences. The second kind of language is called a second language which is English. This language is typically learnt in the classroom from a teacher. There are some crucial differences between these two types of languages. The first language is learnt unconsciously. Therefore, it is imbibed at a very early age. There is no need to being conscious to attain the rudiments of this language. However, the second language is the result of a conscious learning process. It does not come naturally. This explains why almost all people face some amount of difficulty while they handle English language. Accents can be charming, but they also can impede workplace communication: All of the above scenarios demonstrate a foreign accent communication barrier. Although certainly not a disorder, accents can disrupt the work environment. Accents evolve when English is filtered through a mother tongue and native language rules are incorrectly applied to English. Several factors determine the accent and involve many different areas such as stress, pitch, projection, rate, and specific sound productions. In order to overcome the above problems, some suggestions were made and by following the suggestions we can make Business English more effective.

Suggestions:

1. *Memorizing*: Memorizing the key words in English language will make the communication more effective. Knowing the meaning of words is not enough. They aren't useful until we have been through the whole learning cycle. This implies that we have to understand the word, know how to use it, memorize it and be able to recall it when needed.
2. *Improving writing skills in Business English*: From business cards to invoices, basic contracts, agreements and e-mails, understanding key elements of business communication in English is an important area. We need to review the use of formal and informal expressions; grammar and usage for proper business communications. Paragraph should centre on a particular feature of the topic that forms the main text. That is to say, we are putting across a specific thought or suggestion. While the first sentence sets the tone of the paragraph and gives an idea of what will be discussed, every paragraph that follows should not have the same exact first sentence. We should vary the way in which we start a paragraph. Each sentence in a paragraph should be properly connected to the sentences that go before it. Each paragraph should be consistently related to the text as a whole and not disconnected to other paragraphs. Hence it is necessary to have a continuous flow from one paragraph to the next.
3. *Improvement of speaking fluency*: Social conversation and telephone etiquette are paramount to effective business communications. Business people need to talk with clients, customers or personnel from company branch offices abroad in English. Correct and fluent speech and use of idioms and expressions will aid in maintaining good relations with clients and customers outside of your country and in other cultures. It will also aid those who work in company foreign branch offices to better understand each other's speech. Speaking with more fluency will also give a boost to executives' confidence.

4. *Correction of pronunciation problems*: All too common errors in saying complex numbers, using prepositions and grammar points such as proper use of regular and irregular verbs can be corrected to improve our pronunciation. Sessions of practising phonetics and correction of individual pronunciation problems using personalized instruction will allow rapid improvement if effectively administered.
5. *Elimination of common errors*: Whether we have problems in grammar, use of expressions, prepositions or verbs, we can work individually on our biggest problem areas one-by-one to minimize or eliminate them. In speaking, in writing or with poor listening comprehension, guided practice and judicious use of simulations will soon give us noticeable improvement, more confidence and better communicative business English.
6. *Improve Vocabulary quickly and easily*: Vocabulary or lexis consists of words, phrases and expressions-the very building blocks of language. The more lexis we know the better and more precisely we will be able to communicate proposals, ideas or plans to customers and clients. There are a number of easy, simple ways we can increase our vocabulary quickly and effectively for maximum improvement in the shortest possible time. Areas that will substantially aid in building our functional vocabulary as quickly as possible include Knowledge of affixes (prefixes and suffixes), Identification and use the verb, tenses of English, Knowing how to change the parts of speech of a word, Understanding words with multiple meanings, Using true and false cognate vocabulary correctly, giving concise business presentations that promote your company.
7. *Experienced, Skilled native speakers indispensable for Business Organizations:* Organizations need to recruit experienced, skilled native speakers who help the English language learners to develop and practise activities in speaking with confidence, developing listening comprehension skills, writing business correspondence and comprehension of business English documents of all types. A generous variety of prac-

tice activities and exercise types should be made available to suit the needs, interests and abilities of executives and staff.

8. *A business English executive training program* that addresses these major areas will allow executives, administrative or other key personnel to quickly develop fluency and confidence in their English language skills. Careful review of proposed program aspects will help to ensure that the expectations of the company and personnel will be met to their satisfaction. Better business English communications can be a real boon to growing client base, expanding potential customer contacts and engaging in effective international business communications.
9. Assistance from Corporate communication consultants: Foreign accent communication barriers are frustrating to the individual who speaks English as a second language as well as their listener. Many people do not know where to turn for help. Most of these employees are extremely intelligent and highly educated. Frequently, their vocabularies are more extensive than the typical native speaker and their grammar is acceptable. They have taken years of English as a Second Language classes but it is their actual English pronunciation that is holding them back. Corporate communication consultants can assist these speakers to improve their spoken English skills. Everyone benefits from improved communication. The employee gains self-confidence, reduced frustration, and increased productivity. Co-workers experience increased harmony and team cohesiveness. The customer gains timely results and satisfaction. And the employer benefits from improved profitability as well as lower employee turnover.

Conclusion

None of us are 'born great' at communicating with others. Communication is a skill. It can be learned quickly and we can learn these skills. All we need to do is keep reading and doing hard work which improve communication in any relationship and heal almost any communication problem, challenge or issue in Business as well as our relationships.

Bibliography

Andrew D. Mile, 15 ways to improve communication in business English, 2007 from www.slideshare.net

Dennis Rivers, 2007. *The Seven Challenges Workbook,* A Guide to Cooperative Communication Skills for Success at Home and at Work,

Deborah Mecklinger, *The Elegant Email: Ten Tips to Help You Communicate More Effectively, 2009.*

www.barcelonaenglish.com

www.madridenglish.net

www.englishphone.biz.

English for Postgraduate Engineering Students

K. KIRAN KUMAR and V. SRI RAMA MURTHY

Koneru Lakshmaiah University (KLU) has signed several exchange agreements with colleges abroad and the number of Indian exchange students visiting colleges abroad is increasing. However, the number of foreign students coming to KLU is still somewhat below expectations. This situation has triggered a discussion concerning measures to attract more foreign students. One such measure has been the feasibility of continuing English throughout the Engineering course. However, there has been very little discussion about the English language skills of engineering students. Recent research in India indicates that the current proficiency level of English of our students is far below what is expected when they enter higher education and engineering colleges. As there is no/less credit given to English courses, it is reasonable to assume that the language skills of future engineers will not have improved drastically by the time they leave engineering colleges. In view of the current general trends of increased internationalization and number of student exchange programmes on the one hand, and the apparent need for improved English language skills on the other, this paper describes various didactic approaches that may improve the English language competence of engineering students. The approaches have been tried on students within engineering areas such as Industrial Production Engineering, Mechanical Engineering, Biotechnology Engineering, etc.

Rationale

Thomas N. Huckin and Leslie A. Olsen say, "Scientists and engineers may be technically brilliant and creative, but unless they can convince co-workers, clients, and supervisors of their worth, their technical skills will be unnoticed, unappreciated, and unused. In a word, if technical people cannot communicate to others what they are doing and why it is important, it is they and their excellent technical skills that will be superfluous. From this perspective, communication skills are not just handy; they are critical tools for success, even survival, in 'real world' environments."

The truth in this statement becomes even more pressing in view of the current increasing internationalization of trade, commerce and industry. As English has become the lingua franca of international relations, tomorrow's engineers will need English language skills that are far above the skills that most engineering graduates have today. Recent research in India indicates that "the current Proficiency level of English is far below what is required of students entering higher education or engineering colleges. English is taught in primary and secondary schools. In engineering education, today, there is no importance given to English. It may therefore be assumed that the English language skills of future engineers in India will not improve drastically during their four year studies for the bachelor degree, even if all of the course books they read are in English."[2]

In an enquiry it is found that their current English language skills to be 'satisfactory' in their future profession. The total number of English hours should indicate that there is a potential for developing the students' language skills. However, after having listened to their use of English in class, it is our impression that the potential is not fully exploited and that the students overestimate their English language skills. Improved English language skills will enable engineers to keep abreast with recent developments in engineering areas. This is important in a 'life-long-learning' perspective as it may enable engineers to develop competences needed in new areas of engineering and for job opportunities in an international environment. It is equally important for engineering companies to have an engineering staff with good English language skills. They not only make good representatives but may also become an important asset in meetings and negotiations with foreign companies.

The need for improved English language skills among engineering students calls for strategies that develop adequate language skills that are related to their profession. It has been argued that introducing bilingual instruction or lectures in English are feasible alternatives for developing English language skills. Supporters of bilingual education have come up with numerous arguments in favour of using this method of instruction. However, the scepticism against bilingual education is also growing. Those in favour of using English as the language of instruction in higher education argue that the students' language competence will indirectly be improved. Their main reason for introducing lectures in English is, however, financially motivated. The two approaches are not designed for language learning in particular; they are primarily 'subject-oriented' and not 'language-oriented'. They may to some extent help develop the students' language skills and increase their vocabulary. However, as the language competence needed by our future engineers should be related to their profession, a language learning approach should be based on the activities that are relevant and typical of their profession in an international context. A language learning programme for engineering students will therefore have to improve not only the language skills as such, but will also have to enhance their cultural awareness so as to enable them to communicate adequately with colleagues from other nations.

Syllabus and Learning Material

Basically, the overall aim of an English language course for engineering students should be twofold: To develop the students' overall communicative competence and to lay the Foundation for further learning and refinement of language skills. In this respect, the syllabus, the learning targets, choice of learning material and didactic approaches should be relevant for the students' area of engineering. The teaching of English should be implemented in situations and contexts that are authentic; that mirror 'real-life' as closely as possible to enhance the importance and relevance of the classroom activities so as to ease the transfer of knowledge and skills to future real life situations. Learning targets commonly describe knowledge and skills areas of a subject. Assessment and grades express the level of the knowledge and skills that the students have achieved. Tests are used to offer the students an opportunity to demonstrate the level of knowledge and skills they have acquired. Tests and learning targets are closely linked. It goes without saying that the more precise the description of learning targets is, the easier it is to develop tests. Descriptions of learning targets should be precise with respect to skills and knowledge areas. Often it may be necessary to break down main learning targets into more detailed sub-targets and also to add examples to describe the targets accurately. Precise descriptions of learning targets and accurate linking between learning targets, assignments and assessment criteria will help students in their language learning and it will also make it easier for teachers when they design assignments.

The learning targets may consist of two main areas; the knowledge areas and the skills areas. The knowledge area has commonly included knowledge about countries such as the UK, the USA, Australia and the like where English is the national language. The learning targets have traditionally required the students to acquire knowledge about these countries, their history, people(s) and customs, for example. However, due to increased globalization, cultural knowledge as a learning target should be included and related to other countries, particularly countries that it is reasonable to assume that the engineering students will visit in the future as engineers. Cultural knowledge is important, and perhaps equally important as language skills, but need not be taught as a separate subject. It can be acquired when necessary and relevant. Information related to culture can be found on the Internet or in books and students should be asked to apply such information in various exercises. The overall aim of including cultural knowledge in a language course for engineering students should be to raise their awareness of the fact that people from different countries express themselves differently due to their cultural background. Language mistakes can be corrected or compensated for on the spot. Lack of cultural knowledge and awareness cannot. Networking and collaborating with colleagues and between students at other colleges may be a feasible means to acquire knowledge about other countries. I have tried it a few times, but not with the result I had hoped for due to various constraints. There is first of all the time difference between the colleges. This constraint may be overcome if students collaborate asynchronously. The greatest obstacle is the difference between the subjects the students are doing and the overall workload they have. Collaboration requires synchronization with respect to choice of subjects and didactic approaches, and should be planned between the teachers before the students are involved.

The skills area consists of four skills: Understanding written and oral communication, being able to communicate orally and in writing, in formal as well as in informal social settings or contexts. However, in most communicative situations and contexts, students will have to use their cultural knowledge. Language expressions are cultural expressions; they will contain and render implications that are culturally conditioned. They will indicate something about the culture you come from and the cultural knowledge you have about those you are talking to.

The learning material should cover the learning targets listed in the syllabus. Learning material for engineering students should primarily consist of authentic texts (i.e. texts written by engineers, for engineers, on engineering subjects but for other purposes than language instruction), and preferably written by native English speakers. As the students in their future profession will meet these types of text, the texts should be relevant for the particular area of engineering that the students are studying. The learning material should include documents, illustrations and graphic presentations used in contexts and situations that are typical of the students' area of engineering. Depending on the level of the students' language skills, authentic texts written in a national language and or in English by non-native English speakers can also be used for learning purposes.

Language Skills and Didactic Approaches

Didactics is very much a question of what we want to do in class, when, why and how we want to do it. It is a question of planning, structuring and integrating various activities for the purpose of enhancing the students' learning. The English language skills areas comprise the abilities of understanding oral and written English and being able to use English orally and in writing adequately in different contexts and for various purposes. In my teaching I have focused on developing the students' written language skills within genres such as memos and formal letters, reports (of varying length), writing documentation (as in brochures, manuals, procedure and process descriptions), and writing brief articles for journals, magazines and newspapers. Although there are many varieties of how these documents are set up, conventions and various standards indicate a common lay-out that is widely accepted internationally. Oral presentations and discussions in meetings and negotiations are adequate activities for developing the students' oral skills.

General Didactic Considerations

Learning a foreign language is a matter of language acquisition; students will incrementally acquire, practice and refine their language skills in accordance with their individual needs. Developing language skills is a matter of how to activate the students optimally in their work with adequate material, exercises and assignments in the classroom. Organizing the students in groups (in pairs or in groups of 3 or 4 students) is probably the most efficient method to activate all students as much as possible during class. Content specific English language course will inevitably cover the same formal aspects of English as we may find in a 'General English' course. Moreover, working with relevant authentic texts is highly motivating for the students.

In our classes we do not teach grammar 'for grammar's sake'. The students lack the 'meta-knowledge' of grammar and are in general mainly concerned with getting their language 'correct' without having to learn about grammar as such. Teaching grammar for grammar's sake will have no effect on developing their oral or written skills: "The study of traditional school grammar has no effect on raising the quality of student writing. . . . It will . . . do them a gross disservice[4]" Instead, the teacher should encourage students to use 'interactive grammar exercises' available on the Internet individually to improve their formal language skills.

The Authenticity of Classroom Activities

"The ideal authentic setting and context for learning activities within engineering would be to allocate students to a workplace that is relevant with respect to engineering area and to ask students to participate in some of the normal activities of the workplace,[5]" suggests Anne Blakeslee. Still, for most engineering colleges the classroom is where learning activities are organized. It is for this reason important to create an optimal level of 'authenticity' in classroom activities so that students experience the activities as authentic and relevant for their future profession. The activities should give students an understanding of workplace realities, and motivate their language acquisition. Visits to companies and talking to representatives may give students relevant knowledge of workplace writing practices.

Response

Teacher response and guidance during the students' language acquisition process—formative assessment—is an efficient means to inform them of the level of their skills and the quality of their work. Teachers should respond frequently to the students' work and their response should be implemented pedagogically. Responses should focus on a selection of aspects of the students' work and preferably make students reflect on their own work. Moreover, teachers' response should be based on and in line with requirements and assessment criteria. Involving students in setting up the requirements and criteria will enhance their awareness of the learning targets and the expected quality of their work. Student involvement in this respect may have a direct effect on their learning. Similarly, students may be asked to respond or comment on their peers' work. It is my experience that using peer response groups will involve all the students actively and is much more effective with respect to learning than using 'one-on-one' response. As with teacher response, students should have a clear and precise knowledge about the requirements for peer responses. The requirements will vary from one assignment to another but should be in line with some of the learning targets.

Developing Text Comprehension Skills

At work, engineers will read a variety of documents on technical subjects. Authentic documents written by native English speakers can be obtained upon request from local, national or international companies or from the Internet. Authentic documents as those mentioned previously will illustrate the use of vocabulary, sentence construction and lay out, and will give the students the opportunity to study how these elements are used in various types of documents. They may serve as 'models', but should rather—to my mind—serve as resources and examples that illustrate how English can be used in certain contexts and for certain purposes. Text comprehension will require knowledge of lay-out, vocabulary and sentence construction. But comprehension can also be extended by asking students about the context of the documents and their purpose. Authentic texts in national language or written in English by non-native English speakers can be used for language learning purposes. By comparing these texts with texts written by native English speakers, students may become aware of differences between the national language and English. Such a strategy will not merely extend their vocabulary, but may also enhance their awareness of the 'cultural' aspects and differences between the two languages. Moreover, if authentic texts written by native English speakers are used as examples, the students may acquire vocabulary and sentences construction that they may apply when they are writing their own texts on similar subjects and in similar contexts or situations. Thus, learning English becomes an active acquisition of language skills, and the differences between 'classroom' and 'workplace' activities may be reduced considerably which again may enhance the transfer of language skills from the classroom to the workplace.

Developing Oral Comprehension Skills

Developing comprehension skills with respect to oral discourse is an important part of foreign language learning. Oral communication is fast and will require not only a rich vocabulary and knowledge of sentence construction, but also some cultural knowledge about the people you are listening to. As spoken statements are very dependent on culture, situation and context, they should be understood or interpreted within the context they are spoken. Using videos (e.g. TV programmes on technical subjects, companies or product presentations) or sequences from films may give the students knowledge and examples of how language usage is culturally and contextually conditioned. TV-programmes and films in English with no translations or dubbing of what is spoken may be challenging, but is rewarding. The sequences may need to be played several times during which students should be asked to take notes in English and present briefs either in pairs or in front of class. Cultural aspects may be subject for discussions in class.

Developing Oral Skills

Developing good oral skills is a complex activity and probably the most difficult part of foreign language learning. It involves not merely being able to pronounce words correctly, using appropriate vocabulary, and developing a good fluency and sentence construction. It is also a matter of using cultural knowledge and adapting statements to the context, the situation and intention. In meetings and negotiations, applying appropriate language skills as well as cultural knowledge to keep up a conversation is essential. Failure to do so may make or break the communication. Far too often, students use inappropriate language or the 'language of films' uncritically and indiscriminately when communicating with foreigners with no awareness of context or the cultural background of the people they are communicating with.

The simplest activity for developing oral skills is asking students to practise reading out loud in pairs. This activity can be applied to texts, but should also be applied to reading symbols, equations and formulae used in mathematics, physics and chemistry, for example. It is my impression that teachers of English do not always give students time to practise this skill, and lack of fluency in this respect may cause misunderstanding. Activities that aim at developing oral skills can be based on written material at an early stage in the language course, and later combined with comprehension of oral communication. Alternating between developing written and oral skills is efficient for language learning purposes as the two skills areas mutually affect each other. Students may be given an authentic text to study, but instead of asking the teacher for information with regard to vocabulary, sentence construction, use of paragraphs and general lay out, they may first ask their classmates for information in English before they address the teacher for help. They may then be asked to talk about the text (e.g. its background or purpose). This oral activity may be followed up with various types of writing activity (e.g. write a summary or a similar text based on background information given by the teacher).

Oral presentations will involve various activities such as writing, reflection and structuring (e.g. setting up notes). This activity gives the students time to prepare their oral presentation which again has a positive impact on developing their oral fluency. Oral presentations may also cover a wide range of other engineering related subjects (e.g. company presentations, staff and their company positions and responsibilities, product ranges, manufacturing processes, exports and trade relations).

Role play is another activity that students love to do and may be applied to many different situations and settings (e.g. working in pairs like 'guide-tourist', 'instructor-apprentice', 'visitor-information officer'). Role play requires role cards; information that the students will need to act out a particular character. Role cards may contain information about the characters (e.g. age, educational background, job position, situation, context), but students may also be asked to add more information or invent their own characters. Using role play as an activity may give teachers a means to create different 'cultural contexts' in which students may practice their language skills and cultural competence. As most other 'classroom' activities, role play cannot replace a 'real life' situation, but it may give students an opportunity to prepare for such situations.

Videos in the national language can also be used and can be obtained from local or national companies. The sequences shown in class should not be longer than 5-10 minutes; 15 minutes at the most. The oral activities may comprise asking students to do oral summaries of the video (or parts of it) in English, or discussing the subject or product presented in the video or asking them to render in English the contents of the video sequence.

Developing Writing Skills

The engineering profession—as with most other professional activities—is becoming increasingly 'writing-oriented'. It is this reason important therefore to focus on developing the students' writing skills. Engineers will have to proofread, correct or edit documents written by others, and they will have to be able to write these types of documents themselves. As indicated above, authentic documents can be used as 'model' documents. To my mind, however, they should be looked upon and used as learning resources which the students should study and use as examples.

This paper addresses the question of how to improve English language skills of non-native English-speaking engineering students; it does not propose strategies for the teaching of technical writing skills or how to teach writing professional documents as in 'technical communication courses'. The focus is on teaching English writing conventions with respect to genres. Good writing—and also technical writing—is situational and contextual. This also applies to various types of text or genres—literary as well as technical genres. Genres establish the conventions that students must learn and practise in order to communicate professionally, and are commonly defined in terms of formal features. Thus user manuals or academic papers have different features, but texts within one genre may also be different due to the context, situation and purpose when they were written. Knowledge about genres and the conventions that characterize or shape them is important because these conventions in many ways set the standards and the features that readers expect to find. Breaking these conventions may disrupt communication.

As communication is a social act involving two parties, language activities which ask students to address someone, should contain information with respect to a receiver or an audience. Different audiences—and different intentions or purpose—will demand different communication styles. When doing their written assignments, students should apply their knowledge of text types and be asked to adhere to the conventions that are typical of different texts. It is not unreasonable to spend more time on developing writing skills than on the other three skills. The advantage with writing activities is that they give the students time to reflect and check what they are writing so as to be able to correct it. Writing is also an activity that supports the development of oral skills. Writing exercises—and preferably short ones—should be given frequently and should be on relevant technological subjects (e.g. brief summaries of research article, newspaper articles, technical reports, minutes of meetings, product presentations). During the writing process, the groups write, revise and edit the documents several times in line with responses from teacher, peers or peer-response groups. Avoid giving long lectures or talks in class. Instead, allow the students to explore material and inquire or seek information with respect to the problems they have. If the students are working with documents (e.g. a user manual) written in their native language, they may be asked to render—not to translate—the contents of documents in English. This activity gives the students a bit more freedom to paraphrase than a 'word-for-word' translation. As a follow-up, they may be asked to use the rendered text to write a similar document as the original one in the national language using the appropriate writing conventions. The final stage may be to study, collect and use relevant vocabulary from similar documents written by native English speakers in their own document. This series of activities will make the students focus on the language used by native English speakers and the context and purpose of their own document.

Conclusion

Offering our engineering students the opportunity to develop adequate and comprehensive English language skills is increasingly becoming a necessity. Failure to do so is doing our students a disservice as they will need these skills in their studies as well as in their future profession. Various strategies have been launched in this respect. Although bilingual instruction or lectures in English are feasible alternatives for developing English language skills, the two methods are primarily 'subject-oriented'. In order to develop the language skills of our engineering students, a compulsory English language learning programme be incorporated in their studies. The language programme should have as its overall aim and focus the development of the language skills that engineering students will need in their future profession as engineers. As engineers will communicate—orally and in writing—for different purposes and in different contexts and situations, the language programme should allow for activities that are as close to authentic, real life situations as possible. Similarly, the use of authentic learning material may enhance their language acquisition and offer the students an opportunity to develop a language competence that they may further refine in their professional life.

References

1. Huckin, Thomas N. and Olsen, Leslie A. 1991. "Technical Writing and Professional Communication for Nonnative Speakers of English," McGraw-Hill International Editions, P. 3.
2. Hellekjær, Glenn O.2005. "The Acid Test: Does Upper Secondary EFL Instruction Effectively Prepare Norwegian Students for the Reading of English Textbooks at Colleges and Universities?" A dissertation submitted at the Faculty of Humanities, University of Oslo, Norway, p. 72.
3. McArthur, Tom, 2006. "World English and world Englishes: Trends, tensions, varieties, and standards," in *Language Teaching*, 34, 2001, pp.1-20, http://ltsc.ph-karlsruhe.de/McArthur.pdf Accessed March.17
4. Hillocks, George, Jr., "What Works in Teaching Composition: A Meta analysis of Experimental Treatment Studies," *American Journal of Education*, November 1984, pp. 133- 170.
5. Blakeslee, Ann M., "Bridging the Workplace and the academy: Teaching Professional Genres through Classroom-Workplace Collaborations," in *Technical Communication Quarterly*, spring 2001, groups) of technical subjects. Vol.10, No 2, pp. 169-192.

Teaching Language Learning Strategies to the Undergraduate Students: A Case Study in ELT

J. MADHAVI

Language is a purely human and non-instinctive method of communicating ideas, emotions and desires by means of a system of voluntarily produced symbols.

Edward Sapir

There are three functions of language. They are as follows:

i. Informative function: To convey information.

ii. Expressive function: To express feelings, emotions or attitudes and evoke similar responses in the community\audience\other person.

iii Directive function: To cause or prevent actions.

Nature of Language and its Influence on Teaching

Man is the only living being who is gifted with the ability to speak/ communicate with his fellow beings, thus sharing his ideas, expressions, feelings etc. This power of language helps him to influence others and establish relationships. Every language is unique and has a world of its own regarding the set of sound patterns, set of grammatical signals, of syntax or vocabulary. Therefore the learner of the language has to make strenuous efforts to master it.

Proper understanding of the nature of language and the way it is learnt results in good teaching and sound educational policy. For i.e. it has been found that language system has led to selection and grading of structures and vocabulary. Language is primarily speech and this led to the oral work in classroom teaching. Since language changes from time to time, the teaching of descriptive grammar is preferred to prescriptive grammar.

Presents Status of English in India

English occupies an important place in the educational system and life of our country. It is an international language, which opens worldwide chances for employment and is responsible for cultural give and take. English forms a window on the rapid progress of technology and scientific knowledge that is constantly taking place in the world. English is a link language in India. It forms the basis for communication between the people of different states. The trade between two states is carried out mostly through English. Thus the importance of English is widely recognized in India.

Methodology in Imparting Language

The old and new teaching methods have sometimes amalgamated to form a new method or approach in teaching language. The educationalists put forth many methods and approaches to overcome the falling standards of English in India. They also suggested in selecting the best method on the basis of the learner's as well as the teacher's needs.

There should be something lacking behind this poor learning of English language. The learners are not encouraged to participate completely in a class. Indian teachers do fail to recognize the methods, which the learners want to adopt in learning. The teacher should not be a focal agent spreading knowledge widely but should be a mere facilitator. Researchers too say that the learners must be given a chance and freedom to apply their own ways in learning. This will surely lead to the successful learning of the language. As a result the learners try to find out easy ways, tricks or methods to make their learning easy. These methods or ways employed in learning are otherwise known as strategies. By applying these strategies the learners learn the language perfectly and remain in their memory forever.

Thus, instead of learning the language by depending completely on the teachers and his/her own selected methods, it is better to learn the language by applying their own methods seeking a little help from the teacher. Therefore, it is the responsibility of all the teachers in English to train the learners in strategies so that both teaching and learning becomes successfully effective and easy. A learner-centred approach is more effective in the context of teaching language. This led to the study of the actual means or strategies employed by the learners during the process of learning. An innovative teacher should always identify, encourage the strategies, which his/her learners use, and promote an effective use of new strategies by the students.

Language Learning Strategies

"Learning strategy is a choice that the learner makes while learning or using the L2 that affects learning." (Vivian Cook 1991). Learning Strategies are divided into General Learning Strategies and Language Learning Strategies.

General Learning Strategies

Danseraeu's Taxonomy of Strategies

According to Donald Danseraeu, the research studies on learning strategies can be divided into two broad categories. They are a) The primary strategies and b) The support strategies.

Primary strategies include

i) Identification
ii) Comprehension
iii) Retention
iv) Retrieval (Utilization).

Support strategies are further divided as follows:

i) Establishing an appropriate learning attitude.
ii) Concentration (in the presence of distraction, fatigue, frustration etc).
iii) Monitoring and checking the primary strategies.

Language Learning Strategies

Apart from the research studies, which attempted to identify the major strategies employed by people for learning any subject in general; there are studies that focused on language learning strategies

O'Malley's and Chamot's Classification of Strategies

On the basis of their extensive research on learning strategies within an overall model of L2 learning based on cognitive psychology, O'Malley and Chamot (1990) classified three main types of strategies used by L2 students. They are:

i) Meta cognitive strategies.
ii) Cognitive strategies.
iii) Social strategies.

Rebecca Oxford's Classification of Strategies

Rebecca L. Oxford (1990) provides a detailed discussion of different languages learning strategies and suggests how these strategies can be applied to the four basic language skills (i.e., LSRW). Major varieties of language learning strategies are cognitive, mnemonic, metacognitive, compensatory (for writing and speaking), affective and social.

Rebecca Oxford classifies language-learning strategies into two broad categories: i) Direct strategies. ii) Indirect strategies

The direct strategies are further sub-classified into memory strategies, cognitive strategies and compensation strategies whereas the indirect strategies are divided into meta-cognitive strategies, affective strategies and social strategies. Again each of the three in the two broad categories is further divided. This may be shown in a table as follows:

Direct strategies.	Indirect strategies:
a) Memory strategies:	a) Meta cognitive strategies:
i) Creating mental linkages.	i) Centring your Learning.
ii). Applying images and sounds.	ii) Arranging and planning
iii) Reviewing well your learning.	iii) Monitoring and evaluating your learning.
iv) Employing action.	

b) Cognitive strategies:	b) Affective strategies;
i) Practising.	i). Lowering your anxiety.
ii) Receiving and sending messages	ii) Encouraging your self.
iii) Analyzing and reasoning.	iii) Taking your emotional temperature
iv) Creating structure for input	

and output

c)	Compensation strategies	c)	Social strategies:
i)	Guessing intelligently.	i)	Asking questions.
ii)	Overcoming limitations in speaking and writing.	ii)	Cooperating with others
iii)	Empathizing with others.		

The first major class, Direct Strategies for dealing with the new language, is like the performer in a stage play, working with the language itself in a variety of specific tasks and situations. The direct class is composed of memory strategies for remembering and retrieving new information, cognitive strategies for understanding and producing the language and compensation strategies for using the language despite knowledge gaps. The performer works closely with the Director for the best possible outcome.

The second major class, Indirect Strategies for general management of learning can be treated as the Director of the play. This class is made up of metacognitive strategies for coordinating the learning process, affective strategies for regulating emotions and social strategies for learning with others (Rebecca Oxford, 1990). In this new learner-centred approach, the teacher has to encourage the students to take on the functions of the Director at least overtly, which have been reserved earlier for the teacher.

Elaine Tarone (1980) emphasizes social aspects of communication. She sees three overall types of strategy communication, production and learning. All the above strategies can be shown in a tabular from as below.

Socially Motivated Strategies for Solving Natural lack of Understanding (Tarone, 1980):

i. Paraphrase (approximation, word coinage, circumlocution).
ii. Falling back on L1 translation, language switch, appeal for assistance, mime.
iii Avoidance.

Psychologically Motivated Strategies for Solving the Individual's L2 problems of Expression (Faerch and Kasper1984):

1. Achievement strategies:
a. Cooperative strategies (similar to list above).

b. Non-Cooperative strategies.
i) Code Switching.
ii) Foreignerisation.
iii) Interlanguage strategies (substitution, generalization, description, exemplification, word coining, restructure).

2. Avoidance Strategies:
a. Formal (phonological, morphological, grammatical).
b. Functional (actional, propositional, modal).

3. Archistrategies to Compensate for Lack of Vocabulary (Eric Kellerman et.al 1987).
i) Approximative (substitutes one word for another).
ii) Analytic (describes the properties of the object in question).
iii) Linguistic (uses something from the L1 instead).

Advantages and Features of Practicing Learner Strategies:

i) They contribute to the main goal, communicative competence.
ii) They allow learners to become more self-directed.
iii) They expand the role of teachers.
iv) They are problem oriented.
v) They are specific actions taken by the teacher.
vi) They involve many aspects of the learners not just the Cognitive.
vii) They support learning both directly and indirectly.
viii) They are not always observable.
ix) They are often conscious.
x) They can be taught.
xi) They are flexible.
xii) They are influenced by a variety of factors.

Thus it is clearly understood that strategies organize information into usable, meaningful units, although the repertoire of stored and available strategies may differ from person to person. How can teachers make use of learning strategies? Weaker students always depend mostly on the teacher and are least able to fend for themselves. Partly this can be achieved through "Learner training," equipping the students with the means to guide themselves by explaining strategies to them.

There are different approaches followed by the learners in learning L2. The strategies adopted by them may be cognitive, metacognitive, social, affective, etc. There are many advantages in following the methods, which give scope to the new strategies. Learners can employ many strategies at a time so that they make their learning easy. All the above-discussed strategies make the learner more self-directed, goal-directed, controlled, and self-sufficient, etc. The four basic skills (LSRW) do involve some of the significant strategies. For instance, Reading process involves three main strategies. They are Predicting, Confirming and Integrating. Reading, Reading Evaluation and Reading-Instruction form the major elements in reading curriculum.

Strategy Training-Background

Teaching strategies entail giving training to the learners in adopting different strategies and helping the students to use them in their learning and making learning more easy and effective. These in turn, help them to develop their basic language skills viz. listening, speaking, reading and writing. The main purpose of giving training in this area is to make the learners learn English as a language rather than a subject.

By the end of the 1970s, researchers started recognizing that simply by using certain memory aids, it is not possible to wipe out the inefficiencies in learning and problem-solving. Thus, there was a great emphasis on the monitoring and regulatory activities of cognition and the introduction of these higher-order operations viz. information-processing theory, Process-based information, etc. as also strategy training studies.

From the information-processing viewpoint, learning becomes the process of learning, which involves

i) Paying attention to what is to be learned;
ii) Learning by rote or by understanding concepts and processes;
iii) Controlling the rate or the quality of learning; and
iv) Being aware that learning has taken place.

Using an information processing approach, the notion of individual differences in learning becomes a relevant and important concept. Moreover, we can examine the automatic or conscious processing of information by students and catalogue their strengths and weaknesses, not in terms of learning outcome, but by reference to the cognitive systems that mediate learning.

Information Processing Approach (IPA)

"IPA which is a major theoretical and practical framework describes how humans think. It describes the attainment of concepts and reasoning skills in terms of how we acquire, organize, store and retrieve information. Information processing theory allows for the diagnosis of learning difficulties in terms of both cognitive and affective variables" (Ashman and Conway, 1989). It has been studied about different instruction-based approaches. These methods or approaches will definitely help the teacher to carry out the strategy-training program easily, effectively and successfully. The selection of strategies is highly dependent on the needs of the learners.

According to Meichenbaum's Verbal Self-Instruction Model, a teacher can instruct the students to work through a series of self-instruction steps to facilitate learning and problem solving. This model has been widely used to meet the needs of the students who experience difficulty in L2 acquisition.

The unique contribution of information processing comes from identification of individual strengths and weakness in the use of the storage, retrieval and organizational mechanism, that is, the processes, strategies and skills that operate as cognitions. Gelzheiser's training program provides explicit skill training, use of incentives to encourage proficiency, to enhance self-regulatory activity among the learners.

Meichenbaum's Five-step training sequence throws light on both cognitive and behavioural influences. Strategy training, in general, is a cognitive influence that allows students to learn an appropriate strategy to deal with specific problem. Identification and Development and Assessment of the trainable learning strategies and their effectiveness in using these strategies are followed in a stepwise manner by Dansereau in his training sequence program.

Frank Richardson's Model of training strategies includes eight stages, like setting of specific goals for the cause of learning/ training, initial self-assessment skills and preparation, on-going self-evaluation or self-correction etc. There are six different types of activities involved in training each strategy, namely, simulation, strategy instruction, strategy application, etc. Most of the research studies established a positive impact of training in the use of the learner strategies.

Strategies Development and Its Use

This is the main teaching phase of some of the modern approaches, such as, PBI, principled approach, and a communicative approach. Strategy development in regard to PBI will focus the attention towards a playful behaviour, rather than curriculum content. In adopting this approach, there is no point of minimizing or dismissing content. Rather, it is acknowledged that the teacher will have completed a task analysis that will ensure that the content presented is at the appropriate level. The intention is to emphasize how the integration of content and teaching strategy is achieved.

The strategy Development phase involves a three-step cycle: state the specific plan; enact that plan; restate the plan. The teacher continues the cycle until the students are able to demonstrate their ability to use the plan and appropriate coding strategy on blackboard or work sheet examples. The teacher should determine the level of proficiency required to more to the next phase of instruction.

Competencies vary participant to participant and among the groups. The complexity of the situation demands a different approach in which the specific and the general (or common) needs are first. Analyzed in detail and then, a syllabus designed to equip learners with language skills that would be used not only in predictable situations but also those situations which the learner would meet in his life time. This is what has been termed as- 'Strategic Competence'.

Strategy development and strategy use is directly proportional to the language proficiency. That is, greater the strategy use, higher the language proficiency levels. Language strategies are teachable and the effectiveness of the strategy instruction appears to relate itself to cultural background, beliefs, content and presentation of the instruction. Strategy instruction should be integrated as a part of the regular class. Many factors influence the strategy use, namely, motivation, learning style and personality type, career orientation, etc.

The learners try to adopt the strategies according to their requirements and needs. The learner needs may be classified as academic, personnel and professional needs. When these needs are noticed and considered important, then only the active participation of the students is possible which give scope to the birth of new strategies. Simulation and Gaming is considered as an active language teaching strategies and these promote student's initiative, motivation, self-direction and skill.

A Model Programme in Training Learner Strategies

In teaching strategies a teacher can adopt different methods. The method, which is followed in this study, can be demonstrated as follows. Prepare a short-term study programme for teaching or training in learner strategies in one or two colleges. The learners of second language (L2-English) are divided into two homogenous groups. That is, the learners of both the groups are on par in every aspect such as, age, class, etc. They are: i) A controlled group, and ii) An experimental group.

At first both these groups are tested. The results are to be compared. The performance of both these groups is found to be more or less same. Later the experimental group will be provided with training in learner strategies. After a short gap a common test is administered to both the groups and their performances will be compared. The hypothesis underlined this study is that learners trained in using learner strategies will perform better in the examination than those learners (controlled group) who did not receive any training in learner strategies.

Primary data will include the details of the proposed experiment and results of the performance of the learners and related works, research articles on learner strategies. Secondary data will be drawn from books, dissertations and articles in journals in the field of English Language Teaching (ELT).

Strategy Training-Present Case Study

Taking into consideration all that has been discussed in previous chapters, the learners were practically given an opportunity to make use of the newly learnt as well as their previous strategies in the process of language learning thus developing their language competence. The learners were given freedom in choosing any type of strategy i.e. either cognitive or metacognitive or any thing else. But it was taken care that they arrive at an acceptable solution.

Learner's Performance:

As discussed under methodology in chapter three, the same process has been applied in testing the students regarding the language skills, such as listening, writing and reading skills. The first test was administered for both the groups of ECE- Branch neither of them were given any training in strategies, on the same day and in successive periods, to develop their listening skill. After correction of the responses/answers it was found that the results were not up to the mark. Even the most intelligent student made simple mistakes. From the next day onwards only ECE- A group had been given training in strategies, which were to be employed in the process of listening.

The students, then, were asked to discuss their performance in test-1 looking at the corrected papers. The students were suggested some strategies to be used or followed while listening. Some of these strategies suggested are: they should make themselves relaxed and comfortable, calm and attentive while the selected material is read out. At this moment the teacher also takes care that the students are motivated properly so that they can participate actively in the classroom.

In the process of selecting the materials there had been a gradual increase in the quality and intensity of the material.

After a gap of ten days, the second test was administered to the experimental group or the trained group ECE-A and the controlled group or the untrained group ECE-B. Later, on correcting the papers of both the groups it was found that the students of experimental group ECE-A improved more than 70% in the second test when compared to the test-1, while the controlled group ECE-B marked up to 45% only. There was hardly any improvement in ECE-B, the untrained group. The same method was applied in testing the reading and the writing skills also.

Interpretation

The strategies that were discussed with the trained group and those, which the students used while listening, are as follows:

- At first the class should maintain silence.
- Everyone must make himself or herself feel comfortable and try to be attentive.
- While listening they should be careful in grasping some important words.
- It may be impossible to write down the important words or phrases as they are. Therefore, their own abbreviations and certain symbols can be used some times.
- They should listen to the passage carefully and decide the theme that is being discussed in the passage.
- It is important to remember all those points or words, which are concerned with the main topic.

These strategies helped the experimental group in acquiring new technology to be successful in the second language class compared to the controlled group, which is unaware of these strategies.

The strategies were discussed with the trained group and those, which the students used while writing, were as follows:

i) Find out the tense used in the paragraph after reading it thoroughly.
ii) Then find out the word in the paragraph to confirm your answer.
iii) Do you think that this paragraph describes a process, which is not time bound?
iv) Find out the subject used here is time bound or not time bound.

v) Find out whether the sentences of the paragraph are in passive voice or active voice.

The students of the experimental group were trained in the above-mentioned strategies for about a week. During this program the same test i.e. test-1 was conducted and the results were above the average. The students too were showing interest in applying strategies in writing. They also started thinking to find out many more new strategies to employ them in the process of effective learning. After a gap of ten days another test i.e. test-2 was administered to both the groups. The anticipation of solving the test exercise correctly, efficiently and quickly was found in the students of the trained group rather than the untrained or controlled group. The reason for this sort of behavior is due to the lack of knowledge in applying strategies in language learning.

As a result of the cues provided, almost all the students of the experimental group successfully answered the exercise. They used the cues that were discussed with them.

The strategies followed in solving the reading exercises are as follows:

- What is the central idea of the passage?
- Pick out few words that confirm your answer.
- After reading the passage do you find any resemblance with your experience in the college?
- Skimming the questions would help to find out the theme of the passage.
- After reading the passages try to understand the meaning of certain difficult words on the basis of the content. This would be possible through the translation of the sentences of the passage into the reader's own words.
- The student must see that his/her predictions about the passage are confirmed. Then they must try to remember the information that is passed on and try to integrate all the relevant points to confirm their answer.
- If the word socializing is to be defined, firstly it is under stood that the word has some close link with the society. On this basis it is easier to answer the question.

- Narrator actually wants to say, most indirectly that the questions like true or false, tests the student's concentrating power. Skimming and scanning are to be followed to answer such type of questions.
- The exclamatory marks, capital letters in the middle of the sentence, quotations, etc., will stress the meaning, which the narrator actually wants to reveal.

Before the second test in developing writing skills was conducted, the first test was discussed with the experimental group. They were given training in strategies. As a part of this the cues or strategies that would be applicable in solving test-I paper were also taught. Regarding the first test the students were provided with the certain cues. After receiving training the students followed the same process in answering the questions of test-2. There was a lot of improvement in these students when compared to the students of controlled group. Similarly, the students too were enthusiastic in adopting/using different strategies to solve test-2 paper.

Strategies used to improve the Listening Skills of the Students

- At first the student should be motivated to the possible extent, so that he or she shows eagerness and anxiety to learn the language. As a result they come to the class regularly and can participate actively in the process of learning L2.
- Casual strategies include being silent, concentrating etc. Never take notes when the material is readout. This may cause confusion in understanding what is read out and there will be a chance of missing some important information.
- Empathetic strategies: As the material is readout, it would be better to close the eyes for it helps to concentrate deeply on the theme of the material. There is no need to worry about the meanings of the new or difficult words in the material. Instead try to point out the topic that is discussed and answer the questions on general understanding.
- Intensive strategies: Once the idea of the general topic is known, then try to listen for more details, such as, a specific

name of a person or place and several other activities that are discussed besides the definitions and examples mentioned.

- Selective strategies: In the initial stage of listening, if the learner finds it unclear, there is a chance to get to the main idea or theme of the material by reading the questions based on the material.
- Body language cues and Visual cues: The theme and also the meaning of some of the words and sentences can be predicted from the body and visual movements.
- Listening comprehension section is designed to test the learners' listening ability at first, and reading ability next. That is, after listening to the material, the learner is supposed to answer the comprehension questions. In this context, he or she, instead of reading the whole answer-choices, can skim through them and whichever word appears more than once in the answer choices will give a cue about the theme of the paragraph and will help the learner to answer the questions easily, with the given time.

Strategies used in improving Reading Skills of the Learner

The major reading strategies like predicting, confirming and integrating are considered first and all other strategies that are discovered from the fragments of those strategies only. These strategies have been discussed in detail in the second chapter. Besides these the other strategies in which the training was given are as follows:

- The first strategy to adopt is that, read the passage carefully and note down some of the important points or words from it.
- While skimming the passage, the learner has to look for the names of the persons, places, events, dates, etc.
- Read out the questions given and also the answer-choices, if there are and try to answer as soon as you feel it to be correct.
- Since time keeps ticking, the learner skims the questions and answer those questions first which he or she knows.
- The meaning of the difficult words can be predicted by learning the meanings of the prefixes and root words. For example: Take a word 'International'. Here the prefix is 'inter' and its

meaning is 'between'. Therefore the meaning of the word 'international' would be 'between the nations'.

Strategies Used in Improving Writing Skill

Sequencing of ideas, use of linkers at right places, writing down the topic sentence clearly, maintenance of unity and coherence of the paragraph, the form of tense used, singular or plural form of the words, etc. are some of the most commonly adopted strategies in writing. The writing strategies in which the training was given, in addition to those, which have been discussed under writing skill development, are as follows:

- Firstly, read the question thoroughly and try to understand what is to be written.
- Secondly, underline the topic asked and the main words that tell what to write and how to write.
- Thirdly, when the perspective is clear then proceed for writing. After writing the answer, scan it quickly.
- Read the whole passage thoroughly and find out whether the given passage is time bound or not. If it is not time bound then simple present tense should be used.
- Consider the voice of the sentences; accordingly write the correct form of the words.

Methodology of Evaluation

Strategies were taught to the students to improve their language skills by taking some of the examples and providing them the thought cues wherever it was necessary. For example: To identify the meaning of certain word in the given passage for reading, the learner has to see whether the word is free of suffixes or prefixes. If yes, then through the content given in the passage the meaning can be guessed intelligently. Here, comes the use of compensation strategies.

If the word is suffixed or prefixed for example, in the word 'International' the meaning of the prefix 'inter' is 'in between'. Therefore the meaning of the word can be guessed as "in between the nations."

For any task to be solved i.e. if a learner is to be tested in Listening skill, then it is to see that the learner gets trained to make himself comfortable and relaxed and could concentrate more if the eyes are closed. After the passage is readout, s/he has to answer the questions followed. The cognitive strategies play a vital role here. Before answering the questions the learner must analyze and reason out the correct answer.

If the learner reads a passage consisting of difficult words and moreover if the passage is describing a thing or an event then the learner at first should translate the sentences into his own words and think or imagine the thing or an event that is described. By applying memory strategies s/he will be quite successful in understanding the passage.

Before the learner goes for a task, s/he must carefully plan about how to proceed, what to learn first then next and so on and think of the shortest, easiest and fastest method of learning. The metacognitive strategies play an active role in such situations.

After preparing a systematic plan for effective learning, s/he must be cool and confident without any tension or frustration. Self-encouragement is necessary besides asking and discussing the answers with others in learning.

Based on the above points the learners were encouraged to solve exercises that provided a large scope for adopting and following some of the known strategies in solving the problems correctly. During this, some hints or thought cues must be provided to guide them passively.

In this research the strategies dealt were different from those strategies, which are employed to learn the content that is, poetry, prose or grammar. The learners were given training in those strategies, which can be adopted to develop the four language skills. All the strategies discussed in this context are applied in a way to improve the language skills, such as listening, reading and writing. The hypothesis, which said that the learners who received training in strategies would perform better than those who did not receive any training in strategies, has been proved to be satisfactory and correct.

After conducting tests with great care and on the basis of the learners' performance, it can be concluded that those who received training in strategies can learn the language quickly, easily and effectively. A student can think of using strategies only when he or she is mentally prepared, that is, the student should be motivated first, so that he or she can actively participate in the L2 classroom. It is also found that classroom learning, which is only a part of the students' education, is just the beginning. Learning should always push the student beyond the classroom and stimulate him or her to explore that which has yet to be revealed. And this can be achieved only by the successful use of strategies in learning.

Results and Pedagogical findings of the Study

In this study, it was found important to note that there is the anticipation of the learners towards learning English as L2. This can be achieved through proper motivation. Motivation is nothing but encouraging the students to participate in the class completely. That is, a deep interest should be created within the learners so that they themselves show eagerness in learning L2 as quickly as possible. This motivation may be instrumental or integrative.

Once the learner is motivated, the teaching would become definitely easier and effective. Within the L2 class, due to the learners' active participation, there will be a scope for implementing new strategies. By using these strategies, the learners seem to be more interested than before and are found very much enthusiastic to learn English. Motivation along with the other two cognitive domains has an important impact on students' learning and successful problem solving.

The important point to be remembered here is that the teacher must be equally active, motivated, enthusiastic besides possessing profound knowledge of strategies as well as efficient enough to carry out the process of imparting training in strategies successfully. The teacher would be successful to the utmost in a teaching situation where there is a broad scope for the golden independent opportunities for the learners to learn L2 on their own, using their own methods or strategies. The teacher must be a mere facilitator and guide the students wherever it is necessary and direct them towards success in L2 class passively or indirectly. In this type of atmosphere, it was found that the learners, who formed the centre of the class, were independent and this freedom enjoyed by them showed a very good impact on their learning.

The teacher playing a passive role would definitely encourage the students to play an active role in the class. The students provided with training, had performed very well in the test when compared to those who did not receive any training in strategies. In the listening task, the motivated learners followed wherever possible, all the available strategies, which would make them successful. In the listening section the teacher should adjust the volume/tone before s/he begins. This can help in attracting the learners' concentration fully.

To improve the reading skill, the learners need intensive practice in reading a variety of materials, including newspaper, magazines and short excerpts from the textbooks. Moreover, they need to check their comprehension and time themselves carefully. In this reading section, learners try to use more time on reading the passages and less time in reading directions.

In improving writing skills, the selection of topic should be helpful for the learners so as to order their thoughts in a proper way. The learners must prepare a study plan to bring about the unity, coherence and cohesiveness in their writing, especially in essay writing. Instead of wasting time in thinking about how to complete the test, it is better to use every moment to organize and write. Grading systems are to be developed by the teachers, which makes them more alert to their teaching situations.

As it is learnt that training or teaching learner strategies will help the learners learn L2 without much difficulty, it is necessary to train the learners in using strategies and an intensive research is necessary in this direction. Though the research has been in progress but it has to go a long way to get deep rooted in order to make L2 learning easy and successful. It was found that the learners when worked in groups promoted the excessive use of existing strategies and the invention of new strategies thus making L2 class very interesting, enjoyable, encouraging and effective.

Since the present research work was carried out with heterogeneous groups of students of varying degrees of proficiency, some of the strategies worked successfully with some of the students. The learners were divided into three levels:

Level One: This includes below average students who require more time to be trained in strategies. They were able to solve the task by making use of memory strategies under direct strategies category. They are as applying images and sounds, creating mental linkages, reviewing and employing action. They also used affective and social strategies under indirect strategies category. These students needed more training in practicing strategies.

Level Two: This includes the average students. These learners were active enough to understand what was taught quite easily and quickly after receiving training in strategies. They took less time to employ strategies in language learning compared to level one students. Most of these learners used metacognitive, affective and social strategies under indirect strategies and cognitive and memory strategies that come under the direct strategies category. They performed better in the tests administered after the training program.

Level Three: This includes above average students. Some of the learners of this level performed better in the tests conducted even before they received training in strategies. They hardly committed any mistake. They even tried to predict some of the strategies that were not taught such as, in writing task, some of the students suggested that if the word is a verb and it is not time bound then the blanks in the sentences can be filled with the words in simple present tense. These learners adopted almost all the strategies of two categories and employed them easily and effectively in the process of learning.

From the above, it can be learnt that the training program in strategies entirely depends on the students' level of proficiency and knowledge of L2. Therefore, it is recommended that the weak students or the below average students should be trained separately providing sufficient time for practicing the use of strategies in language learning. Later these three levels of students can be mixed up where the above average students can be asked to help the weaker students.

Suggested method of teaching strategies to in-service/ prospective teachers

Firstly, a teacher must be active and comfortable to motivate the students. Teaching a motivated class is always more effective. Secondly, the teacher must help the learners indirectly in the process of learning. That is, a passive role of the teacher would definitely lead to the active participation of the learners in an L2 class. In this situation, the learners also feel self-secured and a sense of responsibility assigned to them is felt.

The teacher must be equally active, motivated, and enthusiastic besides possessing accurate knowledge of strategies as well as efficient enough to carry out the process of imparting training in strategies successfully. The teacher would be successful to the utmost in a teaching situation if there is a broad scope for the opportunities for the learners to learn L2 on their own, using their own methods or strategies.

Conclusion

In this study, it was found that the students were more concerned with how to learn rather than with what to learn. They were found interested in the communicative dimensions of language learning rather than with the grammar of the language. They were concerned much with the discourse errors rather than the sentence errors. Also, as a result of the awareness of their purpose of learning English, as a second language, students were more eager to seek opportunities to use English beyond the classroom.

It can be concluded that an awareness and use of the strategies would definitely help the learners to be successful in the L2 class. Theoretical aspects, such as, the various types of strategies and the intensive training in strategies were observed to be affective with respect to the results. Regarding the hypothesis, which said that those who trained in strategies were more successful and performed well in the tasks administered than those who did not receive any training in strategies, it can be said that the hypothesis is valid. Through constant practice in using as well as in acquiring knowledge of strategies, the L2 learners can develop their four language skills and can excel themselves in this regard. It was found that when a learner is motivated positively and the teacher is only a facilitator, s/he finds a lot of scope to think of new strategies independently and avail the opportunity of using them extensively in their language learning, thus making the language learning easy and effective. English is the key to the storehouse of knowledge. Therefore all teachers should be able to teach English well with the use of different, suitable strategies. The students need to be so trained that they try to learn the language independently with the aid of effective learning strategies.

Bibliography

Anderson, J. 1983. *The Architecture of Cognition.* Cambridge, Mass: Harvard University Press.

Asher, J.J. 1966. "The Learning Strategy of the Total Physical Response: A Review." *Modern Language Journal* 50, pp.3-17

Agnihotri, R.K., & Khanna, L.A., ed. 1995. "English Language Teaching in India: Issues and Innovations." *Research in Applied Linguistics.* Vol. 2. New Delhi: Sage Publications.

Allwright, R.L.1977. "Language Learning through Communication Practice." *ELTDocuments* (British Council) 76/3. Reprinted in Brumfit and Johnson, 1979.

Bialy Stock, E. 1981. "The Role of Conscious Strategies in Second Language Proficiency." *Modern Language Journal*, 65. pp. 24-35

_____. 1990. "Communication Strategies: A Psychological Analysis of Second Language Use." Oxford: Basil Blackwell.

Black, C. and Butzkamm, W. 1978. "Classroom Language: Materials for Communicative Language Teaching." *ELT Teaching Journal*, Vol. 32, No. 4, pp. 270-74.

Brooks, Nelson. 1960. "Language and Language Learning" 2nd ed., New York: Harcourt, Brace and World.

Brown, H. 1987. "Principles of Language Learning and Teaching" (2nd ed.), Eaglewood Cliffs, N.J.: Prentice Hall.

Bialystok, "Communication strategies." E. Blackwell, Oxford. 1990.

Cohen, A.D., & Weaver, J.S.1998. "Strategies-based Instructions for Second Language Learners."

Carver, D. 1984. "Plans, Learner-Strategies and Self-Direction in Language Learning System." pp. 123-31.

Colman, A. 1982. "Game Theory and Experimental Games: The Study of Strategic Interaction." Oxford: Pergamon.

Carter Ronald & Nunan David, ed. "Teaching English to Speakers of Other Languages." Cambridge University Press, pp.166-72

Cook, Vivian.1991. "Second Language Learning and Language Teaching." Edward Arnold, ed. Hodder & Stoughton. Great Britain. pp. 72-82.

Crookall, David and Oxford, R.L. 1990. Simulation, Gaming and Language Learning. New York: Newbury, pp: 109-17.

Chamot, A.U. 1987. "The Learning Strategies of ESL Students." Wenden and Rubin, ed., 1987.

Chamot, A.U. et al. 1987. A Study of Learner Strategies in Foreign Language Instruction: First Year Report. Rosslyn, Va.: Interstate Research Associates.

Chamot, A. and Malley, M.J. 1994."Language Learner and Learning Strategies." N. Ellis, ed., 1994.

Corder, P.S. 1983. "Strategies of Communication." In Faerch, C. and G. Kasper, ed., *Strategies in Interlanguage*, London: Longman.

Dulay, H. 1975. "Creative Construction in Second Language Learning and Teaching." In Burt, M. and Dulay, H., ed., on TESOL 75: "New Directions in Second Language Learning, Teaching and Bilingual Education," Washington, D.C.: TESOL.

Dansereau, D.R., Long, L.G., McDonald, A.B. and Atkinson, T.R. 1975a. "Learning Strategy Inventory Development and Assessment (AFHRL-Tr-75-40. Contract F41609-74-c-0013). Lowry Air Force Base, Colo.: Air Force Human Resources Laboratory.

Goodman M. Yetta & Burke Carolynn. 1931. *Reading Strategies: Focus on Comprehension.* USA Printing Press.

Kohli, A.L. 1970. "Techniques of Teaching English." 12th ed. New Delhi: J.C. Kapur, Dhanpat Rai & Sons. pp. 2-69.

Krishnaswamy, N. & Sri Raman, T. "English Teaching in India." T.R. Publications. pp. 43-70.

Kumar, Arvind. 2004. "A Textbook of Environmental Sciences." New Delhi: APH pp. 94-95.

Lakshminarayanan, K.R. 1999. *A Textbook on Effective Technical English.* Chennai: Scitech Publications. pp. 20-22

Mowla, Shaik. 2001. *The Techniques of Teaching English.* New Delhi: Neelkamal. pp. 1-25.

Naiman, N., Frolich, M., Stern, H. and Todesco, A. 1978. "The Good Language Learner," Research in Education Series No.7, Toronto: The Ontario Institute for Studies in Education.

Nunan, D. 1988. "The Learner-Centred Curriculum." Cambridge University Press.

Nunan, D. 1989. "Designing Task for the Communicative Classroom." Cambridge University Press.

O'Malley, J.M. & Chamot, A.V. 1990. "Learning Strategies in Second Language Acquisition." Cambridge University Press.

Oxford, R. 1985. *A New Taxonomy of Second Language Learning Strategies.* Washington DC: ERIC Clearing House on Languages & Linguistics

_____. 1990. *Language Learning Strategies.* Boston: Heinle & Heinle.

Oxford, R.L. 1990. *Language Learning Strategies: What Every Teacher Should Know,* New York: Newbury House/ Harper & Row. pp. 16-21.

Oxford, Rebecca. 1992. "Research on Second Language Strategies," *Annual Reviews of Applied Linguistics*, pp. 188-205.

Richards C. Jack & Renandya A. Willy, ed. 2002. *Methodology in Language Teaching: An Anthology of Current Practice.* Cambridge University Press.

Rubin, J. 1981. "Study of Cognitive Processes in Second Language Learning," *Applied Linguistics*, 11, pp. 117-31.

Rubin, J., & Thompson, I.1982. "How to be a More Successful Language Learner." Boston: Heinle & Heinle.

Renandya, W.A. & Jacobs, G.M. ed.. *Learners and Language Learning.* Singapore: SEAMEO Regional Language Centre. Pg. 1-25.

Stauffer, Russell, G. 1970. "The Language Experience Approach to the Teaching of Reading. New York: Harper and Row.

Subba Rao, A. "Learner Strategies: Implications for Learner-Centred Teaching in E.L.T.—A Handout."

Subramaniam, T.K. et.al. 2001. *A Textbook of English for Engineers and Technologists*. Orient Longman. pp. 61-62.

Tickoo, M.L. 2003. *Teaching and Learning English- A Source Book for Teachers and Teacher-Trainers*. Orient Longman.

Wenden, A.L. 1983. "Incorporating Learner Training in the Classroom." In Wenden and Rubin, eds., 1987.

Wenden, A.L., & Rubin, J. 1987b. *Learning Strategies in Language Learning*. Prentice Hall: Eastwood Cliffs, N.Y.

Wenden, A.L. 1991. "Learning Strategies for Learner Autonomy." Eastwood Cliffs, NJ.: Prentice Hall.

Widdowson, H.G. 1978. *Teaching Language as Communication.* Oxford University Press.

APPENDIX

Graphical Representation of Learners' performance in Writing Skill Tasks: B.A (A) I year: Trained Group

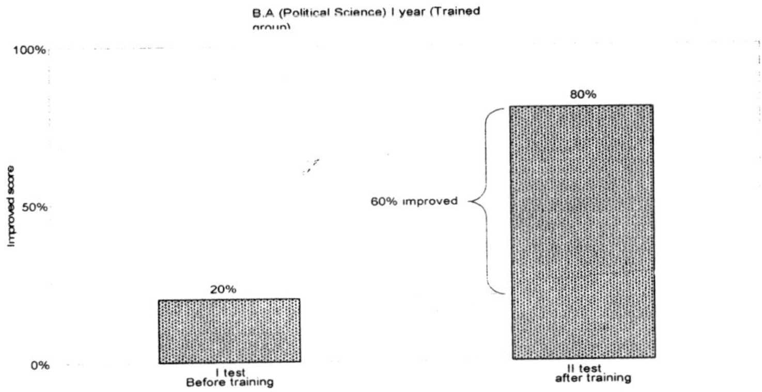

Graphical representation of Learner's performance regarding writing skill tasks

B.A.(B) I year: Untrained Group

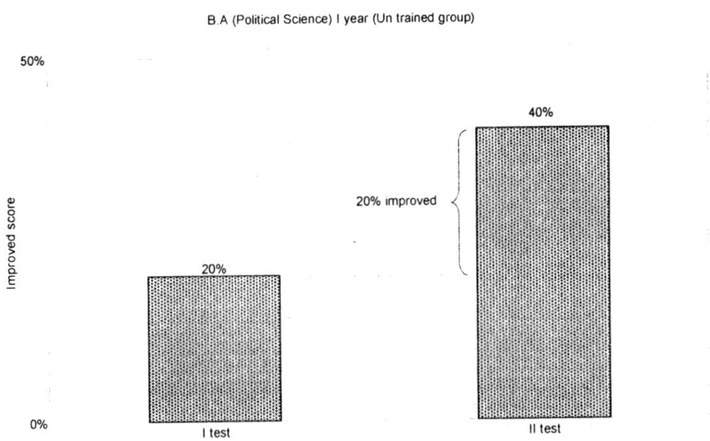

Graphical representation of Learner's performance regarding writing skill tasks

Graphical Representation of Learners' performance in Reading Skill Tasks: ECE-A GROUP: Experimental or trained group.

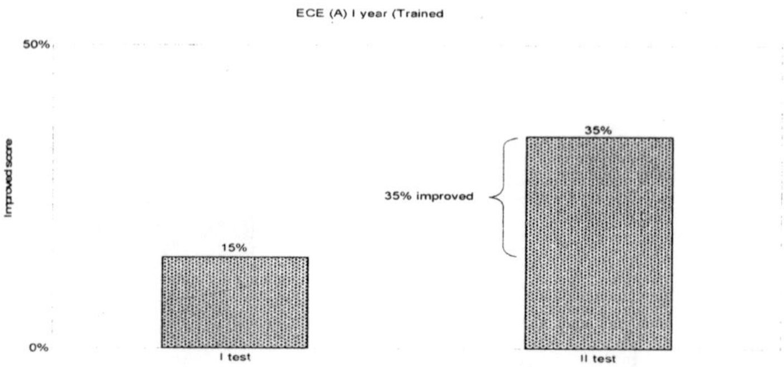

Graphical representation of Learner's performance regarding the reading skill

ECE-B GROUP: Controlled or untrained group.

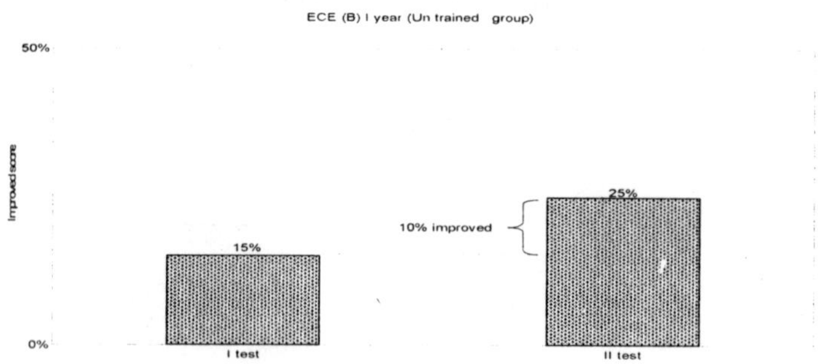

Graphical representation of Learner's performance regarding the reading skill

Graphical Representation of Learners' performance in Listening Skill Tasks: ECE-A GROUP: Trained group

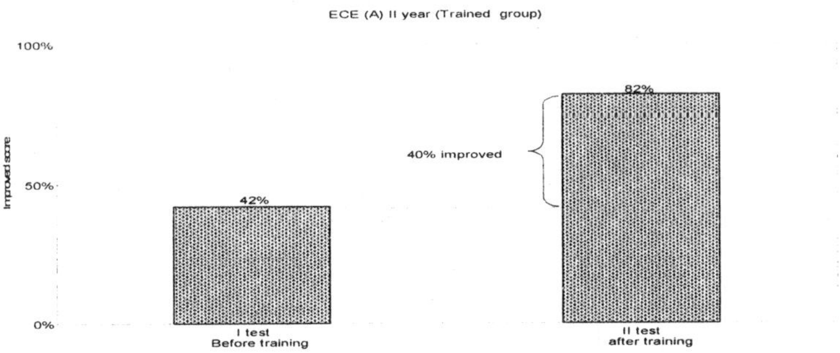

Graphical representation of Learner's performance in listening skill

ECE-B GROUP: Untrained group.=

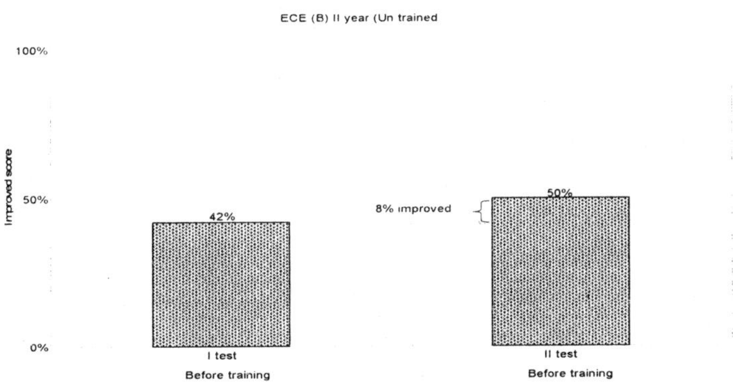

Graphical representation of Learner's performance in listening skill

Teaching English through Mass Media

G. CHENNA REDDY

In today's world, every communication order is ultimately conditioned or influenced by the political system and cultural milieu and the ends and purposes for which it is to be used. With the dawn of freedom, the Indian media were delinked from the apron-strings of British Political and Cultural imperialism.

The Mass Media are a very important component of society. Their use in a developing country like India is considered most crucial in the challenge to mobilize people for development activities. Therefore, there must be a communication policy, and more specifically a mass media policy in each country. Our daily lives are so interwoven with the media that we are scarcely aware of their presence and influence. The modern media of mass communication like newspapers, books, radio, television and video are important sources of information. To these devices like telephones, computers, etc., can be added.

It is a well-known proposition that the media can teach. But our concern here is their role in the teaching of language. It is believed that authentic audio-visual materials teach language in a more efficient way than the conventional classroom "Media" of chalk-and-talk and textbook. We begin with the assumption that media definitely have a positive role in facilitating learning and teaching in general. Well-known attributes of media, such as that they simultaneously reach more learners. Media stimulate learners by motivating them, and they bring the best teacher or teaching team within the reach of all learners, justify this assumption. Media "inform, amuse, startle, anger, entertain, thrill, but very seldom leave anyone untouched." Biagi Shirley (1996).

The usage of media in the class room has always been a challenge, and how to bring various kinds of media in the class room is more than a challenge. Media are a resource to the teachers and the students with creative and practical ideas. Through these instruments a teacher can meet various needs and interests of their students.

Media also provide students with a lot of language practice through activities using newspapers, magazines, radio, TV, movies, books, Internet, etc, and tasks which develop reading, writing, speaking and listening skills. They entertain students and encourage reading English in general, both inside and outside the classroom, promoting extensive reading by giving the students the confidence, the motivation and the ability to continue their reading outside the classroom. We should understand the media, the messages they give and their influence upon us, how to explore this abundant information and create a continuum of the liveliness media create in the life of people and why not in the classroom where students spend a lot of their time.

Newspapers

Newspapers and magazines are informal but provide very influential education. They provide a variety of information. They cover almost all areas of knowledge. Instruction through newspapers introduces variety and element of 'play—way'. The newspapers are very useful for the study of languages. Pupils learn many new words and expressions. They learn how to express themselves and how to follow the expression of others.

Newspapers are the most accessible print media for most people. They are the cheapest reading material. They bring out news about the daily happenings, popular science, historical events, entertainment features, human interest stories, political affairs, trade and economic matters, sports, shopping and many more, giving the reader a panoramic view of human life and society. In short, newspapers are the richest and the most easily available reading material for ali.

For students in the classroom, newspapers can be a source of all subjects. In the language classroom newspapers can be used to reach a wide range of topics and areas from the alphabet to sentence structure, grammar, discourse, techniques, style and all the major composition skills including rhetoric, logic and creative writing.

Newspapers may be used either to add to the supplementary readers or to replace them completely. They are the essence of language learning and teaching, the use of newspapers and materials in the classrooms in India seems to be quite appropriate mainly in terms of quantity. Text books may not match the newspapers in terms of cost and effectiveness.

The daily events, what happens around the teachers and the students are printed in the newspapers. The learners can understand more easily than in the text books. Translations of the same matter can be had in the regional medium newspapers or even from the electronic media to some considerable extent, because the subject matter for the most part will be the same in all media. The learners can perceive the language in action outside their classroom as well, and the parents and other elders may also give unlike the textbooks which require 'specialized persons' to explain them, the news papers can be discussed by anyone who reads them.

Newspapers are full of topical materials. They deal with Politics, Commerce, Mathematics, Science, Religion, Earthquakes, Scams, Cricket, Accidents, Murders, Rape, Theft, Catastrophes, Space adventure, Child prodigies and everything else that happens in contemporary human society. If a bit of that learners' interesting topic be brought into the classroom then the learner will be quite willing to come to the classroom. For centuries the learners have been "creeping like snail unwilling to school" (Shakespeare) largely due to unattractive learning materials in the classroom.

Newspapers are primarily meant for conveying meaning and message. In a second language situation, like India, newspapers are essential means of exposure to communicate through English. The learners can realize how the second language functions in the context.

> Extensive reading may be started with newspapers which contain many communication skills and highly contextualized materials for all higher levels of learners. If the learner does not have interest on news story, he/she can just drop or skip it and go for another one.

> But the learner cannot throw away books or text books as early as an item or a day's issue of a newspaper.

Skimming and scanning can be well taught using newspapers. And these skills are important as a part of second language acquisition. G.C. Ahiya and Prameela Ahiya say: "There is no greater asset to the reader of today than highly developed skill in skimming. Skimming enables a person to select quickly content which he wants to read and discord that in which he is not interested or which is inconsequential to his purpose.

> Most adults develop some skill in skimming newspapers and magazines. This skill can be further developed to a very high degree and used profitably in doing all kinds of reading. Such development, however, requires instruction and practice if it is to function in the best capacity.

Newspapers are also a great source for ESP teachers. They can be used as teaching materials to develop students' language skills. They can be used effectively with a wide range of levels from Elementary to Advanced, either interpreting them or using them as they are. Some newspapers are easy to read, easy to use. The committed teachers can design exercises to develop reading comprehension, critical thinking skills, writing skills, grammar skills, vocabulary, map/chart reading skills, geography skills, social study skills and more. Having a lot of newspapers and information the teachers should be careful with the way how to organize a certain activity using them. So, they are particularly suitable *for mixed-ability classes*, depending on the activity, questions, etc.

In planning a lesson using a newspaper, the teacher should take into consideration the length of the article, paragraph, the complexity of the language, the density of information, the subject-matter and content, the time available and the level of the students. Nowadays, we are living in a period of rapid technological changes in mass communications. Through Internet, we are now able to access thousands of newspapers and magazines worldwide.

Radio and Education

Radio is one of the earlier media to be used in the classroom. Recently there has been a tremendous interest in the use of pop songs to teach, second/ foreign languages. The BBC, for example broadcasts two programmes, "Pop World" and "Pop English" which attempt to teach English through pop songs. Researchers have found that the songs can be used to teach any of the four skills of languages—Listening, Speaking, Reading and Writing.

R.G. Reynolds says: "radio is the most significant medium for education in its broadest sense that has been introduced since the term of the century. As a supplement to class room teaching its possibilities are almost unlimited. Its teaching possibilities are not confined to the five or six hours of the school day. It is available from early morning till long after mid night. By utilizing the rich educational and cultural offerings of the radio, children and adults in communities, however remote, have access to the best of world's stores of knowledge and art. Some day its use as educational instruments will be as common place as text books as block boards."

Radio plays an important role in developing people's imagination, in creating pictures in the mind through the power of words, it stimulates the imagination to fill in the visuals, etc. The listeners see the drama in their heads. Thus, when radio is used in the classroom it helps students to promote their imagination, to voice their creativity.

A lot of radio programs contribute to language learning. Besides getting new information and entertainment, in language classes, radio helps the pronunciation, the intonation, the pitch of voice, etc. These might be successful if we undertake adequate preparation and design carefully graded tasks. Students gain a feeling of satisfaction from having understood something of an authentic broadcast; we can see the joy in their faces. They develop greater confidence in their ability to cope with English as it's spoken outside the classroom.

Institutes of English and Foreign Languages in Indian broadcast many programmes to teach English Language radio. Many state governments provide T.Vs and Radios to the schools and Colleges. Radios and TVs are frequently used in Indian schools to learn knowledge. English and Foreign Languages University, Hyderabad, designed many English programmes to High School students in Andhra Pradesh. Such programmes help the students to learn correct pronunciation, intonation and grammar. Radio lessons in English are heard in hundreds of high school classrooms in Andhra Pradesh.

Television and the Classroom

Television has a tremendous potential for mass education and human resource development. In a gigantic country like India the problem of providing education to all is a huge task. Here the role of mass communication in general and T.V in particular is therefore very significant. In Indian context, Doordarshan has to be conscious of its role. Today there is scarcely a country which is not utilizing television with a view to achieving its culture, social, political and economic development. Television gives information by transmitting programmes through space satellites to people all over the world. Media men often view T.V as an electronic magic carpet, the 20th century's creation of the technological revolution, the great instrument of persuasion, and the most powerful weapon for social change. The scope of T.V programmes can be broadly visualized from three angles, i.e. .information, education and entertainment.

Television is the most potential instrument in educating masses and helpful in narrowing down the gap of progress between the developing and developed countries of the world. T.V. can be an important central media in providing functional, formal and non formal education to the masses. Television helps in enforcing the public understanding of social, political and scientific advancement of a country. TV programs may be used as warming-up activities, pre-activities for the coming issue, as supplementary materials for a certain topic, for up-to-date information, to update the information in the textbooks, etc.

Many programmes are designed to teach English Language through television. English and Foreign Language Training Institutes in India prepare different types of programmes to teach English for Indian learners. The B.B.C has designed several of programmes to learn vocabulary, pronunciation, grammar etc. The students of many schools and college get benefit from such programmes.

Internet for Teachers and Students

First, we have to have computer skills in ordering to bring this kind of Media to our classrooms. There is a separate course for computer skills in our curriculum but this is not enough. More attention should be paid to training courses that help students apply various ways in using computers and Internet in the classroom.

Internet is not merely a source of authentic material in English but also a source of information for all sorts of topics we may want to discuss in the classroom and at the same time a source of professional knowledge for teachers in the form of bibliographies, articles, courses and conferences. But to get all these we need to have some practice and experience. It is often that we spend a lot of time searching the Internet, and we feel that we are wasting time and finding nothing that we really wanted. So, it is crucial to have some tips about the ways how to search the Internet, especially the key words of research.

Internet helps students and teachers to compare and classify information, to induce and deduce ideas, to analyze errors, to abstract concepts, to analyze perspectives, to gather information, to work in teams, etc. The Internet is an excellent tool for locating the latest news not yet published. Information on the Internet has three characteristics that distinguish it from traditional classroom materials such as books, supplementary readings, videos and films. The information on the Internet is *extensive*, *dynamic* and *readily accessible*. Acknowledging these characteristics will provide a better

Internet is nowadays considered to be the greatest innovation in Information Technology. The number of the Internet users increasing dramatically everyday. The benefits and uses of the Internet for education are growing with every passing day. Internet can make education more attainable to more people. It can promote improved and new type of learning. The use of internet in the classroom is a challenging task. Today schools and universities are spending a lot of money for this technology. It is the "the Age of

Internet." Currently computers are being used in the classrooms in our country, but still a lot of schools do not have computers and Internet access. Universities, some high schools and thousands of individuals are connected to the Internet. Some teachers have Internet access in their classrooms.

One can browse a mine of information through Internet. The information can be available in various languages. But no other language is near to English language to obtain information through net. Different types of language learning programmes are available through net. Many such programmes are designed by the B.B.C. The users of Internet, especially in English, are increasing day by day.

Conclusion

Multimedia helps us (teachers) teachers make teaching and learning visual (easy for visual learners). A picture not only tells a thousand words but it also helps students improve their thinking and observation skills, it promotes imagination, etc. Radio (playing the audio) helps auditory learners learn better. Listening to the tape and then having the script is a clear combination that helps visual and auditory learners. By using various kinds of media in the classroom, we can enhance students' understanding and promote it where necessary.

Media can help with many issues such as: motivation, clarity, recycling, drafting, revising, editing, variety, mixed-ability classes, updating information in the textbook, giving life and colour to classroom procedures and methods, thus at the same time helping the students improve accuracy and fluency. Internet has three main educational uses. It serves as a source of information, a place for collaboration, and a place to learn and publish.

The mass media are recognized as the useful tool to teach English language in the classroom. The schools in the 21st century have introduced electronic media in the classroom from Kindergarten. Audio-visual teaching is attracted by the young learners. As English is the essential language of computer, the younger learners pay more attention to learn English first to operate the system to learn various language components.

Many language programmes are designed to teach English language to Indian English learners. Thousands of students are curious to utilize such programmes to improve their Listening, Speaking, Reading and Writing skills in the classroom. The Mass Media, especially electronic media, play a vital role to teach English in Indian classrooms.

References

1. G.C. Ahuja and Prameela Ahuja, *How to Increase Reading* Speed, New Delhi: Sterling, 1979.
2. Biagi Shirley, *Media Reader*, New York: Wardsworth, 1996.
3. Vinod S. Dubey, *Newspaper English in India*, New Delhi: Bharathi, 1989.
4. Jack C. Richards and Theodore S. Rodgers, *Approaches and methods in English language teaching-A Description and Analysis,* Cambridge: Cambridge University Press, 1986.
5. Shakespeare, *As You Like It*. Act I, Scene VII, p. 218, *Complete Works*, London: Hamlyn, 1958.

English for Medical Purposes

JYOTHI HYMAVATHI DEVI

'English for Specific Purposes' has been a distinct aspect within English language teaching. The main aim of ESP is equipping learners with skills to communicate effectively in their work situation. The prime concerns of ESP are—analysis of needs, analysis of text and preparing learners to face situations in their study or work situations. The methodology of ESP takes the inputs of the other disciplines as well. My paper tries to discuss 'English for Medical Purposes' in particular while discussing 'English for Specific Purposes' in general.

ESP had its origins in the 1950s. It began as a movement out of general developments in the world economy in the 1950s and 1960s. During this period, English emerged as the language of science, technology, international business and commerce. Oil crises in early 1970s also accelerated the development of ESP. There are various phases in its development.

Tom Hutchinson and Alan Waters, in their work, *English for Specific Purposes: A Learning-centred Approach* (1987, 19), see ESP "as an approach to language rather than a product." Dudley-Evans and Maggie Jo St John, in their work, *English for Specific Purposes: a Multi-disciplinary Approach*, say, "ESP does not involve a particular kind of language, teaching material or methodology" (Dudley-Evans and John, 2).Therefore, in ESP there is "openness to the insights of other disciplines' (1998, 1). Because of this 'openness', this branch is multi-disciplinary in its nature. Nijole Netiksiene, in his article, 'Teaching English for specific purposes' (2006), says: "The ideas and teaching methods from the classes of general English can be transferred to the classes of English for Specific Purposes." "Marjorie Rosenberg (2004) considers where English for Specific Purposes/Business English and General English overlap" (qtd. in Netiksiene, 80).

As ESP is a movement furthered by materials and teaching, its work involves teaching as well as other work of material production, choosing and adapting etc. Course design plays a pivotal role in ESP teaching. This is the reason why ESP teaching is regarded as extremely varied. Dudley-Evans and Johns (1998, 13) use the term 'practitioner' rather than 'teacher'. According to them, ESP practitioner has five roles to play:

Teacher
Course designer and material provider
Collaborator
Researcher
Evaluator

English for Academic Purposes (EAP) has different specialisms like English for Science and Technology(EST), English for Medical Purposes (EMP) and English for Legal Purposes (ELP).

Medical English includes the needs of different groups like medical students, practicing doctors and consultants in hospitals and also patients. EMP needs are both EOP needs as well as EAP needs. Therefore, Dudley-Evans and John(1998, 49) consider the terms EST, EMP, ELP as "little more than useful umbrella terms derived from teaching situations and the writing of teaching materials."

So with in the English for Medical Purposes, there are English for Academic Purposes and English for Occupational Purposes. EAP includes the needs of medical students to read medical text books and articles, and their need to write essays and short clinical reports. It also includes the nurses' needs to follow their academic courses. The EOP includes the needs of practicing doctors to read specialist articles, and the need of preparing papers and slide presentations for conferences.

Medical language is considered a type of register. In general language usage, written language can be differentiated from spoken, and it is also true of medical language. There are various kinds of medical language. Lankamp R.E., in his work, *A Study on the Effect of Terminology on L2 Reading Comprehension: Should*

Specialist Terms in Medical Texts be Avoided? (1988), made an analysis of medical language in terms of register on the basis of the analysis of register made by Hudson (1980:49, qtd. in Lankamp) and also on the basis of analysis of language for special purposes made by Picht and Draskau (1985:3ff, qtd. Lankamp). According to Lankamp (2), there are three dimensions of variation:

a. Medical specialism.
b. Manner of transmission of the medical message.
c. Relations between participants in the medical exchange.

Medical specialism includes various fields of medicine. Medical language is not a homogenous entity. As quoted in Lankamp (21), "Depending on the manner of transmission, medical registers can be distinguished such as spoken medical language, written medical language, or more specifically written medical language for research reports or medical language in equipment manuals." Five variants of medical language resulting out of its heterogeneity are as follows:

1. The language of medical education (e.g. textbooks, lectures).
2. The language of medical occupation (for example medical journal articles, oral papers).
3. The language of medical journalism (popular medicine, medical encyclopedias).
4. Doctor-patient language (including such as the language of medical instructions of commercial brochures) and
5. Medical technical language (1988, 22).

While structuring courses for EMP, as a first step, it is desirable to make need analyses of the various learners keeping in mind the heterogeneity of the medical language. This would form a basis for the courses. Need analysis is the analysis of linguistics needs. Abel Javier Romo, in his report, titled, *An English for Specific Purposes Curriculum to Prepare English Learners to become Nursing Assistants* (2006) says, "Needs analysis is more than learning what linguistic weaknesses and strengths learners in a course have" (40). Various data gathering instruments and procedures like, observation, interview, questionnaire may be used to perform this analysis. The resultant data can be exploited in designing the courses.

Basic Medical Terminology is one of the most important aspects of English for Medical Purposes. It is the professional language with the help of which the medical personnel communicate. As it is a specialized branch of language, it is to be taught to the learners in need. The learners may be medical students, nursing students, medical practitioners, paramedical staff or the patients themselves.

In medical texts the following types of lexical items are seen: specialist medical terms, common medical terms and sub-medical terms (Lankamp, 34). According to Dudley-Evans and John (1998), uniquely medical items are encountered in case conferences. As in any text, medical texts also contain both content words and function words. Content words give the principal meaning of the objects or concepts they denote. Function words include words such as articles, conjunctions, and prepositions etc. which give the grammatical organization to the sentences. Specialized medical terms are formed by mechanisms like affixations and shortenings of the larger terms. Certain affixations in medical vocabulary are: -atis, -itis, -oma, -osis, -ectomy etc. It is in this area that the learners are to be strengthened. As learners in the profession are to be strengthened in the specialized language, the persons who are in need of taking health services are to be strengthened by colloquial medical language.

In the next part of this paper, I attempt to discuss some of the medical terminology. As it was already indicated, affixation makes it possible to produce new terms. It includes both prefixation and suffixation. Therefore, in teaching these terms, the students can be explained the procedure by which the words are broken down.

'Root' or 'stem' is the fundamental word element which gives essential meaning. Suffix is the end part of the word which many medical terms have. Prefix is a small part added to the root word. Both of these modify and augment the meaning of the root or stem. There are terms with one root. For example:

> 'Hematology' is broken into 'hemat-o-logy'. 'Hemat' is the root word for blood and 'logy' is the suffix for "study of." 'o' is the third part, a combining vowel that has no meaning. It is an important connector between root word and suffix. New word formed with the ad-

dition of the suffix and a vowel 'o' is 'hemat-o-logy' meaning "Study of Blood." Similarly, medical terms can also take two roots. e.g. 'Electrocardiogram' can be split into 'Electr-o-cardi-o-gram' which has two roots, two vowels and two combining forms. The meaning of this term is "Record of electricity in heart." In terms where the suffix begins with a vowel as in 'cardi-ac', the combining vowel is dropped. This is also seen in terms such as 'enter-itis'. But, in a term like 'gastr-o-enter-itis', the initial combining vowel 'o' remains even though the second root 'enter' begins with a vowel. Reason for this is that combining vowels connect roots to suffixes and roots to other roots.

Many medical terms have prefixes. They can change the meanings in specific ways. They can modify or augment the meaning of the root or stem:

1. sub-gastr-ic
Sub=below; pertaining to below the stomach
2. trans-gastr-ic
Trans=across; pertaining to across the stomach
3. retro-gastr-ic
Retro=behind; pertaining to behind the stomach

Prefixes may be classified into different categories of meaning basing on how they modify the stem or root:

Prefixes of Location
Prefixes of Time
Prefixes of Amount or Comparison
Prefixes of Colour
Prefixes of Negation
Prefixes of Size and Position

Most suffixes are in common use in English. A few are peculiar to medicine:

-itis-inflammation
-oma-tumor
-osis-condition, usually morbid

Shortening is a procedure by which words are built. It is also called abbreviation by which professional communication can be quickened. According to Edwards (qtd. Sanchez and Conde, 39):

Shortening is considered a very productive word-building process. It is the dropping of the latter part of a word so as to produce a new and shorter word of the same meaning. The strain of modern life is obviously one of the reasons for this development. For example, almost all written material in hospital is written to be read at a glance because consultants read them before they do their rounds, and new nurses to acquaint with their patients. Similarly, the daily ward reports are read by the offgoing nurse in charge to the oncoming staff.

Here are some of the common abbreviations used in a hospital setting:

1. Some abbreviations are read as ordinary words.
   E.g. Polyps-Polymorphonuclear leukocytes
2. In some other, initial abbreviations with alphabetical reading are retained:
   E.g. B.P.-Blood pressure
   P.R. Pupil reaction
3. There are some abbreviations which are shortened forms of written words.
   E.g. Cas.-Casualty
   Caps.-Capsule

Here are some of the commonly used abbreviations and their meanings:

+, & = and
Bili. = Bilirubin
C = Centigrade
D&C = Dilation & Curettage
EBL = Estimated blood loss
# = fracture
gal = gallon
H&H = Hemoglobin & hematocrit
I & D = Incision and drainage
JVD = Jugular vein distention
mono = monocyte
neg = negative
o.d. = right eye
p = after
q2h = every two hours
r/resp = respiration

SOS = (Latin:si opus sit) may be repeated once if urgently required
t.i.d = three times a day
U = Unit
vag = vaginal
w.a. = while awake (Sanchez and Conde, 2001)

Next part of my presentation tries to focus on a particular medical/biological aspect that can be taught to the students by the help of a material design model. This model follows the sample given by Hutchinson and Waters (1987, 110). This is a model prepared for teaching 'human digestive system'. In this, energy/food itself explains how it supports the human system. It is animated; it says:

> Hey! I am your energy, you know! Do you know what kind of support I am giving to you! It is because of me that you are able to live.
>
> Initially, I was in the form of food material like rice, roti, fruits, milk etc.
>
> I enter your mouth happily where I am chewed by your teeth. There, I get mixed up with saliva.
>
> From there, I enter a very long path, later I reach a round shaped stomach.
>
> There, again I get mixed up with many juices and I get myself divided into tiny pieces.
>
> Later, I enter a big tube from which I proceed to a small tube. Meanwhile, in the form of energy, I circulate through out your body.
>
> Finally, the leftovers of me get ejected out. This is my journey!

This piece has no specialized terms but it provides a general comprehension of the concept. Later, this procedure is equated with the actual medical reading of the digestive system where the subject specific terminology is equated with common terms. This activity can further be extended by discussing the subsystems of larger digestive system. Within the broader system of digestion, there are certain sub-systems:

1. Salivary glands which consist of parotid gland, sublingual gland, sub mandibular gland.
2. Stomach which consists of Cardiac orifice, Pyloric sphincter, Duodenum of small intestine.

3. Ascending portion of large intestine which has ileum of small intestine and cecum appendix.

The last portion of my paper has the component of doctor/patient or other medical professional/patient conversations. As the patients are in need of expressing their grievances to the doctors, they are expected to be in a position to use the informal language of the body and mind. The informal expressions related to illness and health help the patients in effectively communicating the doctor.

Conversation between Doctor and Patient

Patient: Good morning, doctor! Can you spare me a few minutes?
Doctor: Certainly! Come in and sit down. Now, what is the matter with you?
Patient: I've caught a cold, and I'm constantly coughing.
Doctor: You aren't running a temperature, are you?
Patient: I suppose I'm not.
Doctor: Let me examine you. . . Your heart and lungs seems to be all right. Now open your mouth wide. . . Now breathe in deeply through the nose. . . There doesn't seem to be anything radically wrong with you. But you are a little run down. Take a complete rest. Get these tablets thrice a day. You should be all right in three or four days.
Patient: Thank you, doctor.
Doctor: Not at all. (www.manaroju.blogspot.com)

Conversation between Doctor and Patient

Dr. Smith: Hello, Sasha. How are you feeling today?
Sasha: I don't feel well.
Dr. Smith: What's wrong? Can you tell me how you feel?
Sasha: Well, I have a terrible headache.
Dr. Smith: Hmm . . . Anything else? Does your throat hurt?
Sasha: Yes, it hurts a little. I have a cough too.
Dr. Smith: Do you have a fever?
Sasha: Yes, I have a low fever.
Dr. Smith: It sounds like you may have the flu.
Sasha: Oh, that's terrible.
Dr. Smith: Don't worry. I will give you some medicine and you will feel better soon.
Sasha: Okay. Can I go to work tomorrow?

Dr. Smith: No. Stay home tomorrow, get some rest, and drink plenty of juice and water.

Sasha: Thank you, Doctor.

Dr. Smith: Okay, take care of yourself and I hope you feel better soon ("Describing Pain and Symptoms")

Here are some expressions for pain and symptoms of ill health:

What's the matter? What's wrong?	How do you feel?	Adjective
I have a headache	I feel sick.	sick/fine (well)
You have sore throat	You feel sad.	sad/happy
She has the flu.	She feels bad.	bad/good (better)
We have a cold.	We feel awful.	awful/great
You have a stomachache.	You feel terrible.	terrible/terrific
They have a backache.	They don't feel well	

("Describing Pain and Symptoms")

Body Part	Description of Symptoms
Nose	My nose is stuffed. I have allergies. I'm sneezing.
Ear	I have an earache.
Eyes	I can't see clearly.
Teeth	I have a toothache.
Throat	My throat hurts. I have a bad cough.
Head	My head hurts. I feel dizzy.
Skin	I have rash.
Neck/Back	My neck hurts. My back hurts.

Chest	I have chest pain.
Arm/Hand	I think my arm is broken.
Stomach	My stomach hurts. I threw up. I vomited.
Foot/Leg/Ankle	I think I sprained my ankle. I think my leg is broken. I think my foot is broken.

("Describing Pain and Symptoms")

Bibliography

"Conversation between Doctor and Patient." *Manaroju.blogspot.com,* n.p., 12-9-2008. Web.3:2:2011.

"Describing Pain and Symptoms." *www.projectshine.org,* MetLife Foundation, n.d. web.24 Jan.2011.

Dudley-Evans, Tony, and Maggie Jo St. John. *Developments in English for Specific Purposes: A Multi-disciplinary Approach.* UK: Cambridge University Press, 1998.

"English for Special Purposes-Introduction." *www.teachingenglish.org.uk/* BBC, n.d. Web. 24 Jan. 2011.

Hutchinson, Tom, and Alan Waters. *English for Specific Purposes: A Learning-centred Approach.* UK: Cambridge University Press, 1987.

Lankamp, Robert E. *A Study on the Effect of Terminology on L2 Reading Comprehension: Should Specialist Terms in Medical Texts be Avoided?* Amsterdam, 1988. Web. 24 Jan 2011.

"Medical Terminology." *www.portervillecollege.edu/* Porterville college, n.d.Web. 24 Jan. 2011.

Netiksiene, Nijole. "Teaching English for Specific Purposes." *Santalka. Filologija. Edukologia* (2006): 80-82. Web. 24 Jan, 2011.

Romo, Abel Javier. *An English for Specific Purposes Curriculum to Prepare English Learners to become Nursing Assistants.* Utah: Brigham Young University, 2006. Web

Sanchez, Vivian AM., and Beatriz Goenaga Conde. "The Use of Shortening in English for

Specific Purposes. A Practical Review for Nurses" *Rev Cubana Educ Med Super* 15(1) (2001): 39-55. Web. 24 Jan. 2011

US Army Medical Department Centre and School. *Basic Medical Terminology.* 100th ed. Texas. Web. 24 Jan. 2011.

Teaching English for Specific Purposes

DEEPAK KUMAR

ESP is a part of language teaching movement LSP (Language for specific purpose) that seeks to serve the language needs of the learners who need language in order to carry specific roles (e.g., nurse, engineer, and technician). These learners require content and real world skills through the medium of second language rather than master the language for its own sake. ESP has developed its own approaches, materials and methodology and is generally seen as a very active movement that has had considerable influence over the more general activities of TESOL.

Definition of ESP

Hutchinson and Waters (1987) see ESP as an *approach* rather than a *product*, by which they mean that ESP does not involve a particular kind of language, teaching material or methodology. They suggest that 'the foundation of ESP is the simple question; why does this learner need to learn a foreign language?' The answer to this question relates to the learners, the language required and the learning context, and thus establishes the primacy of the need in ESP.

Strevens '(1980): "ESP entails the provision of English language instruction:

- Devised to meet the learner's particular needs;
- Related in themes and topics to designated occupations or areas of study;
- Selective (i.e. not general) as to language content;
- When indicated, restricted as to the language skills included."

The key defining feature of ESP. is that its teaching and materials are founded on the results of needs analysis. The first question when starting preparation for teaching an ESP course is almost always: What do students need to do with English? Which of the skills do they need to master and how well? Which genres do they need to master, either for comprehension and production purpose? Various commentators (notably Brumfit (1984) have remarked that needs analysis is not exclusive to ESP and that much general TESOL- especially when following the communicative approach- is based on needs analysis. However, in ESP one can be more precise about learners' needs; their needs are defined by a learning or occupational situation in which English plays a key role. Specific needs can be identified by examining that situation and the texts in detail; in contrast, for students not immediately using English, or about to use it, needs are much more general.

Apart from the primacy of needs analysis, defining features of ESP can be difficult to identify. Robinson, in her first overview of ESP (1980), suggested that limited duration (i.e. an intensive course of a fixed length) and adult learners are the defining features of ESP courses. however, in her second survey (1991) she accepts that, although many ESP courses are of limited duration, a significant number are not (e. g. a three—or four- year programme as part of university degree) and, while it is true that the majority of ESP learners are adults, ESP can be taught at school (even at primary level in English medium Schools where English is not the pupils' first language). Similarly ESP is generally taught to intermediate or advanced students of English, but can also be taught to beginners. The above are optional or variable characteristics of ESP. I would add to this list the idea that ESP may be designed for specific disciplines that ESP may be designed for specific disciplines or professions. The ESP researcher needs to bear in mind and exploit if possible this specific subject knowledge, which leads to classroom interaction and teaching methodology that can be quite different from that of general English. However, in some situations- e.g. pre-study or pre-work courses where learners have not started their academic and professional activity and therefore have less subject knowledge—teaching methodology will be similar to that of general English. The use of distinctive methodology is therefore a variable characteristic of ESP.

We therefore return to the question of the defining features of ESP. Looking closely at the 'specific purpose', ESP materials will always draw on the topics and activities of that specific purpose, in many cases exploiting the methodology of the subject area or the profession(Widdowson 1983). For example, an English course for engineers will use engineering situations to present relevant language and discourse; problem-solving activities (calculations, making recommendations) will probably also be used, since they draw on skills and abilities processed by the students. Similarly, a business English course will use case studies as these are widely used in business training. It should also be kept in mind that ESP is concerned with teaching language, discourse and relevant communication skills.

Thus Dudley Evans and Jo St John, ((1998) see the absolute characteristics of ESP as follows:

- ESP is designed to meet the specific needs of the learner.
- ESP makes use of the underlying methodology and activities of the discipline it serves.
- ESP is centred on the language (grammar, lexis, register), skills, discourse and genres appropriate to these activities.

The variable characteristics are:

- ESP may be related to or designed for specific disciplines.
- ESP may use, in specific situations, a different methodology from that of general English.
- ESP is likely to be designed for adult learners, either at a tertiary level institution or in a professional work situation. It could, however, be used for learners at secondary school level.
- ESP is generally designed for intermediate or advanced students. Most ESP courses assume basic knowledge of the language system, but it can be used with beginners.

Designing a course is fundamentally a matter of asking questions in order to provide a reasoned basis for the subsequent process of syllabus design, materials writing, classroom teaching and evaluation. We need to ask a wide range of questions. We need to know:

Why does the student need to learn?

Who is going to be involved in the process? This will need to cover not just student, but all the people who may have some effect on the process: teachers, sponsors, inspectors etc.

Where is the learning to take place? What potential does the place provide? What limitations does it impose?

When is the learning to take place? How much time is available? How will it be distributed?

What does the student need to learn? What aspects of language will be needed and how will they be described? What level of proficiency must be achieved? What topic areas will need to be covered?

How will the learning be achieved? What learning theory will underline the course? What kind of methodology will be employed?

Stages in Course Design

According to Hilda Taba's technical (linear) model of curriculum development (1962); these are the following steps:

Step 1: Diagnosis of needs
Step2: formulation of objectives
Step3: selection of content
Step4: organization of content
Step5: selection of learning experiences
Step6: organization of learning experiences
Step7: Determination of what to evaluate and of ways and means of doing it.

Dudley Evans puts it in the following stages: Needs analysis—Objectives—Syllabus—Materials—Methodology—Evaluation

Needs Analysis

Needs analysis is the process of gathering and interpreting information on the uses to which language learners will put the target language (TL) following instruction; and what the learners will need to do in the following situation in order to learn the target language. The results of needs analysis are used in language programme planning to make decisions about appropriate learning objectives, syllabus content, teaching and assessment methods, learning materials and resources.

Needs analysis involves the collection before and during instruction of both *objective* information (relating to the learner's biographical data, learning purposes and language proficiency) and *subjective* information (relating to learner's attitudes, preferences, wants and expectations).

A variety of procedures are used to collect information for needs analysis. These range from traditional research instruments to informational classroom methods, and include:

- Questionnaires which may be administered to language learners themselves and/ or to other people who are familiar with the context in which learners need to use the language;
- Structured interviews (often used in conjunction with questionnaires) involving a series a series of set questions relating to needs;
- Group discussions with learners;
- Collection and linguistic analysis of authentic spoken and written texts which are typically found in the future context of language use;
- Language tests and assessments;
- Case studies of individual learners.

Needs Analysis: (From: Dudley-Evans and Jo St John, 1998)

1. Professional information about the learners: the tasks and activities learners are/will be using English for—*target situation analysis and objective needs*
2. Personal information about the learners: factors which may affect the way they learn such as previous learning experiences, çultural information, reasons for attending the course and expectations of it, attitude to English-*wants, means, subjective needs.*
3. English language information about the learners: what their current skills and language use are-present situation analysis-which allows us to asses.
4. Language learning information: effective way of learning the skills and language in learning needs.

5. What is wanted from the course?
6. Information about the environment in which the course will be run- *means analysis.*

Objectives

Defining objectives allows us to operationalise the aims and questions the presentation of the contents of a course, but the role of objectives in teaching and learning languages is greater than this, since the information of objectives, i.e. describing them and identifying one from another also means to have attained them. The course objectives based on analysis of learner needs are specified as;

- General objectives
- Specific objectives

Syllabus

One of the main purposes of syllabus is to break down the mass of knowledge to be learnt in manageable units. It should satisfy the needs. We need to be aware of the different roles that the syllabus plays, so that it can be used most appropriately. In particular we need to recognize its ideal nature and, therefore, its limitations as an indicator of learning. The syllabus could be Structural, Situational, Functional, Notional, Skills-specific, and Task-based.

Materials

We can start by asking ourselves the question: what are the materials supposed to do? In defining their purpose, we can identify some principles which will guide us in the actual writing of the materials.

(a) Materials provide a stimulus to learning. Good materials do not teach: they encourage learners to learn. Good materials therefore contain
 -interesting texts;
 -enjoyable activities which engage the learners' thinking capacities;
 -opportunities for learners to use their existing knowledge and skills;

-content which both teachers and learners can cope with.

(b) Materials help to encourage the teaching-learning process, by providing a path through the complex mass of the language to be learnt. Good materials therefore should provide a clear and coherent unit structure which will guide teacher and learner through various activities in such a way as to maximize the chances of learning. Thus structure should help the teacher in planning the lessons and encourage in the learner a sense of progress and achievement. On the other hand, materials should not be so rightly structured as to produce a monotonous pattern of lesson-the curse of so many materials.

(c) Materials embody a view of the nature of language and learning. Materials should truly reflect what we think and feel about learning process.

(d) Materials reflect the nature of learning task. In the heyday of structuralism, it was assumed that the knowledge of structure was the same as knowing a language and that repetition led to learning. Materials writing was a simple task of isolating structure, writing a text exemplify it and pattern drills to practice it. But now we need to take a more humble view and recognize that language learning is a very complex and little understood process. Materials should try to create a balanced outlook which both reflects the complexity of the task, yet makes it appear manageable.

Evaluation

ESP is accountable teaching. ESP learners and sponsors are investors in the ESP course and they want to see a return on their investment of time and money. The managers of the ESP course are accountable to these investors. This accountability has produced a demand for more and better evaluation procedures. Two levels of evaluation have been brought into prominence:

(a) Learner assessment. As with any language course there is a need to assess student performance at strategic point in the course, for example, at the beginning and at the end. But this assessment takes a greater importance in ESP, because ESP is concerned with the ability to perform particular communica-

tive tasks. The capacity to asses proficiency is, therefore, central to the whole concept of ESP. the results of this kind of evaluation, for example, enable sponsors, teachers and learners to decide whether and how much language tuition is required.

(b) *Course evaluation.* A second important form of evaluation is the evaluation of the ESP course itself. This kind of evaluation helps to assess whether the course objectives are being met-whether the course, in other words, is doing what it was designed to do.

These two forms of evaluation are not always distinct. Evaluation of the learners reflects not just the learners' performance but to some extent the effectiveness of the course too. An ESP course is, after all, supposed to be successful: it is set up in order to enable particular learners to do particular things with language. If it consistently fails to meet the objective, then something must be wrong with the course design: the objectives may be too ambitious given the resources available; the analysis of the learners' initial competence may be wrong; the methodology may be inappropriate. Evaluation of the learners is unlikely to indicate exactly where a fault lies; it will at least indicate the exercise of a fault somewhere. More precise diagnostic evaluation can be used to trace the fault.

Bibliography

Breen, M.P. 1987. "Contemporary Paradigm in Syllabus Design." *Language Teaching* Vol. 20, no. 2 pp 81-92.

Clark, J.L. 1987. *Curriculum Renewal in School Foreign Language Learning*. Oxford: Oxford University Press.

Richards, Jack and Willy A. Renandya. 2002. *Methodology in Language Teaching: an anthology of current practices*. Cambridge: Cambridge University Press.

Brumfit, C.J. 1984. *General English Syllabus Design.* (ELT Document 118). Oxford: Pergamom.

Hoadley, Ursila and Jonathan Jansen. 2002. *Curriculum: From Plan to Practices' Learning Guide*, ed. John Gultig and Andendorff. Oxford: Oxford University Press.

Tom Hutchinson and Alan Waters. 1987. *English for Specific Purpose.* Cambridge University Press.

ESP as a Tool for Professionals of Business and Finance: A Needs Assessment and Survey

N. LAKSHMI

English has emerged as the global language for trade and commerce in the last few decades affecting many key aspects of business and finance in the modern world. English language which entered India as a result of colonial expansion has now become the standard for all important official communication not only in India but in many countries of the world. English has emerged as a major language for business and finance all around the world. People wishing to do business globally need to have a good command of spoken English. The ability to write clearly in English is also the key as many forms of business communication from e-mails to presentation and marketing to important business contracts are written in English.

Communication as a tool with English as the medium continues to establish itself as indispensable to organizational growth and progress. English has become the language of the corporate world and has become accepted across nations. Command over basic elements of the language benefits professionals in a number of ways. Through this paper, an exploration has been made to design a few concepts to sharpen the techniques and skills in English usage in business communication.

Challenging technologies at the workplace make it all the more necessary for the workforce to acquire integrated skills relating to the subject and language. A lawyer can use English to attend court exchanges, engineers can use technical English proficiently to submit reports etc., since the characteristic features of English application are recognized much earlier in these fields. When we consider the demands of trade schools all over the world, it caters little in extent to the market needs outside. So, we need English for Specific purposes to counter such problems. Here comes the role of ESP or English for Specific Purposes. The ability to communicate effectively in Business English is now a required skill for many employees worldwide. Financial English will provide you with greater confidence when discussing financial documents and data. It increases verbal fluency for face to face negotiation and the confidence to produce professional written reports in English. A Financial and Business English course is suitable for anyone whose job requires a solid command of Financial and Business English and is particularly a remedy for in-company accountants, banker's internal auditors, financial managers, directors etc. Financial and Business English can be looked at for the following:

1. Key financial and business language use and relevant terminology.
2. Revision of financial and business terms as in financial statements, central banking, retail banking, marketing of services etc.
3. Drafting clear accurate and concise written reports.
4. Skills for negotiations.

Financial and Business English has emerged as the most useful form of English all over the world by virtue of its richness, variety and complexity in applications. The corporate world always likes professionals with a strong foundation of English.

English for Specific Purpose: Definition

English for specific purpose, or ESP for short, is a pedagogy in which the syllabus, contents and methods are determined according to the needs of the learners' specialized subjects who want to enter or choose specific professions. ESP is classified as Scientific English, Business English, Financial English, Legal English, Medical English, Tourism English, and many other categories. The intention of categorization was to use English to carry out professional work in certain work environments. ESP focuses on meeting the actual needs of the students keeping the content in mind in relation to specialized industries. ESP supports the development of the student, his language, his knowledge and skills. To get a more exact definition we can refer to the definition given by Dudley-Evans with the specific characteristics mentioned by him:

Absolute Characteristics

1. ESP is defined to meet specific needs of the learners.
2. ESP makes use of underlying methodology and activities of the discipline it serves.
3. ESP is centred on the language appropriate to these activities in terms of grammar, lexis, register, study skills, discourse and genre.

Variable Characteristics

1. ESP may be related to or designed for specific disciplines.
2. ESP may use, in specific teaching situations, a different methodology from that of General English.
3. ESP is likely to be designed for adult learners, either at a tertiary level institution or in a professional work situation. It could, however, be for learners at secondary school level.
4. ESP is generally designed for intermediate or advanced students.
5. Most ESP courses assume some basic knowledge of the language systems.

ESP—A Needs Assessment

ESP students are adults who are already having some familiarity with English and are learning the language to communicate with a set of professional skills and to perform job-related functions. An ESP program is built on an assessment of purposes and needs and the functions for which English is required. It emphasizes on teaching language in context a little away from the teaching of grammar and structure. An ESP program might deal with development of conversational skills in students who are studying English in order to become tour guides or for preparing students for work in technical fields. Being able to use vocabulary and structure in respect to the major fields of study like computer science, accounting, business management, tourism etc., help them to easily understand and enhance their ability to learn English in a better manner. ESP always integrates subject matter and English language instructions.

In teaching EFL (English as a Foreign Language), all four language skills are stressed equally but in ESP a needs assessment determines which language skills are most needed for professionalized students. English for specific purposes has two distinctive features: First, learners have a clear objective of learning which is need based, learners need to meet in some disciplines the use of English language ability and the other, to have a special content which is oriented towards achieving success in the respective field.

This paper analyses the needs of ESP learners by producing an ideal course design for students of business and finance and provides a few general strategies to teach ESP to specific professionals too.

Objectives of an ideal course design for business students:

1. Subject matter: The organizing of programs on an hourly, daily, weekly basis with activities of vocabulary and reading based on texts of management and finance. Knowledge of the subject enables the students to identify the real context for vocabulary usage.
2. Set Goals and clear objectives: Set short-term goals and long-term goals and short objectives for assessing the students achievements.
3. Learner based environment: Teacher should create a learner based environment to build the learner's confidence by motivation.
4. Reference to context: English should be presented in authentic contexts to make the learners acquainted to identify it with their fields of specialization.

ESP—Finance and Business: A Course Design—Overview

In order to develop one's skills, the incorporation of LSRW skills strategically is a must condition. Let us see how the four LSRW skills can be suitably imparted to develop communication in ESP learners.

Listening: Language which is not understood is just noise and it isn't just any form of language acquisition. To improve language skills, listening comprehension is an effective form. The cloze exercise is a good way to check the students' listening comprehensive abilities. Give them a short passage with some words deleted from it. Read the passage aloud twice. If they are unable to fill the words, then they are unable to make sense of the passage. Let the students work out passages like these and let them focus their attention on these language structures. Make the students take dictation exercises. Recognition of missing words, identifying the tone of the comprehension and identifying the denotation and connotation of the words used can be done by practising listening to small documentaries.

Speaking: To develop spoken skills, one needs to take time to hold conversations in the ESP classroom. However, for each and everyone to speak is not possible in a classroom situation. But other techniques like listening comprehension, role playing, use of flow charts etc. can be done. Listening helps to increase ability to speak; role playing stimulates a conversation and flowcharts helps to figure out to draw an outline of a situation. The objective is to carry on a short conversation advancing fluently with few errors and appropriate answer for the information required.

Activities

- Debating can be used to stimulate ability to converse freely.
- Small JAM Sessions can be held on familiar topics on business or finance like depreciation, assets, marketing, product etc.
- Interpretation of picture or diagrams can be done (fig. of role of auditor, types of banking etc).
- Role playing activity can be started by showing flow charts describing different steps.
- Explaining about a known topic (explaining a balance sheet, explaining the use of journals etc).

Reading: Reading is the primary channel through which your students will progress in English. The reading program should include simple identification skills (decoding), higher level cognitive skills such as analyzing, synthesizing and predicting. Materials should include newspapers, magazines, articles etc. Both intensive and extensive reading skills should be inculcated. Intensive reading by a close analysis of a short passage can be used to develop vocabulary, grammar skills and comprehension. Extensive reading indulges a faster reading of longer passages to develop understanding of writers' organizational strategies, to improve reading speed and to focus on main ideas. To improve oneself in spoken skill, one needs to read more of business magazines, newspaper columns and advertisements to get the flavour and vocabulary used. Vocabulary should be taught only in context rather than as word lists. Grammar is best taught in connection with writing. Comprehension checks can be built into reading as well as listening exercises. Certain points should be noted to give reading texts:

1. Length should be brief rather than long text.
2. Density of information should proceed from familiar to unfamiliar.
3. The text should follow a logical pattern of events.
4. Texts which offer concreteness are better to speculative texts.
5. Opinions from the text should be drawn.
6. Distinguish main ideas from supporting details.
7. Summarize the text.
8. Understanding information directly stated or implied.
9. Scanning to locate specific information.
10. Deducing meaning from lexical items from context.

Writing: Learners should focus their writing skills on the basis not only on the English grammar structure but on the usage and comprehension of the language in relationship to context. In speaking the opportunity to monitor usage of grammar is lesser when compared to writing and the grammatical forms which should be observed and learnt are those that control sentence level functions such as question form, negation, relative clause formation and other structures involved in subordination and coordination. Students should be given assignments to check paragraph features such as tense continuity, parallel structure and connectors.

Structural errors like subject-verb agreement, articles, word order problems, present tense, verb +ing form, passive voice, spelling and punctuation should be observed as they occur in their assignment. Students should be able to compose paragraphs on familiar topics.

Activities

- Exercises should include dictation, cloze exercises or fill-in-the-blanks. They help to hypothesize and to recognize relationships between sentences.
- Sentences combining exercises like combining two simple sentences help to support co-ordination and coherence.
- Reordering jumbled sentences helps build understanding paragraph structure.
- Note-taking exercises to practise recording information.
- Outlining main points helps them to make and plan their own patterns.
- Summarizing exercise helps them to express information in their own words.
- Writing descriptions helps them to improve vocabulary and contextualization.

Strategies for Learning ESP

1. Focus on Learning: The ESP student has a particular purpose and focus for learning. People learn languages when they have opportunity to understand and work with language in a context which they find interesting. English should be presented in authentic context to acquaint the learners with the particular ways the language is used in functions that they will need to perform in their specialty fields.
2. Subject matter knowledge: Knowledge of the specialty area enables the students to identify a real context for the vocabulary and structures of the ESP classroom. In this way, the learners can take advantage of what they already have in their minds regarding their area of study and at the same time learn English.
3. Adult learning abilities: The adult in the ESP classroom has a language learning ability which is more than the normal students in an academic classroom. Educated adults have a be-

havioural pattern which allows them to expand vocabulary, modify linguistic behavior and become more articulate in correspondence with situations and new roles.

4. The students of ESP need to build on the vocabulary of English for Specific Purposes and have to master the stylistic discourse structure, language features and expression patterns.
5. Students find that professional vocabulary, longer sentences, hard core concepts and theories are hard to be understood. Hence, it is better to start teaching them professional phrases in the beginning with introduction to professional terms, grammatical features of these sentences used and then analyzing discourse structures.
6. ESP teachers should take the initiative to devise a variety of teaching methods, creating an active classroom atmosphere to fully mobilize the initiative of the students. The learning approach should be positive.
7. ESP teachers' role is to enable learners to develop their language skills within a business context. Teachers of Business English are first and foremost the teachers of English.
8. Business English differs from teaching General English in the choice of contexts for listening and reading texts and in the choice of lexis in grammar and vocabulary exercises. "Can you explain how a balance sheet works?" is a question which supposes the answer in simple English. The answer to this question provides the teacher of ESP with plenty of diagnostic data about the weaknesses in the learner's grammar, gaps in their vocabulary and pronunciation problems. The teacher in his role as language provider can do the necessary correction and provide the correct word or phrase where necessary.
9. Learners can be asked to give a presentation about their particular product; describe their company or talk about their current research. The teacher can give guidance at the preparation stage and then give a feedback on performance.
10. It becomes a teaching and learning process for both the ESP teacher and the learner. A great deal of information about a wide range of business processes can be acquired and explained.

Small Survey

Skills needed for MBA Professionals

Content	Rate
Speaking	50%
Listening	20%
Reading	10%
Writing	20%

We focused on the skills of speaking, listening, writing, reading, translation or decoding and examination or analyses as the criteria. The MBA students focused on the need of abilities in speaking, listening and writing English as urgent, with speaking ranking the first.

Skills which improved as a result of ESP

Contents	Rate
Speaking	30%
Listening	15%
Reading	30%
Writing	25%

Is ESP practical

Contents	Rate
Highly practical	24%
Practical	61%
Not quite practical	13%
Unpractical	2%

The results show that the practicality of ESP teaching was confirmed by 85% of the students.

Rate of improvement of language abilities

Contents	Rate
Listening	10%
Speaking	25%
Reading	50%
Writing	15%

Difficulty of an ESP Course

Contents	Rate
Very difficult	8%
Difficult	51%
Moderate	38%
Easy	3%
Very Easy	0%

More than half of the students felt the course difficult. It is a bit beyond students' level at present since it is new to Indian students. However, along with the advance of English level of the newly enrolled students, the course tends to become moderate in the near future.

Rate of improvement by an ESP Course:

Contents	Rate
Greatly improved	8%
Improved	51%
Not significantly improved	38%
Not improved	3%

Of the samples, 59% confirmed that their ability in professional communication had been improved; however there were still 41% of the students who thought otherwise.

Recommendations on the basis of survey

We can conclude that students have a definite target need for English at a professional level and it is necessary to deliver ESP course to postgraduates. Most postgraduates desire to improve their abilities in English listening, speaking and writing, but they neglect the importance of style and rhetoric in advanced reading. An ESP course is highly practical and useful to raise students' ability in professional communication chiefly in the aspect of reading and writing, but not so significantly in speaking. Listening and speaking can be improved by making them listen to live channels like the BBC and a few educational instructional channels like the Discovery, NDTV Profit, CNBC etc. Instructors of ESP also need to improve their teaching methods and keep themselves up-to-date. Student-centred approach should be adopted in teaching and the mutual communication between teachers and students should be emphasized in class to raise students' oral ability in professional communication.

Conclusion

We encounter a lot of problems to teach English for Specific Purposes such as suitability of teachers to teach for a particular profession; difficulty in selecting teaching material; establishing the assessment standards and so on. The students should take advantage of every opportunity to have an English language experience—see a movie, go to a lecture etc. The students should be advised to a news program on BBC etc. Students should take inspiration by reading for pleasure books in English like novels and short stories. Books like Business World, Business Concepts for English Practice, Fluency Squares etc. are helpful books in improving English for Business and Finance.

The current college English teaching curriculum also needs to be changed a little in order to accommodate the new challenges or new technologies of the workplace in a changing world. A suitable Needs assessment and an ideal course design along with an authentic survey lie at the very heart of the best practices for an effective and accountable ESP course.

Bibliography

Main, Jeremy (1983) "The Battle for Quality Begins" ed. R. Speegle and W.B. Giesecke, *Business World*, OUP: London.

Bates and Evans (1976) "General Science," *Nucleus: English for Science and Technology Series*. Longman: London.

Dudley-Evans, Tony (1998). *Developments in English for Specific Purposes: A multi-disciplinary approach.* Cambridge University Press: London.

Era of Globalization: Vision and Values for the English Teacher

K. NARASIMHA RAO

Globalization has been defined as the intensification of worldwide social relations which link distant localities in such a way that local happenings are shaped by events occurring many miles away and vice versa" (Giddens 1990: 64). Globalization refers to the expanding connectivity, integration, and interdependence of economic, social, technological, cultural, political, and ecological spheres across local activities. In an increasingly globalized society, empowered individuals communicate across cultural and national boundaries as citizens of the world.

Globalization began in 15th century Europe, when Europeans began to map and colonize the world and gained momentum in the latter part of the 20th century. It is viewed as a "'work in progress' which is unequally developed in different parts of the world. A steamroller of late modernity, it is defied as taking away all that is authentic and meaningful in our lives. It is seen as an egalitarian process and an extension of American imperialism.

In a sense, Television and the Internet supply us with a huge amount of information functioning as observation windows or surveillance cameras through which we can always see what is happening and how people live throughout the world. Paul Virilio in *The Information Bomb* uses the phrase, "the globalization of the gaze" (18). It seems that people speak as if the world has already been homogenized. This feeling is also connected with the teaching of English as the common global language. In short, there is a sense that because this is the age of globalization, you must learn to speak English. English competence is a powerful tool to survive the age of the globalization. English ranks second among languages of the world as to its number of native speakers. It comes after Chinese, which has the greatest number of native speakers.

English is a language with speakers who have acquired it and use it as a second language. English which is second in its number of native speakers in the world at present occupies the first place in its economic strength, while Chinese which has the highest number of native speakers in the world ranks seventh in its economic strength. German which is the tenth language in the world in its native speakers ranks third in economic strength. Japanese is an excellent example of being a giant in terms of its economic strength, but unlike English and the US, lacks in terms of power of being widely used in all spheres of life.

David Crystal (1997) in *English as a Global Language* attests this spread of English language worldwide since it is the most taught foreign language all over the world and has produced more pidgins than any other foreign language. Being known as the best source of borrowing loan words from other languages, it is also the language of "higher communication" in the fields of science and technology.

The perception of English as an International language necessitates a shift of emphasis in pedagogy that has been realized by scholars in different countries. Larry E. Smith (1978, 1983) and Nunan (1999), Talebinezhad and Aliakbari (2001) looked into English as an International Language (EIL) as the proper model for teaching English in the era of globalization. With a large number of people speaking varieties of English, the British and American accent no longer stand as the models of pronunciation. Students need to be taught intelligible pronunciation and a tolerance towards the different varieties of English. They also need to be "alerted to lexical variety within standard Englishes and shown how English can express cultural identity which is not that of an English or American culture."

The seven underlying concepts for Teaching English as Foreign Language (TEFL) that would serve as a blueprint for English education in the 21st century are:

- learner centred curriculum
- communicatively designed

- proficiency-based approach to use the language effectively for purposes of practical communication.
- integration of the four skills from the beginning of instruction
- connecting EFL instruction with other disciplines
- fostering a high level of intellectual function promoting learning skills of more general application (e.g. analysis, memorizing, drawing of inferences).
- flexible and eclectic way of presenting contents

The idea of "focus on the learner" suggested by Richards and Oller (1975) greatly changed the roles of language teachers in their classrooms. The teacher can no longer be only a lecturer in a language class. We have to take other roles like materials adaptors, facilitators, consultants, and evaluators. In cooperative learning, the teacher must know the management techniques. He or she has to understand five principles underlying learner contribution in an external syllabus: 1) learner commitment, 2) learners as materials writers and collaborators, 3) learners as problem solvers, 4) learners as knowers, and 5) learners as evaluators and assessors. In brief, the teachers have to pay more attention to the students and get them involved in the teaching and learning process.

Shifts of emphasis need to be made in the teaching of English skills especially in reading and writing. It is rightly contended that the practices in the skill of reading, especially among young people who grew up with computers, are shifting from the page to the screen. This shift requires different psycholinguistic processes that are related to decoding information from the screen instead of the page. This necessitates changes in the teaching of reading subskills such as skimming, guessing words from a context and scanning. Of special importance is the combination of texts with graphics, images and audio-visual content to convey a message.

The writing skill has been given little emphasis worldwide. When it is given emphasis, that emphasis comes in the framework of "putting on paper grammatically correct sentences." This was sufficient to the learner before the information revolution of the 1970s. The rise of informationalism and the widespread use of computers and the Internet call for the need for effective written communication. The following writing sub-skills are needed:

- Integrating texts, graphics and audio-visual material into a presentation
- Audience orientation dispensing with jargonish communication.
- computer-mediated communication—email writing and various forms of synchronous real time communication

In higher education if one of our goals in language teaching is to prepare our students to be qualified world citizens, the ability to use English and the Internet is one essential quality. English teacher should envision the administering of the following skills, competencies and qualifications that enable the students to acquire better quality and build their competency levels.

a. Skills: conceptual skills, operating skills, technical skills, management skills, human skills, and communication skills.
b. Competencies: English proficiency, computer literacy, analytical ability, innovation, and critical thinking.
c. Qualifications: Meet international standards, adopt the attitudes of life-long learning, and have positive attitudes towards learning and working. In addition, they should be able to work in a team.

Therefore, to help the students at the higher level, to become equipped with the skills that both academic and business sectors require, English skills, computer skills and knowledge of cultures need to be integrated into language courses. To meet the international standard and in designing a language course, one must consider the local needs as well as regional and global needs.

Goal 1: To use English to communicate in social settings.

Goal 2: To use English to achieve academically in all content areas.

Goal 3: To use English in socially and culturally appropriate ways.

In terms of materials development, different types of materials such as texts, newspapers, tapes, CD-Rom, Internet, etc. should be used where appropriate, to encourage both learning and acquisition in the classroom and outside the classroom. Teachers can supplement their teaching by using IT tasks such as CALL activities, e-mail writing tasks, web-based projects, electronic student portfolios, etc.

In addition, the roles of the teacher and learner will change according to the new teaching paradigm. The teachers have to act as teachers, facilitators, mentors, as well as assessors and evaluators, whereas the students have to be learners, collaborators, problem solvers, thinkers, as well as assessors and evaluators. It should be remembered that "There is no intellectual growth without some reconstruction, some reworking" (Dewey 1938:64). Adopting the attitude of life-long learning may assist us to reach our common goals. As English educators, we need to explore how globalization is (re)shaping and (re)defining literature and language:

- Literature is broadening in terms of authors, audiences, genres, and modes of representations. Readers have an expanded set of possible identities, discourses, subjectivities, communities, and modes of interpretation.

The corpus of print literature is expanding almost exponentially because of the number of works either being written in English or being quickly translated into English. Prospective teachers of English, as well as English educators, must now be much more attuned than they were in the past to works being written by major authors outside the United States or the British Commonwealth.

Non-print literature—television and motion pictures—is an invaluable literary asset in providing viewers with a sense of verisimilitude about the diverse physical and social worlds of the characters. For a given historical period, geographic setting, or futuristic world, television and film can realistically depict the eating habits, clothing, means of transportation, class system, work habits, societal concerns, religious practices, and family life in the context. In short, English educators and their students should recognize the strengths of both non-print and print literature in providing a sense of the outward and inner worlds of persons different from themselves.

- Language is changing the role of English in global contexts, resulting in uses and forms that diverge from a single standard. Communicators have multiple Englishes to mesh for rhetorical purposes within and across cultural discourse practices.

While researchers and teachers of English in the US have been stating for over thirty years that the formal teaching of grammar in isolation from the teaching of writing is simply not effective in a globalized world, this statement becomes more relevant than ever. There is not one English, but a plethora of world Englishes through which our students could communicate (Canagarajah 2006). These world Englishes may vary according to the culture or nation in which they are spoken and resultant convergences with that nation's native language.

Teaching media literacy is more important than ever as students grow up in a world where they encounter media messages hundreds of times daily, from advertisements on websites to billboards, TV, radio, and popular music. It is important that they become critical, meta-aware readers of media texts so that they can be thoughtful, critical agents in a world where they are increasingly encouraged to be passive consumers of information, materials, and goods.

As information technologies and a so-called "flattening" world (Friedman, 2005) make global communication and collaboration more ubiquitous, teachers of reading, writing, speaking, listening, and viewing are being forced to change the way they instruct their students. Twenty-first century literacy educators must broaden their curricular horizons and align their teaching with the real-life multicultural and multimodal communication needs of their students who increasingly live and work in a globalized society. Through such critical literacies, students can communicate and collaborate across cultural and national boundaries through technologies that afford them unprecedented ways to reinterpret, appropriate, and negotiate texts in order to participate more fully in local and global communities.

The teaching of English in the era of globalization has put more demands on the teacher of English. Apart from teachers playing an important role in increasing the students' motivation, the students are to be given a shift from knowing to doing in order to bridge the gap between the curriculum and the requirements of the job market. The teachers in this noble task have to concentrate their energies to conduct research, develop instructional strategies, overcome stereotypes, disseminate ideas, arrange workshops and seminars, make teaching relevant to world realities, link ELT professionals worldwide, and establish links with professional association.

In the future, today's youth will be required to actively address economic, environmental, and cultural problems that could have widespread and long-term consequences for themselves and their world. In order to be active problem solvers, they should be able to think with clarity, imagination, and empathy. Literacy instruction is one avenue through which such contemporary critical thinking might be taught. By teaching literacy skills through social-cultural methods of language study, global rhetorical approaches to writing, and juxtaposed multimedia representations, students can begin to think critically and globally in a world that, increasingly, will require a politically and socially active citizenry.

Bibliography

Canagarajah, S. (2006). The Place of world Englishes in composition: Pluralization continued. *CCC*, 57 (4), 586-619.

Crystal, David (1997) *English as a Global Language*. Cambridge: Cambridge University Press.

Dewey, J. 1938. *Art as Experience*. New York: Minton, Balch.

Friedman, T. (2005). *The World is flat: A brief history of the twenty-first century*. New York: Farrow, Straus & Giroux.

Giddens, A. 1990. *The Consequences of Modernity*, Cambridge: Polity Press.

Graddol, David. et al (1997) *English: History, Diversity and Change*. London: Routledge.

Pennycook, A. 1994. *The Cultural Politics of English as an International Language*. London: Longman.

Richards, J.C. and Oller, J.W., ed., 1975. Focus on the Learner. New York: Newbury House Publishers.

Virilio, P. (2000). *The Information Bomb*. London: Verso.

Weaver, C. (1996). *Teaching grammar in context*. Portsmouth, NH: Boynton/ Cook.

Widdowson, H.G. 1978. Teaching Language as Communication. London: Oxford University Press.

Internet Sources

http://globalization.about.com/library/weekly/aa040401a.htm

http://www. tesol.org/pubs/articles/2002/tm12-3-09.html

http://www.jceps.com/?pageID=article&articleID=95

http://www.cal.org/ericcll/digest/0013ESLstandards.html

http://www.ncte.org/cee/2007summit/globalization

Communication Skills for Engineering Students in English Language: A Study on First Year B.Tech Students

B. NEELAMBARAM and M. JAYARANJAN

It is often said that students are the best judges of the curriculum, course structure and teacher performance. A needs survey conducted by B. Neelambaram & M. Jayaranjan among the students of I/IV B. Tech Course at V.R. Siddhartha Engineering College, Vijayawada, on the language skills reveal that communication skills are among their top priorities.

In the globalized context and present scenario, students of Engineering and Technology need a specific set of language skills for their success in education and career. English for B.Tech students poses a challenge to them. Industries are also voicing their concerns about the need for better communication skills among students of Engineering. Therefore, English for Engineering students should be framed to suit the requirements of the evolving curriculum and the world of work outside college.

Rationale

The current system of Board of Intermediate Education in Andhra Pradesh, does not prepare students well enough for entering into the first year of an undergraduate programme in Engineering and Technology. The recent trends in the world, such as globalization, have stressed the need to develop communicative competency in the individuals.

The professional profile of a modern qualified engineer should include well-developed communication skills and English language proficiency to help him/her achieve success in the cut-throat competitive global arena. In the process of educating future engineers, special emphasis on English becomes necessary. In order to identify their English language needs, the researchers designed and administered a questionnaire.

Objectives of the Study

The survey was conducted with the following objectives in view:

1. To find out the language needs of the Engineering students
2. To discover students' expectations regarding their teachers of English

Theoretical Background

EAP (English for Academic Purposes) researchers, such as Christison and Krahnke, 1986; Ferris, 1998; Ostler, 1980, have surveyed L2 students enrolled in subject-matter courses to ascertain their perceptions about the relative importance of language skills and classroom tasks for academic success (Stoller 2001). Ostler's early study showed that students felt the greatest need to develop the ability to read textbooks (indicated by 90% of respondents), followed by the need to listen and take notes (84%), ask questions in class (68%), write research papers (58%).

Huckin and Olson (1983), while speaking about the importance of communication skills, refer to the survey conducted by the American Society for Engineering Education to determine which academic subjects are most needed for engineering careers in industry. Responses were received from 4057 experienced engineers. The results show that communication skills rank above any other type of skill, capturing five of the nine most needed categories. Other items in the list are technical writing, public speaking, working with individuals, working with groups and talking with people.

The Language Studies Unit of the Curriculum Development Cell, IIT, Kanpur conducted a national survey in 1990 for the purpose of identifying English Language Needs for Technical Education. This survey was funded by the Department of Education, Ministry of Human Resource Development, New Delhi. Data was collected on the nature of language-related needs of technical students across the country to provide an objective database for developing a more learner-centred curriculum. Basing on the findings, the following courses were developed: 1. Introduction to Technical Communication 2. Advanced Technical Writing.

Research Tool and Methodology

A survey was conducted on 50 B. Tech Degree students at V.R. Siddhartha Engineering College (Autonomous) affiliated to JNTU (K) with the aim to identify the students' language needs. A close-ended questionnaire with fourteen categories, supplied with specifications for each category, was administered. The respondents were students of the first year, studying at the following departments: Mechanical Engineering, Computer Science and Engineering, Electronics and Communication Engineering.

Questions 1 to 7 are related to personal information. Questions 8 to 14 tries deal with information on the needs of the students and their expectation of English teachers.

The students were asked to choose the options in the questionnaire in the order of priority. Their responses were pooled, tabulated, and final rank for each category was computed.

Findings

The main objective of the survey was to find out the perception of the students of Engineering and Technology of the kind of language skills required.

The responses to the research questions of the survey were:

Q. No. 8: Do you think you that need to improve your proficiency of English even at this stage of your Education?

98% of students said YES and only 2% of the students said NO

Q. No. 9: What are your needs pertaining to English language learning?

Out of 7 language skills and sub skills option 'B' i.e., Speaking Skills and option 'G' Grammar and option 'A' Listening Skills were ranked the highest. Speaking Skills received the highest importance from the students' perception, 50% of the students opted speaking Skills as their first priority. Option 'G' Grammar was opted as the second choice with 18% and option 'A' Listening Skills was opted by 10% of the students

Q. 10. Is the English Language course helpful for your future?

94% of Students answered YES and 6% of Students opted TO SOME EXTENT as their option. The findings indicate that the students are really in need of this course and also think that it will be helpful to their future.

Q.11. Do you think that, you require more attention on any of the following?

a. Listening skills
b. Speaking skills
c. Reading skills
d. Writing skills
e. Pronunciation
f. Vocabulary
g. Grammar

The Students were asked to choose one of the above options and give their priorities in order of preference. Speaking Skills was given the highest priority i.e., 36% of the students opted for it as their first preference. Grammar received second best priority i.e., 24% from the student's perception. Listening Skills, Reading Skills and Vocabulary received equal importance by the students i.e., 10%.

Q. 12Do you think that teachers of English in Engineering College require a special set of competencies?

90% of students stated YES.

Q.13Do you want the teachers of English in Engineering College to be facilitators, who know the strategies of modern classroom teaching and give you a lot of activities in the classroom and make you an active participant?

94% of students stated YES, which is an indication that the students of Engineering and Technology would like to see their English Teachers to be well versed in modern strategies of classroom teaching. Which means an English Teacher in an Engineering college requires technical expertise which will be helpful in moulding the students as a rounded professional.

Q.14. Do you think that a separate English course should be framed branch wise?

58% of the Students said NO and 42% of the students said YES which is a sign that students do not want a separate course according to their branch.

Recommendations

1. The Engineering students surveyed have very clearly indicated which English language skills they needed for their education and future career. Based on the findings, we can design and develop a modern curriculum for Technical English and Communication Skills for Engineering students of Andhra Pradesh.
2. 90% of the students agree that teachers of English in Engineering colleges need a specific set of competencies because of the skills they are expected to develop in their students. Hence, the teachers can be given competency-based training to train the students in a better manner.
3. The fact that the students want their English teachers to be facilitators and trainers in the classroom is a clear evidence of the existing need to rethink the roles of English teachers at Engineering colleges and a sign that teachers have to be adept in modern classroom teaching strategies.
4. Responses to the Question number 9 and 11 clearly indicate that students really want to improve their Speaking Skills.

Conclusion

The participants of the survey, who are Engineering students have given us the data that requires a serious attention. Thus, we recommend that their views be taken into consideration when formulating the English curriculum and developing courses in engineering colleges and universities in the future.

Bibliography

Flowerdew, John and Matthew Peacock, *Research Perspectives on English for Academic Purposes*. London: Cambridge University Press. 2001.

Huckin, N. Thomas and Leslie A. Olson, *English for Science and Technology: A Handbook for Nonnative Speakers.* Singapore: McGraw-Hill. 1983.

Sing, Damayanti, ed. *Identifying English Language Needs for Technical Education,* Survey 2. Kanpur: Language Studies Unit, Curriculum Development Cell, IIT. 1990.

Internet Source

http://dialnet.unirioja.es/servlet/articulo?codigo=918880

QUESTIONNAIRE
FOR B.TECH STUDENTS

Note: Kindly put a tick mark (√) in the relevant boxes, except where a descriptive answer is required.

1. Name of the student:
2. Branch:
3. Age:
4. Sex: Male ( ) Female ( )
5. Mother tongue:
6. Name of the college:
7. Affiliated to: J.N.T.U ( )

8. Do you think you need to improve your proficiency of English even at this of your Education? Yes ( ) No ( )

9. What are your needs pertaining to English language learning? If you think that more than one option is required, please indicate it by using numerals (1, 2, 3 . . . etc) in descending order of their usefulness.

a. Listening skills ( )
b. Speaking skills ( )
c. Reading skills ( )
d. Writing skills ( )
e. Pronunciation ( )
f. Vocabulary ( )
g. Grammar ( )

10. Is the English Language course helpful for your future?

Yes ( ) No ( ) To some extent ( )

11. Do you think that, you require more attention on any of the following? If you think that more than one option is required,

please indicate it by using numerals (1, 2, 3 . . . etc) in descending order of their usefulness.

h. Listening skills ( )
i. Speaking skills ( )
j. Reading skills ( )
k. Writing skills ( )
l. Pronunciation ( )
m. Vocabulary ( )
n. Grammar ( )

12. Do you think that teachers of English in Engineering colleges need a special set of competencies? Yes ( ) No ( )

13. Do you want the teachers of English in Engineering College to be facilitators, who know the strategies of modern classroom teaching and give you a lot of activities in the classroom and make you an active participant? Yes ( ) No ( )

14. Do you think that a separate English course should be framed branch wise? Yes ( ) No ( )

ESP: Reading Skills in Technical students

A. PADMAJA

In Andhra Pradesh, there are approximately 650 engineering and technical colleges, allowing an annual intake of nearly 1.8 lakh students. Then naturally the question of quality looms large. Already the situation is grave as a recent Nasscom McKinsey study has revealed that only around 10 per cent of the Andhra Pradesh's fresh engineering graduates are "actually employable." It might be noted that the low quality of basic skill sets of reading and writing might be one of the glaring reasons for the poor performance of the students of our state. In the modern age of information, reading is a fundamental survival skill. Reading has always been an important part of the learning process in college classrooms. Students' performance is directly proportionate to the student's ability to read. However, the amount of student reading is declining, affecting the classroom performance of the students.

Some of the reasons for the lack of interest can be low self-confidence, lack of reading comprehension skills, disinterest in the research topic and subject matter, and underestimating the significance of completing the required reading.[1] Here, I would like to explore how teachers can improve the reading comprehension ability.

Reading is a process of constructing meaning by interacting with text; as individuals read, they use their prior knowledge along with clues from the text to construct meaning. According to the National Reading Panel (NRP), "The ability to read requires proficiency in a number of domains such as 'phonemic awareness', 'phonics', 'fluency', 'vocabulary' and 'comprehension or reading comprehension'." It indicates connectivity of many things during reading and also all the concepts mentioned will help for effective reading.[2]

Research indicates that effective or expert readers are strategic (Baker & Brown, 1984a, 1984b). Reading is mainly a decoding process where the decoder decodes the encoded message. It has been rightly called as "psycholinguistic guessing game" by Kenneth Goodman. This means that they have purposes for their reading and adjust their reading to each purpose and for each reading task. Strategic readers use a variety of strategies and skills as they construct meaning (Paris, Wasik, & Turner, 1991). A strategy is a plan selected deliberately by the reader to accomplish a particular goal or to complete a given task (Paris, Lipson, & Wixson, 1983; Paris, Wasik, & Turner, 1991). When students are able to select and use a strategy automatically, they have achieved independence in using the strategy. Along with the strategies that expert readers use, they also use a number of comprehension and study skills. It is clear from research that readers develop the use of strategies and skills by reading and writing and being given the support they need to grow in these processes (Wells, 1990).[3]

The two strategies which have a significant impact on reading the text are cognitive and metacognitive strategies. Cognitive strategies are seen as mental processes directly concerned with the processing of information in order to learn, that are for obtaining, storage, retrieval or use of information. Brown (1994) defines cognitive strategies as specific learning tasks which involve more direct manipulation of the learning material itself. In general, studies in cognitive strategies reveal the use of bottom-up and top-down. Goodman (1998) refers to the bottom up model as the 'common sense' notion. In this approach, reading is meant to be a process of decoding; identifying letter, words, phrases and then sentences in order to get the meaning. On the other hand, Carrell (1998) termed reading process as "an active psychological guessing game." Top down rejects the notion that identification of letters to form words, and the derivation of meaning from these words is efficient reading. On the contrary, it assumed that efficient reading requires the readers to make predictions and hypothesis about the text content by relating the new information to their prior knowledge and by using as few language clues as possible. It is further assumed that the readers can confirm whether the hypothesis was correct or otherwise by sampling the text. Both bottom-up and top-down theories formed the Models of Reading.

Cognitive strategies are useful tools in assisting students with learning problems. The term "cognitive strategies" in its simplest form is the use of the mind (cognition) to solve a problem or complete a task. Cognitive strategies may also be referred to as procedural facilitators (Bereiter & Scardamalia, 1987), procedural prompts (Rosenshine, 1997) or scaffolds (Palincsar & Brown, 1984). Cognitive strategies provide a structure for learning when a task cannot be completed through a series of steps. For example, algorithms in mathematics provide a series of steps to solve a problem. Attention to the steps results in successful completion of the problem. In contrast, reading comprehension, a complex task, is a good example of a task that does not follow a series of steps. Reading comprehension is an area where cognitive strategies are important. A self-questioning strategy can help students understand what they read. Rosenshine states that the act of creating questions does not lead directly to comprehension. Instead, students search the text and combine information as they generate questions; then they comprehend what they have read. The use of cognitive strategies can increase the efficiency with which the learner approaches a learning task. These academic tasks can include, but are not limited to, remembering and applying information from course content, constructing sentences and paragraphs, editing written work, paraphrasing, and classifying information to be learned. In a classroom where cognitive strategies are used, the teacher fulfills a pivotal role, bridging the gap between student and content/skill to be learned. This role requires an understanding of the task to be completed, as well as knowledge of an approach (or approaches) to the task that he/she can communicate to the learner.[4]

Some definitions of metacognition are: (i) "Metacognitive theory deals with cognitive self-knowledge, that is, what individuals know about their own thinking (Kellog, 1994)." (ii)The emergence of metacognitive theory has given a clear understanding of the complex phenomena which involves learners' awareness and the controlling process during learning. (iii) Flavell (1976) describes metacognition as one's knowledge concerning one's own cognitive processes and products or anything related to active monitoring of consequent regulation and orchestration of these processes. Metacognition is a form of cognition which involves active control over cognitive process. There also appears to be a strong relationship between reading strategies used by readers, metacognitive awareness, and reading proficiency. In essence, successful readers appeared to use more strategies than less successful readers and also appeared to be using them more frequently. (Baker & Brown, 1984; Garner, 1987; Afflerbach, 2002).

Metacognition's basic tenet is that by understanding what the mind is thinking during learning, an individual will be able to focus his strengths and improve upon his weaknesses when trying to comprehend a text. An awareness of knowledge can be described as cognition, while metacognition is a deeper, more involved process that utilizes that knowledge, and applies strategies when cognitive processes fail to serve the learner in tackling a piece of writing. The first step to improving reading skills through metacognition is to avoid distraction. The mind can be easily distracted away from a piece of writing due to the external environment, but people can re-train their brains to identify the interruption, and then refocus on the task at hand. One way to do this is to perform an interior dialogue, focusing on the brain processes as they occur. For example, as an individual is attempting to tackle a text, he or she might find thoughts of other projects or social obligations creeping in and blocking out the comprehension that should be taking place. It is important to note this interruption, become aware of the types of distractions that are most common, and to re-train the brain to ignore these and focus on the text.[5]

Yet another new technique has been developed by researchers Janette K. Klingner, Sharon Vaughn, and Jeanne Schumm for students with learning disabilities who are in general education classrooms. CSR integrates word identification, reciprocal reading, and cooperative learning to enable struggling readers can use to decode and comprehend as they read the content area text. The four strategies used are the

1. Preview: before reading the students brainstorm the prior knowledge and predict what will be learned.
2. Click and Chuck: Students identify words or word parts that were hard to understand (called "clunks"). A sequence of "fix-up strategies" is used to decode the "clunk." These strategies are: (a) re-reading the sentence for key ideas, (b) looking for context clues in the sentences before and after, (c) looking for prefixes or suffixes, and (d) breaking the word apart to find smaller words.
3. Get the gist: Students learn to ask themselves: What is the most important person, place, or thing? What is the most important idea about the person, place or thing?
4. Wrap up: After reading, students construct their own questions to check for understanding of the passage, answer the questions, and summarize what has been learned.

Conclusion

It rests with the teachers on how they employ different strategies to promote the reading skills among the learners/students. I as a teacher first try to evaluate their level of reading by holding a simple test. Then, after assessing the level of reading ability, I have tried to promote the reading skills among the students with the help of different strategies by devising suitable exercises. Well, I might say that the outcome is often not very encouraging. One of the reasons can be the non compliance on the part of the student. But it again depends on the teacher's motivation in motivating the students.

References

1. Simon A. Lei, Kerry A. Bartlett, Suzanne E. Gorney, Tamra R. Herschbach. "Resistance to reading compliance among college students: instructors' perspectives" *College Student Journal*, June, 2010.
2. http://www.articlesbase.com/self-improvement-articles/how-to-develop-reading-skills-297612.html#ixzz14fF2SE4d
3. http://www.eduplace.com/rdg/res/literacy/st_read0.html

4. An Introduction to Cognitive Strategies, *Special Connections*, http://www.specialconnections.ku.edu/cgi-bin/cgiwrap/specconn/main.php?cat=instruction&section=cs/main
5. Morrow Licia, *How to improve reading skills through metacogtion*
6. http://www.helium.com/items/1443955-reading-skills

Bibliography

Lessard-Clouston. Michael, "*Strategies and Success in Technical Vocabulary Learning: Students' Approaches in One Academic Context*," *Indian Journal of Applied Linguistics* vol. 34, no. 1-2, Jan-Dec 2008

Cubukcu Feryal. Enhancing vocabulary development and reading comprehension through metacognitive strategies, *Issues in Educational Research,* 18(1), 2008 1

http://www.specialconnections.ku.edu/cgi-bin/cgiwrap/specconn/index.php

http://en.wikipedia.org/wiki/Metacognition

http://charityguide.org/volunteer/fewhours/adult-literacy.htm

Role of English: 'Classroom to Career'

V.R. PRANUTHI

It is a de facto that English is now the dominant or official language in almost 70 countries and is represented in every continent. English undoubtedly is the sole universal language which allows communication via electronic means that avoids subsequent confusion. The Twentieth century has witnessed numerous technological inventions and developments which have brought about a drastic change in communication. The following quote justifies the prominence of English - 'Most of the scientific, technological and academic information in the world is expressed in English and over 80% of all the information stored in electronic retrieval systems is in English' (Crystal. D, 1997). In India, people going from North to South for education or business mostly communicate in English, which has become a link language. Keeping this in mind, the Parliament has also recognized English as an official language in addition to Hindi. All the facts of history and developments in present day India underline the continued importance of learning English in addition to vernaculars.

This paper focuses on the role of English in education and career with a special reference to the fields of Tourism and Hospitality and is written taking into consideration the Bangalore University Curriculum for the students of these courses. The protuberant fact is that there has been a remarkable gap between the academics and the industry as far as English as a language for communication is concerned. The underlying fact is that this gap, results in discouraging levels of employment in the above mentioned industries which are largely people oriented. ESP holds unique importance because of its usage as the most popular lingua franca.

This paper throws light on four aspects with regard to classroom teaching:

i. How important is English for the students of Tourism and Hospitality?
ii. What is being taught in the classroom (with respect to Oral and Written Communication)?
iii. Does what is being taught suffice what the industry expects from a potential employee?
iv. What aspects need to be implemented in the curriculum to mitigate the gap between the academics and the industry?

How important is English for the students of Tourism and Hospitality?

Let us look at the importance of English in Tourism and Hospitality industries before we begin with its relevance to the students.

These industries being largely global foreign languages play an invaluable role when dealing with the people of other countries. Language, so far as we know, is something specific to humans, that is to say it is the basic capacity that distinguishes humans from all other living beings. Language therefore remains potentially a communicative medium capable of expressing ideas and concepts as well as moods, feelings and attitudes. The historical circumstances of India (having been ruled by the British for over two centuries) have given the Indians an easy access to mastering English language, and innumerable opportunities for advancement in the field of science and technology. It is spoken by more than 300 million native speakers, and between 400 and 800 million foreign users. It is the official language of air transport and shipping; the leading language. of science, technology, computers, and commerce; and a major medium of education, publishing, and international negotiation. English is a means not only for international commerce; it has become increasingly essential for inter-state commerce and communication. English thus is very essential for the professionals of tourism industry.

English as a *Lingua Franca:* A *lingua franca* is a language systematically used to make communication possible between people not sharing a mother tongue, in particular when it is a third language, distinct from both mother tongues. (Wikipedia)

Tourism, especially when International, involves people from various countries which makes it difficult to communicate with each other in the absence of a lingua franca. English, especially in India is the most popular lingua franca, which is on par with our National Language.

Importance of English in Internet usage

According to Forrester, Research it is known that English dominates the Web, with more than two-thirds of the Web's pages being in English. According to a study by Vilaweb, a Web site in the language Catalan, Japanese is the second most popular language of Web sites. This shows us that English is the most accessible language for people who access the net.

Web Pages by Language

Language	Web Pages	Percent of Total
English	214,250,996	68.39
Japanese	18,335,739	5.85
German	18,069,744	5.77
Chinese	12,113,803	3.87
French	9,262,663	2.96
Spanish	7,573,064	2.42
Russian	5,900,956	1.88
Italian	4,883,497	1.56
Portuguese	4,291,237	1.37

The number of web pages/sites in English itself is an evidence to show that it is the most accessible language on Internet. There are large numbers of people who decide on their travel plans by searching online. Internet can provide direct contact making it easier to create customized packages by linking with several companies' website. The factors contributing to the success of travel website are lower distribution costs, higher revenues and larger market share. It also complements other traditionally used information sources such as travel agencies. The tourism development corporations of states are spending a lot of resources developing and continuously improving their websites for making them attractive and user friendly. It is seen as a fast moving sector influenced by individual choices about what to visit and where to stay. It is also to be noted that majority if the online communication occurs in English.

Having discussed the major influence of English on Tourism and Hospitality, let us try to evaluate its relevance with the students. This could be understood better by taking it under two categories:

1. Oral Communication: Oral communication plays the basic role in making the customer or the client feel comfortable when he wants to get some information regarding his travel or the services that he looks forward to have. Good communication skills would be the first qualification for him to get into a job in these industries. Without good command over English it is almost impossible for anyone to excel in his career in today's world. Command over English doesn't necessarily mean using multifarious and flowery language but being able to communicate what is necessary in the right manner. For example, when we talk about the functions of a travel agent, he plays the role of a guide in convincing the customer who walks into the travel agency looking for suggestions regarding his travel. The travel agent should not have communication barriers nor should he have his Mother-tongue influence on his English. Time is money in today's world. So the travel agent has to be clear and precise in his conversation.

   Examples for Oral communication:

- Face to face, e.g. serving a customer, guiding a tour group
- Telephone, e.g. taking a booking, giving information

2. Written Communication: We live in an age of information overload! The ease of sending electronic documents has added to the problem. The paperless office may sound good in theory but in practice, it means people have to filter through a lot more written information to extract what they want. It is the mode of formal Communication. In travel and

tourism industry, where one needs to be meticulous and very alert in his work, it is necessary to have a record of all his transactions. This is possible through written communication alone.

Examples of written communication:

- responding to a letter
- sending an email/fax
- writing an itinerary
- Travelogue writing

What is being taught in the classroom (with respect to Oral and Written Communication)?

As mentioned already, this paper is written considering the Bangalore University Curriculum. Though there is a paper on Communicative English it is not very specific to these courses alone. It is a common syllabus for the Bachelors Degree students when it comes to General English. When the syllabus is not subject-specific it ultimately does not fulfil the exact purpose of the student. It is thus observed that the syllabus is not very compatible with the standards of the industry. The curriculum covers aspects like regular Prose, Poetry and Non-detailed along with the communication skills. English is taught only for four semesters out of the six for U.G. students. For the Masters Degree students English is nowhere in the curriculum at all.

Does what is being taught suffice what the industry expects from a potential employee?

It is now clear-cut that the industry expects the potential candidates to have excellent oral and communication. It is observed that majority of the students, who are excellent at academics are poor at Communication and Soft skills fail to get through the interviews. Especially in industries like tourism and hospitality, the employers now look into the proficiency of the candidate in -oral and written communication skills in English. Most of the students are not able to overcome the jargons, their mother-tongue influence and the like which hinder their communication. It is an obvious fact that one could soar up to great heights only when he overcomes the barriers of communication.

What aspects need to be implemented in the curriculum to mitigate the gap between the academics and the industry?

It is the need of the hour that there has to be a revolutionary change in the curriculum as far as English is concerned. It has to be made more subject-specific. In support of this statement let me quote some examples:

When asked for the meaning of what a parkway is more than 80% of the Tourism students answered that it is a place where we park our vehicles whereas the actual meaning is a broad landscaped highway. It is not uncommon for our students (Indians) to mistake it that way, since we are not familiar with the using such a term. English sometimes is a confusing language too!! One principle would not work with all the words all the time and this is what which makes it very confusing. Let me cite an example, the plural of box is boxes but ox becomes oxen!! So it is not entirely the mistake of the student to take it in a wrong sense. Sometimes it is beyond the logics to understand or teach English. You just need to follow the principles without a thought which makes it all the more difficult for students, the primary school-going children in particular.

Concerning the changes that have to be implemented

- The syllabus should be framed in a subject-oriented manner.
- It should include the terms and terminology of the specific field.
- It should include academic assignments which review the oral and written communication skills in English

Reviewing oral communication skills in terms of:

- Pace
- Tone
- Formality/informality
- Overall clarity of information
- Reading and Listening Skills

Reviewing written communication skills in terms of:

- Spelling, punctuation, grammar
- Use of terminology/jargon

- Formality/informality
- Overall clarity of information
- Report writing
- Keeping it simple

➢ Computer Based Tests (CBTs) have to be implemented in all the semesters.

➢ English has to be inculcated in the curriculum for the Masters Degree students as well.

➢ It is very important to revise the fundamental principles in the First Semester, pertaining to their respective courses, instead of expecting the student to be proficient enough.

Thus, it is understood that for the students to be excellent professionals, classroom is the platform to acquire the abilities required by the industry. Needless to say, English for Tourism plays an instrumental role in shaping tomorrow's professionals thereby shaping the future of Tourism and Hospitality industries.

References

1. Kate Williams. Communication in Organisations. (28.01.2011)
2. Adam Jaworski, Annette Pritchard. Discourse, communication, and tourism (28.01.2011)
3. Kavita Chavali and Dr. Subrat Sahu. Comparative Study of Tourism Websites in India—with special reference to South India.
4. http://www.clickz.com/clickz/stats/1697080/web-pages-language (23.01.11)
5. http://en.wikipedia.org (27.01.11)
6. www.david-kilgour.com/mp/sahla.htm (26.01.11)
7. http://www.usingenglish.com/teachers/articles/importance-english-language.html (26.01.11)

A Study on Perception of Management Students towards the Importance of Professional English Learning

CH. RAVI VARMA, M. SRAVANI and MD. JOHN BASHA

Introduction

There is no disputing that the global spread, popularity and range of use of English are unparallelled and unchallenged. It is an official language in over 50 countries, and nearly all international organizations of any standing use English extensively as either the only or main language of official communication. A working knowledge of English is also highly desirable if not a requirement in a number of world organizations, fields of knowledge and occupations. In communities where it is not indigenous, its learning is highly encouraged and promoted. It is often referred to variously as the window to the world, the key to science and technology, the language of international participation and even the key to power and influence. It is also accepted as the official language of international aviation and maritime communication, and the most popular medium of cyber communication.

It is impossible to determine the actual number of 'speakers' of any language not merely because the number of speakers at any given time never stays constant, but also because the features or attributes that qualify a person as a 'speaker' are hard to define precisely. Even so, scholars estimate that there may well be close to 1.5 billion people in the world who can be counted as English proficient to some extent, which amounts to nearly a quarter of the world's population. It certainly has the largest and perhaps the most versatile vocabulary, which even at this moment is rapidly increasing. English is also a 'free-wheeling' language in that unlike some other modern languages, correctness and acceptability in norms are based on popular usage and not arbitrated or controlled or circumscribed by official bodies or institutions or academics.

Growing Importance of English in Business Management

Largely depending on the intention for which learning is intended, Business English can refer to the study of business English vocabulary used in the fields of trade, business, finance, or international relations. If the study focuses on techniques on business presentations, negotiations, correspondence, writing and other skills needed for business communications, then it can be classified as the study of Business English communication skills in the workplace. There is really not much difference between the two classifications, as vocabulary and communication skills work together to achieve a common goal to develop or enhance both written and verbal English skills for business or career advancement purposes.

The rapid growth in technology for global communications notwithstanding, there are still many companies and individual professionals who fail in their quest for business or professional success. And oftentimes the failure primarily lies on one of the most basic foundations of making business relations the language spoken. Undoubtedly, the English language is the global language for business and having a good command of English will definitely give one who is eyeing globally competitive business or career a clear edge. Any communication problem, whether personal or business, translates to losses, zero result in negotiations, incompetence for global business, or will just simply leave you ill-equipped to carry out international business.

Objectives of the Study

In this regard the Main objectives of the present study are:

- To determine the importance of English learning for Management students.
- To assess the level of Professional English learning skills required for career growth.

- To assess the importance of professional English in corporate company.
- To analyse perception levels of Management students towards English communication.

Scope of the Study

The present study is an attempt to assess the perception levels of Budding Managers towards the importance of Professional English Learning for career growth, survival, grievance handling etc. The present study mainly focuses on determining and analyzing perception levels of MBA students towards the importance of professional English Learning skills.

Research Methodology

The research is carried out by taking both primary data and secondary data into consideration. A sample of 100 students from two universities was taken. 17 characteristics were taken and the percentages of perceptions were calculated and by taking a 5 point scale from strongly agree to strongly disagree, scores were calculated and appropriate ranks were given. After assigning ranks to both variables (using scores of students from two universities), by taking rank differences and calculating deviations, rank correlation coefficient was calculated. Thereby t-test is applied to know whether the association between characteristics perceived by students from both universities is significant or not.

Data Collection Methods

We used the questionnaire as a data collection instrument. A separate questionnaire was given to students of both the universities and a five point scale was taken for analysis.

Questionnaire consists of 17 simple statements or characteristics like

1. English is useful to communicate effectively with others
2. English communication is useful for career growth
3. English plays great role in Organizational Development and Growth etc.

which are very easy to answer and researchers assisted respondents to get accurate responses. Respondents were asked to assign

rating to each question and the 5 rating scale is used to record the responses. Options of the 5 Rating scale are:
5 = Strongly Agree 4 = Agree 3 = No Opinion 2 = Disagree 1 = Strongly Disagree.

Sample selection

A sample of 100 students was taken from two universities. 50 students each were selected from Krishna University and JNTUK.

Data Analysis Tools

Spearman's rank correlation coefficient is applied to know the association between the characteristic values perceived by Management students belonging to different Universities.

T-test is applied to know whether the association between the variables is significant or not.

Analysis and Findings of the Study

Table 1: List of statements to determine perception levels of Management students towards the importance of Professional English Learning:

S. No	Characteristics or Statements
1	To communicate effectively
2	Career growth
3	Organization Development
4	Knowledge Management
5	Managing Information system
6	Compulsory for Companies having subsidiaries abroad
7	Effective procurement of Resources
8	Easy and speedy understanding of concepts
9	Content development for HR Managers
10	Good Corporate governance
11	Strengthen relations within the Organization
12	Posting Company details on web portals
13	Study and Research abroad
14	Global Economic linkages
15	To make Convincing Arguments

16·	Promotion of Products & Services
17	To gain Foreign Assignments & Projects

Table 2: Scores and Ranks of Obtained from Krishna University and JNTUK

S. No	Krishna University		JNTU	
	Total score	Ranks	Total score	Ranks
1	213	8	210	7
2	234	2	229	1
3	200	11	202	11
4	204	10	191	14
5	224	4	203	10
6	235	1	228	2
7	196	12	199	12
8	165	15	*184	16.5
9	218	5	217	4.5
10	186	13	189	15
11	171	14	198	13
12	230	3	205	9
13	215	7	218	3
14	212	9	215	6
15	163	16	*184	16.5
16	161	17	217	4.5
17	216	6	206	8

*Scores of 8th and 15th characteristics are equal.

Table 2 depicts that highest scores were obtained for 2nd and 6th characteristics i.e. "Professional English Learning is essential for Career Growth and Professional English learning is compulsory for companies having subsidiaries in foreign countries." The students of both the universities gave First and Second preferences to 2nd and 6th characteristics.

Management students of Krishna University gave least importance to Role of English language in promotional activities of Products and services where as Students of JNTUK gave least importance to 8 and 15 characteristics i.e. for making convincing arguments and for easy understanding of concepts, Professional English Learning is not compulsory.

Table 3: Correlation coefficient for perception levels of Management students (JNTUK and Krishna University)

No	Characteristics	JNTUK Students (X)		KU Students (Y)		(X-Y)	(X-Y)2
		Score	Rank	Score	Rank		
1	To communicate effectively	210	7	213	8	-1	1
2	Career growth	229	1	234	2	-1	1
3	Organization Development	202	11	200	11	0	0
4	Knowledge Management	191	14	204	10	4	16
5	Managing Information system	203	10	224	4	6	36
6	Compulsory for Companies having subsidiaries abroad	228	2	235	1	1	1
7	Effective procurement of Resources	199	12	196	12	0	0
8	Easy and speedy understanding of concepts	184	16.5	165	15	1.5	2.25
9	Content development for HR Managers	217	4.5	218	5	-0.5	0.25
10	Good Corporate governance	189	15	186	13	2	4
11	Strengthen relations within the Organization	198	13	171	14	-1	1
12	Posting Company details on web portals	205	9	230	3	6	36
13	Study and Research abroad	218	3	215	7	-4	16
14	Global Economic linkages	215	6	212	9	-3	9

15	To make Convincing Arguments	184	16.5	163	16	0.5	0.25
16	Promotion of Products & Services	217	4.5	161	17	-12.5	156.25
17	To gain Foreign Assignments & Projects	206	8	216	6	2	4
	=∑d2						**285**

Spearmen's Rank correlation method is applied to determine the relationship between perceived values of Management students of two universities.

Correlation Co-efficient:

$$\rho = 1 - \frac{6 \sum d_i^2}{n(n^2 - 1)}.$$

The Rank correlation coefficient between the preference ratings assigned for perceived attributes (JNTUK and Krishna University) is 0.6507 which is fairly high.

The Combination of the Hypotheses to test r is:

H0: rs = 0 (the Means of the two variables are not associated)

H1: rs = 0 (the Means of the two variables are associated)

The t statistics is:

$$t = r\sqrt{\frac{n-2}{1-r^2}}$$

The table t value, at half of the significance level (α/2 =0.025) and 15 degrees freedom is 2.131.

The calculated value of t statistic (2.9406) is more than the table t statistic (2.131). Hence Null Hypotheses is rejected. This means the rank correlation coefficient of JNTUK and KU Management students is significant.

Conclusion

Governments across the world have in the last few years embarked on ambitious educational reforms which will integrate English more deeply into the Curriculum. English will cease to be a foreign language for many, perhaps most, as it will be considered as a 'basic skill', to be learned by everyone alongside other 21st century skills especially 'Business Management'. This language is the basic need of any corporate; so to get into any MNC one must have good communication skill on top of everything.

Bibliography

Donald R. Cooper & Pamela S. Schindler, *Business Research Method,* Tata McGraw Hill, New Delhi, 2008.

R. Panneerselvam, *Research Methodology.* PHI Learning. New Delhi, 2009.

C.R. Kothari, *Research Methodology Methods and Techniques* (2nd Edition) New Age International. New Delhi, 2008.

Kitty Locker and Stephen Kyo Cacz Marek, *Business Communication* (3rd Edition), Tata McGraw Hill, New Delhi, 2009.

Penrose/ Rosberry/ Myers, *Business Communication for Managers* (5th Edition) Thomson South Western India Edition, New Delhi, 2009

Websites

http://toeflgencligi.blogspot.com/2008/11/importance-of-english.html

ESP through Verse

G. SUNDARI

> There are at least two learning benefits that can be derived from studying poetry: The appreciation of the writer's composition process, which students gain by studying poems by components, developing sensitivity for words and discoveries that may later grow into a deeper interest and greater analytical ability.
>
> Murat Hişmanoğlu

Poetry could be used as a significant tool in fostering certain ethical principles, whose specific purpose would be to provide ethical education along with inside learning, critical thinking and self reflection in and among the learners opting for technical education.

While discussing "Teaching English through Literature," for ESP, Murat Hişmanoğlu, an instructor in UK university states that there are three main kinds of writing that could be based on literature as a model. "Controlled Writing," used mostly at the beginning level; "Guided Writing," at the literal level, that enables students to understand the literary work and third one is "Reproducing the Model," which consists of techniques like paraphrase, summary and adaptation. The adaptation herein lies in comprehending a slice of the essence of life and certain ethical principles that enhance their Life Skills, inevitable in human life.

Poems are authentic texts, which motivate the learners of the target language to adapt their personal knowledge and experience which relates to the topic. The communication in this context is genuine because they voice their own experiences. Giving poems to learners in an Engineering stream is to make an attempt of a creaky rusted engine to start moving. At the outset, the activity took off in fits and starts and to my delight turned around to the concept that I intended to introduce to them in the classroom. The aim and objective was to fulfill a specific purpose that enables the students to nurture certain ethical principles in their being, to follow in life. As a noted ESP instructor, Paul Fanning stated: 'Ethics may be regarded as the inquiry into the nature of moral actions, while on a more practical level it is the search for the morally good life.'

To facilitate the learners of the present day scenario, I did not think of giving neither the poems of yesteryear's legends nor the ones who have already carved a niche in the field of Indian English poetry. Modern verse facilitates comprehensibility of the learner to voice out his inner voice, I felt. And so, I deliberately chose a slender volume of poems of a poet, who is presently teaching the technical students for a considerable period of time. The volume entitled *Sow the Spring . . .* by Jandhyala Ravindranath, Associate Professor of English, working for Gayatri Vidya Parishad in Visakhapatnam. In this debut volume of 'poems on love, friendship, education, creativity and his pet dogs have been penned during the last seventeen years in moments of inspiration. He states in his foreword to the volume, "Poetry is the heart of the heartless world, property of the propertyless and the prerogative of one and all. It's there in a blade of grass as well as in the memories of the twin towers of New York. It is an answer to the questions which defy answers."[1].

1. Live for Liberty. P. 3
2. Celebrate the Local. P. 5
3. You are not free to be not free. P. 6
4. Balance p. 10
5. To write is to live. P. 11
6. Salutes to TVS, My Teacher. P. 12
7. Homage to page. p. 13
8. Art Empowers. p. 15
9. Mortal Words. p. 18
10. Fit for Poetry. p. 23
11. Anything but Democracy? p. 36
12. Sow the Spring in Your Heart. p. 41

Why can't we join to dismantle the
Structures of oppression? (*Live for Liberty*, p. 1)

Paraphrase

The poet spent much of his time feeling lonely and bored. The poet was in love, and was undaunted by the criticism that he received or faced. He warns us not to underrate his emotions of love and passion. These emotions are like "Tempest" that can create a myriad of feelings. The poet asks his beloved as to why they can't work together to fight against oppression. He even feels that his beloved's smile could bring in new life into his soul whereas her spurning could ruin his life. (D. Sushmita Rao)

> "A noted writer passes away," says a headline
> in a corner of a newspaper
> "He built his house beside a burial ground but
> Home in the hearts of readers . . ."
> People pester, "why write"
> They may as well ask the cows 'Why give milk?"
>
> ("To Write is to Live" p. 11)

Summary

Though a writer passes away, he still lives in the hearts of his readers. Writing, to a writer, is like water to fish. The writer wrote endlessly but never complained. He helped the people around him and gave a new outlook of life to everyone who read. What's the use of writing? One may ask, it is something like what's the use of breathing?

> (A. Jyostna)
> You can't pen a line
> When your pain is proximate
> You also can't write
> When your pain is remote.
> To find the balance
> Is the secret of the art. ("Balance," p. 10)

Paraphrase

One can't write when one is too engrossed in pain. One can also not write when he is insensitive to pain. Finding the balance between pain and pleasure is the art of life. The person who is apt at this art can live life and savour it. Balance is the oxygen of existence. Without balance, life can't be handled. Balance is like a rollercoaster ride, there are ups and downs and the art of finding one's self after that ride is nothing but the art of balancing life. (K. Alekhya)

> Meet not to make fresh wounds but heal festering ones
> Talk not to increase malice but realize life's essence. . . .
> It's never too late to begin anew and to
> Sow the spring in your heart
>
> ("Sow the Spring in your Heart," p. 41)

Interpretation

Spring and "springtime" refer to the season, and broadly to ideas of rebirth, renewal and regrowth. The poet herein refers to the season of changes because he intends to see the kind of change in the attitude of the humans, and so, a season of newness and life. The poet suggests his readers to sow the seeds of spring that enlivens the eternal joys of life at least once in a lifetime. If the seeds are sown in the heart of the humans, they sprout up in fostering humaneness delivering us out of the narrowness of the mind that overcomes the divisions of the humans in various terms like status, race, religion and the like. Thus the poem fosters the feeling of oneness and that all of us have to live in peace and harmony on earth. (G. Sundari)

My earnest reason to select the volume for the activity was that poetry has many an imperative meaning that makes the classroom, teacher-centred. As the present-day language-learning curriculum focuses on learner-centred, I chose the volume as it suited the language levels of the students and that every poem would directly reach out not only to the mind but also to the soul of the learners. The volume presents a substantial number of poems that I felt necessary for the activity, to teach language skills blended with ethical principles which insinuate and motivate the students in the present-day context. This kind of activity-based learning in the classroom by adopting "Reproducing the Model," to teach not only the language skills but also certain ethical principles that supplement the students in inculcating some finer nuances and also to comprehend the submerged truths of/in life.

I feel that poetry is endowed with a kind of universality and suggestive power enabling the reader to notice personal relevance in the printed word. At times ambiguity in poetry may hinder the learners to take interest in reading poetry and so, I chose the above poems as a powerful resource in the classroom context. The authentic examples used in the classroom context helped me to drive in the students' involvement so that, they can even share their emotional responses. The learners herein, constituted their reading experience relevantly to their own lives while interacting with each other. They not only responded collectively to the activity but also personally to the poems and recorded their emotions and thoughts in an enthusiastic spirit.

Interpersonal skills woven with language skills and ethical principles are best learnt when the teacher introduces them not in isolated manner but in an integrated methodology of imparting on the part of the teacher and learning on the part of the students.

Students, in this context appreciated the poet's faculty of composing simple thoughts in the form of metaphorical expressions that connected them between learning and to arrive with a different viewpoint towards the use of target language "beyond the known usages and rules of grammar, syntax and vocabulary, triggers unmotivated readers owing to being so open to explorations and different interpretations."[2]

Poetry very effectively paves the way for learning certain skills imparted as a part of the academic curriculum for, an academically successful student is expected to succeed not only in life but also in career. It is a well-known fact that the biggest challenge a student faces when he is on board, is the ability to work in a team and thus, the activity could be considered as the first step to begin with, in their journey of thousands of miles.

In a group activity students are encouraged to learn because the tasks that they take up are appropriate to their individual levels. Positive interdependence gets enhanced while the students realize that cooperative learning has many a lesson to teach them in life. They end up in making a positive difference in the world they live in, which include courage, inside learning, imagination, innovation, willingness to take risks, the ability to rebound from setbacks and the capacity to empathize with and to work well with others.

The activity was termed as a significant change from a monotonous class work because it involved the learners in such a way that the session would live in their memory and that it surely appears in their mind's eye when they take up the profession of their choice. They practically noticed that poetry gave them a voice to express that lied unheard till then to establish their identity in the group.

The students collectively expressed that this method would help them as a channel for communication by transferring the knowledge that they've gained, to implement their innovation successfully in their real life contexts like building teams and working in/with teams, while getting their senses involved in the learning process. I noticed that this would inevitably make the students become empathetic and sympathetic towards their fellow beings which in turn improved their personality and code of behaviour.

At the heart of the activity, a kind of inside learning takes place that captures their wisdom to put into practice in reality which was indeed a factual realization dawned upon me at the moment. To work on the given poems was a rewarding experience for the students because some have claimed that the verses ignited their creative spirits in a magnanimous manner. According to *The Innovator's Toolkit* by Harvard Business Press:

Creativity plays a role in the innovation process, though one that is difficult to measure. Creativity sparks the innovative idea and it helps to improve facets of the idea as it moves forward. Creativity is needed on both the technical and market sides of the process. It helps the technologist to see new ways of addressing known customer needs even as it helps customer-facing people find new ways of applying or adapting existing technologies to those needs.[3]

I adopted "Reproducing the Model" method because students can use words within their vocabulary to rephrase the things that they see in print or hear aloud. What actually happens herein is that the paraphrases written by the students exhibited their sincere endeavour to make sense of the poem. I felt that the activity provided "a solid basis for the learners to bridge the gap between their receptive and productive skills, offering students the space and time to develop new ideas and insights in a range of contexts."[4] Their imagination was captivated to explore the human communication interpersonally, that constituted sharing of ideas and their comprehending abilities, the aim and objective of my assigning the activity for them, who became creative, critical and analytical that unplugged their horizon of possibilities allowing them to question, interpret, connect with each other while doing the activity that tapped their senses to be more interesting. The Model enhanced their personal growth and encouraged the learners to draw on their own opinions, feelings and personal experiences. The activity aimed at interaction between the text and the reader in English, helping them to make the language more intimate in their practice for, "Any activity based learning makes the students to be aware of the difference between written and spoken English."[5]

Instantly, I gave one of my poems entitled "Let Me Enjoy My Childhood, Ma . . .!" The following lines made a strong impact on the students:

> Enjoy the sunset hues but not the mundane syllables,
> Not to memorise and chant, but to love and create,
> He wanted to chisel beautiful sculptures, but made to convert the
> rocky lines. . . .
> He was conditioned to corporate walls.
> Is that to enjoy childhood. .an exorbitant affair . .?
> He just wanted to be safe and secure
> Not a beast trained to adulthood,
> His fading voice . . . his heart's deep felt desire,
> Screamed beyond the ocean.
> Let Me Enjoy My Childhood, Ma. . .!

G. Sundari, "Poet's Paradise" p. 157

Children are too exhausted these days even to smile because they seem to emerge out of a prison-house by the evening of every other day. Mini Krishnan, who edits literary translations for Oxford University Press, lamented in his article "End of Childhood?" in the popular daily *The Hindu*, that the children are growing up too fast today, egged on by parents who try to live their dreams and aspirations through their young ones. He adds that parents are controlling every moment of their children's lives and they want but designer children who are packed and labelled and finally sold as doctors, engineers, bio-tech professionals rather than helping them to know their intrinsic worth. He questions the parents, "Is the joy of life being deleted while our children are coached and designed for life?" What I feel is that only when childhood is fully lived and its joys fully shared, can one outgrow it and embrace the next stage of life. Let us not dwarf the mental and psychological growth of the children and mar their innocence at an early stage that their likes and dislikes, wishes and desires are brushed aside mercilessly in pursuit of equipping them to participate and perform in the rat race for marks and ranks. As a parent and a teacher, it is time we pause and give a sincere thought on the wonderfully apt lines of Khalil Gibran: "You may give them your love but not your thoughts/ For they have their own thoughts."

The poem sent a wave of uproar in every corner of the classroom because they already treaded on the path bearing the physical weight of books and mental heft of stuffed lessons by the pedagogue. They unanimously felt that the teachers and children should share their views on the topic of overloaded curriculum in the present day education system that it is time for the academics to rethink on the system so that the students would be benefitted with the kind of survival skills to live life in a courageous manner. We, as teachers and parents, should come together and take measures to expand our students' knowledge to their behavioural health, taking care of their stress levels.

My Reaction

It seemed as though these little poems stirred their senses, fed their soul by making them discover their inner voice because individuality and creativity were encouraged in the context. They were overwhelmed by discovering their inner voice that lied unheard till then In factual sense, poems are considered to have value as art that expanded their language skills and awareness pertaining to the same. The exposure that the poems accorded to the students made them look at bigger and better things in life that undoubtedly turned out to be a significant plus in their learning process. They felt as if they were liberated psychologically from their habitual means of mugging up their lessons from the examination point of view.

Follow Up Activity

Once we read and work with a piece of literature, it might naturally lead on to another follow up activity which sometimes sparks off to create wonderful creative writing. I instructed them to use adverbs to pen their thoughts that evoke sensitive feelings at heart. Each group contributed a wonderful poem thus:

Warmly the sun rises in the east
Smoothly the breeze kisses the leaves
Fragrantly the bud blooms into a flower
Brightly the dew drops appear on the petals
Melodiously the bird sings a song
Constantly the greenery grows in the lawn (M. Praneetha)

The students who were experiencing the initial hiccups to learn the language, were eager to pen a thoughtful poem that threw light on the present-day students' life, in the kind of 'characteristic regional English.'

Lightly lightly the sun
Fastly fastly the time
Quickly quickly the college
Softly softly the teachers
Lovely lovely the friends
Jolly jolly the friends
Tensely tensely the exams
Successfully successfully the life. (S. Sarada)

A student went to the extent of addressing a social issue that I grabbed the opportunity to discuss with them some of the issues like the racial attacks on students abroad, Child marriage, Child labour, Right to Education. I intended that these were essential for the progress of society. They realised the value of human rights, relationships, life skills and most importantly the joy of sharing and venting out their hearts' concerns. Sometimes we need to speak out on social issues in order to teach correct principles and ensure the practice of societal harmony in which we live.

Many a burning issue, dealing with some of the new ethical dilemmas as a result of technological advancement, or taken a new form, with the rise of the Internet and Social Networking and copyright infringement of software, are widely discussed all over the globe. To identify ethical issues as they arise, as well as defining how to deal with them, has traditionally been problematic with intelligentsia all over the world.

Situations regarding the copyright infringement of software, music, movies, are widely being discussed, with the rise of file sharing programs such as Napster, Kazaa, and the BitTorrent (protocol) and Cyber Staking. The ethical questions that arise from software piracy are: is it immoral or wrong to copy software, music, or movies? Some have claimed that the Internet is a "democratic technology." Does the Internet foster democracy and freedom of speech? What are the ethical implications of this process on the world? Does the digital divide raise ethical issues that society is morally obligated to change and spread the ability to access different forms of electronic communication? (Source: Wikipedia)[6]

Terrell Ward Bynum, who developed curriculum materials for Computer Ethics as a subject for a university course in 1979, argues: "Various national and international professional societies have produced code of ethics documents to give basic parameters for computing professionals,"[7] in his pathbreaking article entitled *Computer Ethics*. Moreover, he concluded that computer ethics is a set of moral principles that regulate the use of computers that include intellectual property rights (such as copyrighted electronic content), privacy concerns. He also discussed how computers affect society in accordance with their evolvement and the use and abuse of technology through the device. In his view, computer ethics continues to create ethical standards that address new issues raised by new technologies, every other day over the universe.

Probably, this kind of an urge might have been the prominent reason that propelled the JNTU-K university authorities and academics to introduce a subject by name Professional Ethics in the engineering curriculum. The inside learning of this subject particularly, might instill in the students the kind of appreciation and commitment to the universal values and virtues that cement unity and understanding in and among the students as humans living on planet earth.

> Inside Teaching is an important read for policymakers and other decision makers; it is a reminder that genuine education is a complex and fragile process that takes into account the idea that every student is a valuable contributor to the world and not a product to be assembled.[8]

Soft skills, Life skills, Survival skills cannot be included in the curriculum but the prospective corporate employers wish to find them during an extensive interview.

And so, today's TESOLS are tailoring their lessons and materials to prepare students to face the world. In actual sense, all communication in the workplace falls into two broad categories, human communication and electronic communication. Some communication interactions fall into both facilitating the productive workforce in the organization. Everyone is aware of the electronic communication but human communication varies in many aspects when discussed in connection with Gender and the effectiveness of communication. Basically, The good students are the ones who can faithfully repeat what they have been taught in an ethics class. The sole criterion of success in social ethics thus appears to be wholly cognitive. But then, as Ruskin reminds us, education consists not in teaching people what they do not know, but in teaching them to behave as they do not.[9]

All societies have a basic structure of social, economic, and political institutions, both formal and informal. The teacher herein can teach the students on how to live in harmony and peace with the fellow beings and of how these two elements are prominent enough to develop a healthy mind in a healthy body; where the netizens become citizens working towards the realization of a world where all the people come together, regardless of any kind of a background, socio-economic status, race, gender or faith to enable them to enjoy their basic human rights and get equal benefits in the society that they live in. As an ardent lover of poetry, I personally feel that poetry helps students to get good footing, making it easier for them to update their skills, increase their knowledge, and expand their communication background because it includes many types with many different people at the workplace.

Today's prospective employers are spending 25 percent of their expenses on training the students on inter-personal and life skills after recruiting them. Strong Work Ethic should be maintained by the people who work for them. They want them to be reliable, dependable and self-motivated. The ability to adapt and transfer the critical methods of their learning to a variety of working environments and distinctive interpretative skills of the subject is much needed today. The students' involvement in various activities and discussions during the college years make them learn the needed ethical principles in life. In actual sense, literature educates the whole person. By examining values in literary texts, teachers encourage learners to develop attitudes towards them. These values and attitudes relate to the world outside the classroom.[10] The specific goal of the teacher is to cultivate "sound ethical behaviour of the individual person, whether alone, or with others at home, school . . . in the neighborhood or in a foreign country." As a teacher, I honestly consider that, the implication here is that no teaching goes on if the teacher simply "tells" it to the student, or worse if she tries to prevent the student from acquiring any support for her belief. In such a case the teacher does not teach, but indoctrinates. If this is what is meant by indoctrination then we must conclude that indoctrination goes on all the time. The teaching of such subjects as mathematics, chemistry, physics and even languages involves a great deal of factual information for which reasons are not always offered. However, most people would not be bothered by this kind of indoctrination.[12]

The kind of ESP can be suggested as a method for improved learning because poetry employs language to evoke and exalt special qualities of life, and good enough for the present day readers with feelings, are swayed by the vigorous waves of technology. In this connection, computer ethical principles should be given a worthy concern to see the world flourish and shaped in the form of a real ethical society to experience the naturalness of life and its labyrinth of relationships.

The paper throws light on how an English teacher enforces value added measures to attain certain soft skills through a communicative methodology, using poetry as a model for writing, specifically known as "Reproducing the Model," so that today's learners turn out to be tomorrow's technical professionals who embark towards greater international cooperation, surely not with the aid of electronic communication, but certainly with humaneness in communication. My pondering ran thus: 'Be true to yourself and the rest will follow'.

NOTES

1. Ravindranath, Jandhyala. *Sow the Spring*, Published by the author, Visakhapatnam, 2009.
2. Murat Hişmanoğlu. "Teaching English through Literature," *Journal of Language and Linguistic Studies,* Vol. 1, No. 1, April 2005, p. 14
3. Murat Hişmanoğlu., *The Innovator's Toolkit*, Harward Business Press, Boston, Massachusetts. Printed in India by Gopsons Papers, 2009. p. xix.
4. Murat Hişmanoğlu. "Teaching English through Literature," p. 17
5. S. Stern, 1991. "An Integrated Approach to Literature in ESL/ EFL" *Teaching English as a Second or Foreign Language*, ed. M. Murcia, Boston: Heinle & Heinle Publishers, 1991. p. 333
6. http://en.wikipedia.org/wiki/Computer_ethics
7. Bynum, Terrell Ward. "A Very Shory History of Computer Ethics". Southern Connecticut State University. Archived from the original on 2008-04-18. http://web.archive.org/web/20080418122849/http://www.southernct.edu/organizations/rccs/resources/research/introduction/bynum_shrt_hist.html
8. Reviewed by Sergio Mora, Mathematics/AVID Teacher, Montclair High School, Montclair, CA http://findarticles.com/p/articles /mi_qa3614/is_200712/ai_n25137720/pg_2/?tag=content;col1
9. Qtd. R.W. Livingstone. *The rainbow-bridge and other essays in education.* London: Pallman Press, 1959, p. 151.
10. Lindsay Clandfield, *Teaching materials: using literature in the EFL/ ESL classroom.*
11. Republic of Kenya. Ministry of Education, Science and Technology. "Social education and ethics syllabus for Kenya Certificate of Secondary Education," p. 1
12. *Ibid*, p. 11

Mysticism and Language

CH. VENKATA SIVASAI

Introduction

A human being is defined by language. An animal that does not use a language or speak cannot be a human being. Language, of course, is to be distinguished from communication. Many animals and birds have developed communication, though not language. Language is a system of relationship sound and meaning. It is very complex, indirect, round-about relationship. The round-about correspondence between meanings and sounds that one finds in language is what is called syntax. Syntax is the way words are used in a language. But there are imperfections in the use of language, especially words, which might easily have been avoided and are due to man s willful faults and neglects.

Locke on the "Abuse of Words"

John Locke sets forward seven such imperfections. They are

a) We use words when we have no ideas corresponding to them. That is, we may learn to repeat sounds (words) parrot-wise.
b) We use words "inconsistently make the same word stand now for one collection of simple ideas and now for another."
c) We affect a jargon. We make ourselves purposely obscure in order to give our words an appearance of subtlety or to veil the ambiguities which our thoughts contain. This abuse of words, Locke says, one finds all too prevalent in the works of logicians, lawyers and scientists too.
d) We "take words of things" that is, we fall into thinking that if there is a word then there must be a thing corresponding to it.

e) We make words stand for things they cannot possibly signify, as for instance when we make the word "gold" stand for the real essence, such as malleables, etc.

f) We use words whose meaning is clear to us, without making their meaning clear to others,.

g) We use figurative speech, in conversation, in poetry, this is a venial fault, a fault that cannot be excused, since it increases pleasure and delight (emotions and feelings). But in the pursuit of "dry truth and real knowledge," the use of figurative speech is dangerous. Herein lies the chief defect and error of eloquence and rhetoric.

Locke on the "Remedies of Imperfections"

Locke has also suggested possible remedies for these imperfections

We should take care to use no word "without signification." That is, in using a word one should know what idea it signifies

This idea should be known precisely and distinctly. If a word signifies a simple idea it should be clear, if it is a complex, it should be "determinate"

We should respect conventions in the use of language and use of words in strict conformity with the common usage.

If we deviate from the common usage we should show in what way we do so.

We should "use the same word constantly in the same sense." But the case is we are frequently forced to use the same word in slightly different senses, and as far as possible, we should avoid ambiguity.

A little reflection will show that if one were to follow Locke's guidance, one will be reduced to a mere "reasoning" intellectual object, obliterating and effacing and feeling and emotional dimensions of oneself. Then our world will be a world of dry, dreary, desert, full of bloodless categories. In such a "logical" world, there will not be any place for music, poetry and mysticism. Many contemporary language analysts believe that the language of music or poetry or mysticism suffers from the fatal disease of meaninglessness and they uphold scientific language as the epitome of proper meaningful language.

The Nature of Scientific Language

According to logical positivism, the language of science is the only linguistic area most worthy of attention. The early positivists believed that language was meaningful only if it were either tautologies or capable of empirical verification. Logic and mathematics fulfilled the criterion of tautology and science fulfilled the criterion of empirical verification. All other languages - the language of metaphysics, the language of ethics, the language of poetry and music and the language of mysticism - are rejected as unworthy of attention because they are unverifiable and therefore meaningless. Being convinced that science is the only field of meaningful language, the early positivists like Schlick, Netwrath, Feigl, and Cnap diverted their attention on the analysis of science. All other languages are purely "subjective" which cannot be confirmed by common observable experiences. Hence they lack scientific "Objectivity."

What about theoretical terms of science? Are they speculative and unverifiable? To this the positivist says that the theoretical terms can be derived from "observation terms." In this connection Rudolf Carnap advocated his programme of using logical relations to convert or reduce theoretical terms to observation terms. His programme is based on the presupposition that scientific terms are precise and rational in that they can be expressed in logical propositions. On the other hand, speculative metaphysical and mystical terms cannot be "reddened" to observation terms in the strict logical sense. In short, scientific language is precise, logical and can be verified by observation. Mystical or religious language is anything but logical and precise and could be verified by any empirical test. Mystical language is highly ambiguous, metaphorical, unverifiable "directly" and hence unscientific and therefore meaningless.

The Nature of Mystical Language

Mysticism may mean many things to many people. It is very difficult to give a precise, per genus et differentia definition of it. Any attempt to define it will be limited in scope. Mysticism is characterized by "an inner distancing" from the world of language.

It is governed by a "headedness'" which can only be revealed and not reasoned. Mysticism is grounded in the phenomenon of consciousness. An "Interpretation" of mystic experience can be doubted, but the experience itself is indubitable, for the mystic is also certain of the truth of his/her experience beyond the possibility of arguing him/ her out of it. That is, mystic experience is "above reason" or "outside reason." One cannot reject the testimony of mystical experience unless one rejects the whole of mysticism as fraud.

That is, mystic experience cannot be considered as true or false in the ordinary sense in which empirical acts are true or false for they go beyond "the either-or pattern" of the logical understanding. Mystic experience is "poetic truth" and the language of empirical truth is the steno-language, the language of science. In short mystic experience is free from all theories of explanation and proof. A mystic has no proof. He is the only proof.

Since mystic experience is wholly unconceptualizable the method to be adopted for an understanding of mysticism is the method of appreciation and not the method of description. It can be understood only by knowledge by acquaintance. When the mystic tries to communicate what is incommunicable by its very nature, one lands in paradoxical language and sometimes in twilight language or *sandhya-bhasa* which forms the integral part of mystic language.

To say that mystical experience is one "from which words return" is what is called paradoxical, for in it say or speak about the experience by saying that it cannot be said or spoken. Paradox is one of the universal characteristics of all mysticism. W.T. Stace speaks of the essential paradoxically of mystic experience in three words: the pantheistic paradox, the positive-negative or plenum-vacuum paradox and the paradox of dissolution of the individuality. What is involved in the pantheistic paradox is the idea of what has been called the "Identity-of-opposities" or "identity-in-differences." According to Stace, this is an expression of non-rational element in the human kind. In the paradox of individuality one ceases to be individual and yet retain one's individuality.

Mysticism is a state of spiritual impersonality where the sense of otherness disappears but the sense of integrity persists. When something is indescribable one has to remain silent, be in a state of cumma, a state of silence. Cumma is a state of "Imageless liberation" or to use a state of "Choiceless awareness." Tagore says that the trees, the flowers, the blue hills and the stars above ache with a meaning which can never be uttered in language. Mystical language is reflective awareness, a spontaneous insight, an acceptance without proof, a trust without reservations. Bogar defines mystical experience as one beyond Vedanta knowledge. But in the case of mystical experience there is the fullness of experience without stagnation. This fullness of mystic experience is not static, nor does it stagnate; it is always dynamic and full of energy and activity, yet transcendental.

Conclusion

Let us not try to decipher mystical expressions and treat them as non-sensical. As Rudolf Otto has said, mysticism has its own "under logic" and the logic beyond the scope of the logic of science or the logic of positivism or the logic of language. Let us not limit the "given" world of consciousness to scientific experiences only. The "given" world as presented to consciousness comprises not only the outer world of "verifiable" external objects, but also the inner world of spiritual and mystical experiences. Let us not look into "the mouth of the gifted cow" and count its teeth. Let us not reduce our experiences to logical experiences only. To use an expression of Heidegger, let us go "beyond onto-the-logic.

Mystic communication may be termed as "non-logical communication" which is independent of scientific objectivity. As defined by Mukhopadhyaya, non-logical communication is a kind of communication which is independent of both space and time. Even though there is no "scientific evidence" for this type of communication, recent theories of science are prepared to consider and accept it as a "permissive" theory though not a "specific" theory. Physicist Henry Strapp, as quoted by Mukhopadhyay, is right when he says that "non-locality" is the greatest discovery of modern science. Caṅ we conclude that mysticism is phenomenon of non-local, Trans-linguistic communication?

Bibliography

Christ R.J. *The Problems of Perception*, London, George Allen and Unwin, 2nd Impression, 1966.

Locke, John, *An Essay Concerning Human Understanding*, Henry Regnery.1949

Stace, W.T. *Mysticism and Philosophy*, London, Macmillan, 1980.

Suzuki, D.T. *Zen Buddhism*, NewYork, Doubleday.

English for Engineering Students in India

SARMISTHA BAJPAYEE ROY

We have witnessed history as we stood the threshold of the 21st century, bidding adieu to the last and welcoming a new era altogether. This is an era of globalization where man has witnessed tremendous development in the field of technology. With the world turning into one global village, the modern man has developed the need of a global language which could be understood by most people across the globe. There is no doubt that English serves as a link language in establishing connectivity with the world. One of the major forces of globalization in India has led to an overwhelming demand for engineers across the globe. The last few years have witnessed an unprecedented rise in the number of skilled professionals in India, employed by both local and multi-national companies, to service customers across the world. With the whole world becoming one global market and business becoming diverse and result-oriented, professionals are facing new challenges in effective communication every day.

As we know that ESP concentrates more on language in context than on teaching grammar and language structures, engineering students are highly benefitted by this. The ESP primal focus is on the fact that English is not taught as a subject separate from the students' real world; instead, it is incorporated into a subject matter in such a way that it helps them in their practical world and more correctly in their professional life. With improved listening, reading, speaking and writing skills, the technocrats of today can certainly prepare our country to establish itself as a powerhouse of tomorrow's global economy.

ESP (English for Specific Purposes) aims to meet the needs of a specific group of learners. ESP students are usually learners who already have the basic knowledge of English and are actually learning the language to meet the specific demands of their profession and to communicate a set of professional skills effectively. This group of learners may be lawyers, engineers, doctors, or even business administrators. ESP actually serves to fulfill the basic needs of a particular profession. From its beginning in the 1960s ESP has come a long way and today it has grown to become one of the most prominent areas of teaching English language. Initially ESP was designed for a specific group of learners, particularly adult learners, who had some acquaintance with English language. However in the contemporary time, ESP courses can be taken up by eager students at a much early age and at a much lower level of proficiency in English. ESP concentrates more on the English language as a medium of communication rather than on strict grammar and language structures.

Among the varying subjects that it covers like medicine, tourism, business management, finance, journalism, mass communication, administration etc. Engineering is one field where ESP is becoming increasingly popular. With globalization, the demand of engineers across the globe has increased. Hence the need of English as a link language has been acknowledged. As we know that ESP concentrates more on language in context than on teaching grammatical syntax and language structures, engineering students are highly benefitted by this.

English—the Popular Lingua Franca of the World

English for various reasons, primarily due to the British rule in many parts of the world, has emerged as the popular lingua franca. However, the role of English has vastly changed down the years. English is no longer seen as the language of the rulers or as an instrument of promoting British culture and values. In fact it has become a global resource and does not owe its existence or the protection of its essence to any group or nation.

English ranks second only to Mandarin Chinese in terms of the amount of the people who speak it. However, it is second to none in terms of the number of people learning it. Mandarin Chinese is hardly spoken outside the Chinese communities. However in many regions of the world, where English is not the native language, it is still widely spoken and is even included in the curriculum of educational institutions. There are various reasons that account for the widespread popularity of English language: the foremost among them being the fact that, today the USA's influence on world information and technology is dominant. English being their native language is sweeping the world's economic, cultural, educational, social, and the cyber space. It is the official language of air transport and shipping; the leading language of science, technology, computers, and commerce; and a major medium of education, publishing, and international negotiation. English is the primary language used in the World Wide Web and in the business field. It is becoming a global language unlike any other in history.

The Importance of English for Engineering Students in India

One of the major forces of globalization in India has been the significant rise in the demand of engineers. Engineering, much like any other science, is a broad discipline which is often broken down into several sub-disciplines. These disciplines concern themselves with diverse areas of engineering work like civil, chemical, electrical, electronics, telecommunication, mechanical, mining, naval, industrial, aerospace, architectural, nuclear, and computer engineering. With the dawn of globalization and the entire world turning into one global village, business is no longer pole centric. It is rather scattered to different parts of the world. Hence effective communication is the primary challenge to engineers irrespective of their field of specialization. English for engineering students lays stress not only on all four language skills - listening, reading, speaking, and writing, but it also analyses and determines which language skills are most needed by the students. For engineering students, ESP focuses on all four language skills, with special stress on speaking. Effective communication skill is one of the most desired qualities in an aspiring engineer. An engineer requires effective oral communication skill in several formal communicative situations, like meetings, conferences, group-discussions, panel discussions, interviews, teleconferences, video-conferencing, seminars, workshops, and symposiums. English language competence is a significant aspect of an engineering student's academic life and prospective career. Many of the engineering students studying in different engineering colleges (both government and private) in India are from the state boards where English is the second language. These students who have studied all the subjects till the 12th standard in their regional language find it very difficult to manage the engineering subjects which are in English. Some of the students of the state boards do manage to read, write, and understand English easily. But when it comes to speaking, they are not so good. ESP courses bridge this gap since it is designed to meet the specific needs of non-English speakers. ESP is designed to meet the specific needs of learners i.e. Engineers. It combines subject matter and English language teaching. This is highly encouraging and interesting to the students since they are able to apply what they learn in the English classes to their main field of study. Being able to use the vocabulary, structures and ideas of ESP classes to a more meaningful and practical context increases their motivation and their ability of quick learning and easy grasping of the subject matter. Engineering students need to read academic papers and books to enrich their knowledge. For the better understanding of scientific theories, it is important to read the original works, most of which were written in English. The Internet, which is the most convenient way to get information and provides more than 70% of information for higher studies, is also in English. Most of the scientific papers or journals in the world are written in English. The engineering graphs are also marked in English. Moreover, most of the lectures by professors in renowned foreign universities are also conducted in English. Hence, engineering students should at least master the Basic English ability to deal with the countless English lectures, tutorials, labs, projects, papers presentations, and seminars. Moreover who can undermine the importance of English for students aspiring for higher studies? For students who want to pursue M.Tech program in a leading institute of the country, Graduate Aptitude Test in Engineering (GATE) score is a must. Even GATE examination which is technical, has introduced some Basic English in the General aptitude section. Apart from this, engineering students who wish to go abroad for higher studies need to clear GRE (The Graduate Record Examination) and TOEFL (Test of English as a Foreign Language) examination which are purely English paper. These examinations measure the ability of non-native speakers of English to use and understand English as it is spoken, written and heard in English speaking colleges and universities. These examinations measure the English language proficiency of a student by evaluating him on the basis of all four skills—reading, listening, speaking and writing.

I worked in an engineering college in West-Bengal from 2005 to 2008. During my three years of stay in that college, I got an opportunity to witness campus interview and placement procedures from a very close quarter. I observed that despite having good subject knowledge, many of the engineering students could not get through the campus interview of many good companies. This was due to the fact that though they were knowledgeable in their engineering domain but when it came to the language for interpersonal communication many of them were found wanting. Most of the national and multinational companies have an aptitude test and a compulsory English paper with a particular cut off mark at the preliminary level The English paper in these interviews comprises questions related to vocabulary, comprehension, and other aspects of English language. Students who clear the two papers are selected for the technical round. Infosys for instance has a 100 marks compulsory English paper at the preliminary level for freshers. Only students who clear this paper are eligible for the aptitude round. Many companies also conduct group discussions for evaluating candidates for the final round. Group discussion is a very effective method to judge a candidate's communicative skill, knowledge on the subject matter, his personality, ability to work in a team and leadership qualities. This strategy of the companies clearly establishes the importance of English in securing a good job in the industry. A recent survey reveals that a student's chances of getting a good job in the industry are enhanced by two times if he possesses a sound knowledge of English and good communicative skill. The ESP course for engineers focuses on Technical communication. Here Technical communication refers to the entire process of how a person builds his vocabulary, and "puts words together into sentences, arranges sentences into paragraphs, and organizes paragraphs to frame a piece of writing or an appropriate oral discourse to convey technical information clearly and accurately."

In this world of technology, English serves as the uniting element, giving all entrepreneurs and small companies a better chance and greater advantage over those who lack the competence in this language. There is no doubt that, professional knowledge and experience is essential for success, but reaching and staying at the top requires more than just being knowledgeable and experienced. One of the simple reasons why some entrepreneurs are successful and some of them are less successful may lie in their ability to communicate their thoughts and ideas effectively in English. The solution to this problem lies in realizing the importance of learning business English to enhance the ability to communicate effectively and efficiently. The IT revolution and Globalization of business have brought technical communication to the forefront of academia and industry. The primary target of ESP courses designed for engineering is to enable the students to communicate effectively and fluently in English with one's counterpart (a colleague or client) in some distant part of the world like Germany, United Kingdom, Russia, Brazil, France or the United States of America. It is important for a business professional to be able to communicate effectively with overseas business partners. Proficient and proper use of English is of vital importance in today's world. Success in this competitive environment depends not just on acquiring knowledge and technical skills but also on developing effective technical communication skills. Keeping the demands of the industry in mind, ESP courses for engineering students are so designed that they aim at a holistic development of the students; enabling them to contribute their knowledge to the industry and participate in the global technical village through effective communication in English, the technical language of the world.

Conclusion

Winston Churchill observed that the gift of a common tongue is a priceless inheritance. It's our task to safeguard that inheritance. English serves as our window to the world. Herein lies the need to master the language; particularly for professionals who reach out globally to meet the needs and demands of their profession. Effective communication is the key to success. No matter how good your selling techniques are, or how good your marketing proposal is, poor language skills destroy all your efforts. It is important for a business professional to be able to communicate effectively with overseas business partners. Proficient and proper use of English is of vital importance. ESP caters to this need of the engineers. With improved listening, reading, speaking and writing skills, the technocrats of today can certainly prepare our country to establish itself as a powerhouse of tomorrow's global economy.

Bibliography

Lord Chesterfield. *Effective Technical Communication.* Tata McGraw Hill Publishing, 2007. p. 35

http://en.wikipedia.org/wiki/Engineering

http://en.wikipedia.org/wiki/English_language

http://en.wikipedia.org/wiki/TOEFL

http://en.wikipedia.org/wiki/Graduate_Record_Examination

English for Engineering Students: The Need of the Hour

D. SRIDEVI & K. LAZARUS

ESP (English for Specific Purposes) has been referred to as "applied ELT" as the content and aims of any course are determined by the needs of a specific group of learners. ESP is often divided into EAP (English for Academic Purposes) and EOP (English for Occupational Purposes). Further sub-divisions of EOP are sometimes made into business English, professional English (e.g. English for doctors, lawyers) and vocational English (e.g. English for tourism, nursing, aviation, and bricklaying). According to Dudley-Evans (2001), the absolute characteristics of ESP are:

- ESP is designed to meet the specific needs of the learners.
- ESP makes use of the underlying methodology and activities of the specialism it serves.
- It is centred not only on the language (grammar, lexis, register), but also the skills, discourses and genres appropriate to those activities.

ESP practitioners are also becoming increasingly involved in intercultural communication and the development of intercultural competence.

English for Academic Purposes

English for academic purposes (EAP) entails training students, usually in a higher education setting, to use language appropriately for study. It is a challenging and multi-faceted area within the wider field of English language learning and teaching (ELT), and is one of the most common forms of English for specific purposes (ESP).

An EAP program focuses instruction on skills required to perform well in an English-speaking academic context across core subject areas generally encountered in a university setting. Programs may also include a more narrow focus on the more specific linguistic demands of a particular area of study, such as psychology, business or medicine. 1 Programs may be divided into pre-sessional courses and courses taken alongside students' other subjects. In the former case, sometimes EAP courses may be intended to raise students' general English levels so that they can enter university. In the UK, this often means endeavoring to help students get a score of 6 or above in the IELTS examination. In the US, this can mean helping students attain a score of 80 or greater on the TOEFL. Outside Anglophone countries, English-medium universities may have a preparatory school where students can spend a year or two working on their English and academic skills before starting degree courses. English courses running alongside other degree courses may be based on the American English and Composition model, or may employ Content-based instruction, either using material from the students' degree subjects or as an independent, elective-like course.

In common with most language teaching, EAP instruction teaches vocabulary, grammar and the four skills (reading, writing, speaking - including pronunciation - and listening), but usually tries to tie these to the specific study needs of students; for example, a writing lesson would focus on writing essays rather than, say, business letters. Similarly, the vocabulary chosen for study tends to be based on academic texts. In addition, EAP practitioners often find that, either directly or indirectly, they are teaching study skills.

If we observe the present day situation, Globalization is creating a rapidly increasing demand for engineers who have the ability to deal effectively with professionals from other cultures and countries. The English language is de-facto standard in cross national communication among engineers. Students though, interested in learning English various key factors play vital role in distracting their attention from language learning.

Barriers

Many people think that communicating is easy. It is after all something we've done all our lives. There is some truth in this simplistic view. Communicating is straightforward. What makes it complex, difficult, and frustrating are the barriers we put in the way.

Anxiety in Learning a Language

Some people come crossways with many difficulties when learning a second language. It is believed that there are some emotional factors in foreign language learning which affect our learning abilities. These are mainly thought to be intelligence, motivation, attitudes and anxiety. Among these, anxiety stands out as one of the main influential factors for effective language learning. This foreign language anxiety is defined by some authors as "a feeling of tension, apprehension and nervousness associated with the situation of learning a foreign language."

Background

The students are generally a heterogeneous group. They come from different backgrounds. Some are from rural areas and some other are from semi-rural. Generally, the people who study in rural are from vernacular language background. Some students though they study in English medium, because of lack of usage they never come forward to put forth their ideas.

Gender Differences

Some students, while speaking in English, are fearful about their co-students. Especially, the girl students are apprehensive about the boy students' mocking. They assume that the boys may take their English conversation sarcastically and tease them. With that fear they don't come forward to speak.

Lack of Content

Some students are unable to express their ideas, as they don't have any idea of that particular topic. So lack of content makes them timid and weak to speak about the given topic.

The students with all these barriers and filters could not perform well and achieve anything in this world of English, which is essential in the current situation. The internationally recognized English language is inevitable to be learnt. If one wants to achieve success in one's life by settling in a good career, by performing the tasks given successfully, one need to be fluent in English. At least he should use neutral English which is understandable to everybody in the world. Almost all the fields demand English for accomplishment in work as the world has become a global village. Every student must shed off his apprehensions about English and be trained well in it for success. Communicative English is given utmost importance. One may not master grammar and everything, but should be able to make meaning constructions. One need not be fluent in English but must be clear about one's ideas.

Activity-based Learning

Identifying the significance of English, we, the teachers of English, always encourage our Engineering students to enhance their English language skills by assigning various tasks related to LSRW skills: "Activities that involve real communication are essential for language learning. Activities in which language is used for carrying out meaningful tasks promote learning. Language that is meaningful to the learner supports the learning process."

Tasks are proposed as useful vehicles for applying these principles. Although definitions of task vary, it is understood that a task is an activity or goal that is carried out using language, such as finding a solution to a puzzle, reading a map and giving directions, making a telephone call, writing a letter, or reading a set of instruction and assembling a toy: "Tasks. . . are activities which have meaning as their primary focus. Success in tasks is evaluated in terms of achievement of an outcome, and tasks generally bear some resemblance to real life language use. So task-based instruction takes a fairly strong view of communicative language teaching." (Skehan 1996b:20)

"The communication task is a piece of classroom work which involves learners in comprehending, manipulating, producing or interacting in the target language while their attention is principally focused on meaning rather than form. The task should also have a sense of completeness, being able to stand alone as a communicative act in its own right," says Nunan(1989:10)

Pica, Kanagy, and Falodun (1993) classify tasks according to the type of interaction that occurs in task accomplishment and give the following classification:

1. Jigsaw Tasks: These involve learners combining different pieces of information to form a whole (e.g., three individuals or groups may have three different parts of a story and have to piece the story together)
2. Information-Gap tasks: one student or group of students has one set of information and another student or group has a complementary set of information. They must negotiate and find out what the other party's information is in order to complete an activity.
3. Problem-Solving tasks: students are given a problem and a set of information. They must arrive at a solution to the problem. There is generally a single resolution of the outcome.
4. Decision Making tasks: students are given a problem for which there are a number of possible outcomes and they must choose one through negotiation and discussion.
5. Opinions Exchange tasks: Learners engage in discussion and exchange of ideas. They don't need to reach agreement.

The Role of the Learner

A number of specific roles for learners are assumed in this kind of language acquisition. Primary roles that implied by task work are:

Group Participant

Many tasks will be done in pairs or small groups. So, the students are to be ignited to participate in group as well as individual activities.

Monitor

Tasks are employed to facilitate learning. So the students should notice how language is used in communication. Learners themselves need to attend not only to the message in task work, but also to the form in which such messages typically come packed.

Risk Taker and Innovator

Many tasks will require learners to create and interpret messages for which they lack full linguistic resources and prior experience. In fact, this is said to be the point of such tasks. Practice in restating, paraphrasing, using paralinguistic signals (where appropriate), and so on, will often be needed. The skills of guessing from linguistic and contextual clues, asking for clarification, and consulting with other learners may also need to be developed.

The Role of the Teachers

The teachers carry the following roles while encouraging the learners to participate in tasks.

Selector and Sequencer of Tasks

A teacher should select or create the tasks himself/herself and form these into an instructional sequence in keeping with learner needs, interests, and language skill level.

Preparing Learners for Tasks

The proponents of tasks suggest that learners should not go into new tasks "cold" and that some sort of pre task preparation or cuing is important. Such activities might include topic introduction, clarifying task instructions, helping students learn or recall useful words and phrase. o facilitate task accomplishment, and providing partial demonstration of task procedures. Such cuing may be inductive and implicit or deductive and explicit.

Consciousness-Raising

If students are to acquire language through participating in tasks, they need to attend to or notice critical features of the language they use and hear, which is called "Focus on Form." It does mean employing a variety of form-focusing techniques, including attention-focusing pre task activities, text exploration, guided exposure to parallel tasks, and use of highlighted material.

Conclusion

English language skills can be acquired only through active participation in various activities like role plays, group tasks and individual expressions. If we observe the I B. Tech. English Text Book "Step By Step," prescribed by JNTUK, we can strongly say that it encourages the engineering students to participate in various activities like making structures, participating in conversations or role plays, group discussions on various issues like deciding a place to visit and the logistics involved in it etc. Some case studies are also given to introduce and sharpen the students' problem solving skills and decision making skills. Some examples are given to make students composed in any kind of favorable or unfavorable situation. The students are advised to stretch a helping hand to the people in need by having interaction with them wherever they meet. It enlightens everyone about gender equivalence by highlighting the women achievers. The board games and the vocabulary games enhance the students' word power. Life Skills and Core Skills drive them towards enhancing learning skills, communication and make them perfect human beings with good personality. The software industry which offers thousands of jobs prefers to recruit the candidates with good communication skills and life skills. Keeping in view the rising importance of English and because of this activity based text book, there is really a great revolution one can find in student community as everyone is motivated to acquire language skills. This is the need of hour that one should strengthen one's English through determination and active participation to be triumphant in this competitive technological epoch towards which the teachers of English strive and drive the students.

References

1. Jack C. Richards and Theodore S. Rodgers, *Approaches and Methods in Language Teaching* Cambridge Language Teaching Library
2. P. Skehan, 1996b. *Second Language Acquisition research and task based instruction.*
3. Nunan, 1989. *Designing Tasks for the Communicative Classroom.* New York: Cambridge University Press.

4. Pica, T.R. Kanagy, and J. Falodum.1993. Choosing and using communicative tasks for second language instruction. In G. Crookes and S. Gass, ed., *Tasks and Language Learning: Integrating Theory and Practice*. Clevedon: Multilingual Matters.9-34.
5. J. Bell and B. Burnaby.1984. *A Handbook for ESL Literacy*. Toronto: Ontario Institute for Studies in Education.
6. http://en.wikipedia.org/wiki/English_for_academic_purposes
7. Tony Dudley-Evans, (1998). *Developments in English for Specific Purposes: A multi-disciplinary approach*. Cambridge University Press.

Use of Case Studies for Teaching Business English

SHARADA ALLAMNENI and A. VIJAY VISHNU

English is, undoubtedly, regarded as the lingua franca in international business contexts (Louhiala-Salminen, Charles, & Kankaanranta, 2005; Nickerson, 2005; Planken, 2005; Rogerson-Revell,). As the demands for Business English have increased in recent years, a considerable amount of research has been carried out on Business English (Barbara, Celani, Collins, & Scott, 1996; Charles, 1996; Chew, 2005; Eustace, 1996; Gimenez, 2000, 2001, 2002, 2006; Grosse, 2005; Louhiala-Salminen, 1996, 2002; Nickerson, 2005; St. John, 1996).

Coming to management education in India, it is a thriving market, and there are ongoing efforts to address its needs and provide appropriate teaching materials, especially for the teaching of Business English. According to Ellis and Johnson in their book *Teaching Business English* (1994, p. 3), Business English (BE) implies the "definition of a specific language corpus and emphasis on particular kinds of communication in a specific context." The core module in business communication offered to students of Management Education should, therefore, equip them with skills to communicate effectively in English at their workplace. Of course, language teachers have always taught the skills of speaking, listening, reading and writing, but these days English teachers are expected to be able to train business students in the soft skills necessary to perform work functions like meetings, negotiations etc.

However, for teachers who have gone through the regular University courses to acquire their degrees and with no special training may find the teaching of BE to be a daunting task. Changes in the modern business world throw up new words on an almost daily basis and it is often difficult for teachers and textbook writers to keep up.

Moreover, there are socio-cultural barriers a teacher has to pierce through to enable students in acquiring the required language competencies. It is found that, culturally, Indian students are very concerned with accuracy and do not like to make mistakes. They, also, have a tendency to underrate their ability in speaking English. This makes them shy and hesitant to make utterances lest they make an error. The best way to overcome this is through practice, repetition, review and reflection. This calls for both teachers and students to analyse carefully the reasons the students have for studying Business English, to create the right balance between accuracy and effective communication. Teachers need to create a cooperative, friendly and relaxed atmosphere in the class in order to eradicate the students' fear of failing. They must ensure that the courses they run and the individual classes they teach provide plenty of opportunity for students to do meaningful practice and monitor their own progress through rigorous review and reflection supported by the teacher

A lot of resourcefulness is, thus, needed on the part of a teacher while designing classroom activities for teaching of BE. Another area, the language instructor needs to be mindful of is the shift in emphasis from a grammar-based methodology to a lexical one. The teacher's lesson plans should, thus, encompass and pursue a more constructivist, cooperative, and learner centred style. Teacher must reduce his/her role to that of a mere facilitator, discussion partner or ideas generator. Also, the tasks and materials to be are to be strategically deployed towards realization of the desired objective.

To the dilemma, what do teachers of Business English do if they have language learners, who have certain grammatical, lexical or pronunciation problems and for the most part are ill at ease in their L2, confronting most ELT teachers in their classrooms, Case Studies provide a way out. The introduction of a case study provides a democratic situation in the classroom where learners explore opportunities to express themselves freely.

The use of case studies has experienced a recent growth in popularity due to its ability to bring industry specific problems into the classroom while adapting to the learning styles of a diverse student body. According to Kramer-Koehler, Tooney, and Beke [20], these are experiences that "students at all levels in education, and especially those students already enrolled in an engineering or business administration field at the post secondary level need to become aware of, the realities of the scientific and technical workplace where teamwork, and related leadership and communication skills have become increasingly important."

Use of case studies, therefore, offers an authentic tool for teaching not only Business English but also exemplary attributes in the budding management professionals. Typically written in narrative form, case studies are systematically arranged problems reported from life, presented so as to provide a student with data sufficient to help evaluate alternative courses of action. The case usually contains an analytic task rather than simply describe an outcome. The emphasis, here, is on active learning as opposed to passive teaching where the teacher or case writer does all the work. Ideally the case would take the student out to the frontier of his or her comfort zone in terms of technical challenge, familiarity with general business knowledge, and the need to take action on analysis.

However, it is found that many language teachers shy away from using case studies in the classroom situation for many reasons. First of all, they may feel that they will be engulfed in the content aspect of the case study and lose face before their students. Secondly, teachers who are used to a transmission style of teaching may feel that teaching is not really happening. They may not be comfortable with the role shift in their teaching - from teacher to facilitator.

Also, teachers of Business English consider the content-based and task-based approaches as different approaches, when in reality the two seemed to coincide well from the theoretical as well as practical perspective. The task-based method seems to satisfy most of the rationales for content-based instruction. Brinton, Snow, and Wesche (1989) summarized five implicit rationales of content-based instruction: (a) taking into account the eventual uses of the target language; (b) increasing motivation by using content relevant to learners; (c) building on the previous experience of the learner; (d) promoting contextualized use of the target language; and (e) providing comprehensible input (Krashen, 1985a; 1985b).

The task-based approach of teaching Business English syllabus seems to satisfy at least four of the rationales. First, it promotes the eventual uses of the target language by emphasizing the real-world resemblance of the tasks with the purpose of preparing the students for the real-world tasks. Second, tasks derived from the analysis of learners' needs increases learners' interest and motivation (Robinson, 2001). Third, while performing tasks, learners can learn the target language through contextualized and meaningful use of the language rather than learning sentence-level usage of the language. Fourth, tasks presented with gradually increasing complexity provide rich, elaborated, and comprehensible input for the language acquisition to occur (Doughty & Long, 2003).

In addition, this approach to language teaching has been considered more efficient than other traditional language teaching methods for teaching cross-cultural aspects of Business English, as Gimenez (2001) suggested in his study on cross-cultural business negotiations:

> By the same token, it seems sensible to suggest that teaching negotiations to business English learners could be more efficiently tackled by a task-based approach. Tasks which present cross-cultural models to study and examine can be more beneficial than formulaic representations of business negotiations. Such tasks would also warn learners about the dangers of transferring "ready-made" models to international contexts and situations. (p. 187)

The advantages of using the case study approach therefore are numerous. Most importantly, it helps students who are reticent due to lack of confidence, fear of making mistakes, low English proficiency to overcome their inhibitions, disorientation, and thereby hone their language skills. It makes the classroom more learner centric by reducing TTT (teacher talking time) and increases STT (student talking time). The language instructor plays the role of a "coach," a facilitator who even while assuming the responsibility for the conduct of the class still allows students to play their own game. When it comes to the evaluation part of case method learning, the instructor simply has to keep a mental "record" of the class participation of the students and record such participation in a grade book once the class is over

Also, the professional attributes the teacher wishes to foster in the students of Management Studies should influence how they teach with case studies. As a form of Problem Based Learning (PBL), case studies require students to "apply knowledge they have acquired within their disciplines to the solution of authentic, practical situations." Prince [33] defines PBL as, "an instructional method where relevant problems are introduced at the beginning of the instruction cycle and used to provide the context and motivation for the learning that follows. PBL typically involves significant amounts of self-directed learning on the part of the students." Further, to build empathy with decision makers, good case discussions should dwell on the nature of the problem: its imponderables, the dilemmas it creates and the practical effect of making one choice over another. Some of the advantages of using the Case Study approach to teach BE are set out below:

1. To develop critical thinking and reflective learning in the learner.
2. To improve the student's organisational skills - as case studies are sometimes very dense in information, the key is to condense this information into logical sections and organize them so that a clear picture of the problem/issue can be understood
3. To enhance communication skills - case studies can be used to improve the student's written and oral communication. Non-verbal communication skills are also practised by using case studies
4. To train managerial communication skills such as holding a meeting, negotiating a contract, giving a presentation etc. Case studies force students into real-life situations, requiring them to get involved in managerial communication.
5. To encourage collaborative learning and team-working skills in the language learner.

Here the overarching learning objective is the use of business lexis for problem formulation in unstructured contexts and formulation of alternatives, (Viscione and Aragon 1978); therefore the cases selected should offer that learning opportunity. From there, instructors must relate objectives to the level and experience of the students. It should give adequate space for teaching business lexis. According to Ellis and Johnson (1994, p 27) business vocabulary is always absorbed and 'appropriated' better when it is presented in a context. Assessing exactly how much vocabulary students need to acquire is something the teacher needs to determine.

An intrinsically motivating case study involves students in co-operative group preparation. Students embrace the task of discussing a case as a valid, a fair means of measuring their language competence. It brings out their best performance, not their worst. It has authentic language and tasks. It provides optimal feedback to the students. The teacher has to be alert and exercise tact in dealing with students who will not readily participate. They can be brought into the discussion by referring to them by name, especially when there is a fairly straightforward question on the floor. This may serve as a confidence builder. To build the tempo, a few minutes at the beginning of class may be devoted to questions concerning particular aspects of the project. This clarifies the assignment, allows similar questions to be answered all at one time, gives the reticent students a reason to participate and makes for a more meaningful discussion. Thus, a clear outline, creating and maintaining the proper classroom environment, and guiding the discussion rather than dominating it are necessary tasks for the instructor.

With a bit of forethought, familiarity with the prerequisite courses, and ample preparation, case study teaching is interesting and effective provided each student knows what his role is. It is not sufficient just to give the case study to the student and hope that they will understand how to use it. This is a mistake made by many teachers unfamiliar with the case study method. There are many ways of introducing the case study but the language teacher can administer the activity in three parts:

1. Introduction - deals with the preparation of the case study, the introduction of a Problem Solving Learning(PBL).
2. Grouping students - here the class is divided into sections to include meetings, presentations of findings and discussion of recommendations.
3. Debriefing - the teacher gives feedback on language mistakes, managerial skills and the meeting documents and support materials used.

The following steps could be followed during the case study introduction to the class:

1) The teacher should read the case study thoroughly with the students and then take up discussion of any lexical or grammatical issues. The teacher may also like to ask students to represent the background information in a visual form. They could be guided on the use of blackboard or flipchart to get a clear picture of the company background. As shown in the example below, the main information is extracted from the case study, which will then be used later for further analysis.

For Ex:

- **Company Name:** Dabur
- **Turnover:** 400 crore
- **Profit in 2001:** 92 crore
- **Number of Employees:** 4,800
- **Head Office**: Mumbai
- **Product Range:** Health & cosmetics

2) Then, the teacher should provide students with some input on how they should analyse the case study. The problem solving analysis below is an example of how to get the students to analyse the case critically.

- Read the case several times.
- Define the main issues/problems.
- Set out the firm's objectives.
- Identify options open to the firm.
- Draw up some criteria to evaluate the options chosen.
- Select the best option.
- Decide on how the option should be implemented.
- Draw up an action plan to implement the solution chosen.

3) The teacher is also to pre-teach the language required to discuss the case study. There are many publications in the market for teaching meeting skills, presentation skills or negotiation skills. It is important to select the skill you would like to focus on and teach the specific language. If we take meetings as an example, we could do some of the following:

- refer students to websites to read up on the skill being practised. A web search will also reveal number of interesting sites.
- If students have access to libraries, then they can read up on meeting skills in one of the many communication books on the market
- brainstorm some key concepts of meetings such as type of meetings, people at a meeting, verbs, etc
- move on to the language of meetings - provide the students with useful language input for both the chairperson and the participants such as the language of contradicting and disagreeing, interrupting, taking the floor etc.
- familiarize the students with the documents of meeting - the form and content of agendas, minutes and memos.
- divide the class into small groups. The facilitator can either ask them to form the groups themselves or can form the groups based on the class lists.

Students could be divided into two small groups (maximum six students) to discuss different aspects of the same case study. Therefore, it is a good idea to find a case study that has two distinct parts. The teacher must remind the students that they do not have all the information they need to solve the case but based on the information available, they can make recommendations and come to preliminary decisions. The teacher can also inform students that in real life situations in business, one will not have all the facts required to solve a problem.

Of the one-and-a-half hour session given for discussion of the given case study, the class time can be divided into three half hour slots:

- Meeting (30 mins): Groups (A and B) meet to discuss their part of the case study.

- Presentation (15 mins/group): Group A present their findings to the other group and vice versa.
- Discussion (30 mins): all students come together to discuss the findings and make recommendations.

Meeting (30 minutes)

Students are divided into two groups (A and B) of four-six students to discuss their part of the case study. A chairperson is selected to lead the meeting and an agenda is drawn up. Students can be asked to prepare the agenda in advance and ensure everyone has a copy or they can write their agenda on the flipchart. Students discuss and provide recommendations, which they then represent graphically on transparencies or on the flipchart/chalkboard. The teacher should impress on the students that their visuals should be clear, concise and coherent and long sentences are unacceptable. The students should then prepare their presentations. The facilitator should ensure that the chairperson does not monopolise the presentation but lets the other students have equal speaking time.

Presentation (15 minutes/ group)

The findings of Group A are presented to Group B and vice versa. This would take approximately 15 minutes for each group including questions. Students must take detailed notes in order to participate actively in the third part of the lesson. Students will need to clarify the issues their group did not deal with by asking questions and repeating. This section should be treated as information exchange and the facilitator should prevent further discussion of the points presented. In order to include active participation of all students in this section, the teacher, acting as a facilitator could ask the students to share the presentation speaking time equally.

Discussion (30 minutes)

A discussion of both parts ensues whereby the students compare and contrast the various findings and suggestions are made. Everyone is encouraged to participate and a consensus is reached on the main points raised in the presentation.

Finally, the facilitator asks the students to prepare the minutes for the following week. The minutes are prepared in groups of three so that the students can consolidate their ideas on paper.

Debriefing Class

All case study classes need to be debriefed to include the language, the skills (in this case, meeting and presentation skills) and the support documents and written communication (the transparencies, the agenda and minutes).

We will now look at these elements in more detail.

Language: There are various ways to address the mistakes made. The teacher can create exercises from the mistakes or can simply go through the major mistakes and explain the correct form.

Managerial Skills: As regards the meeting and presentation skills, the teacher should provide feedback on how to improve these skills. The feedback should include rapport building, body language, eye contact, etc

Written Communication: Having corrected the written work which resulted from the case study interaction, the teacher can also look at such issues as the difference between spoken and written language and style switching. The teacher also gets ample opportunity to provide targeted feedback on the written documents, visuals, agendas and minutes.

Conclusion

The task thus assigned by the teacher is found to be well received by the majority of the learners. They find the experience to be intrinsically interesting, and educationally beneficial. They get involved in the task, because the tasks give them the feeling of real life situation. However, at the initial stage till the students get acquainted with the various phases of carrying out a Case Study task, there may be some problem. Sometimes, during the discussion the situation may go out of control, where a teacher might need to take over and restore order. On the whole, the case based approach for imparting oral communication skills has proved efficacious in the teaching of Business English. Moreover, indirect benefits are accrued to the students in terms of acquisition of other business skills as they learn to apply techniques of data analysis, different quantitative and qualitative research methods etc.

References

Bonet, P. (1997). *"Applying the Case Study Approach to Students of Business English." Applied Languages: Theory and Practice in ESP*. J. Piqué and David J. Viera, ed. Valencia: Universitat de València.

Brinton, D.M.& M.A. Snow & M. B. Wesche. 1989. *Content-based second language instruction* [M]. New York: Newbury House.

Castler, K & Palmer, D (1989) *Business Assignments - Eight advanced case studies with video*, Oxford University Press: Oxford.

Daly, P. 2002.Methodology for Using Case Studies in the Business English Language Classroom. http://iteslj.org/Techniques/Daly-CaseStudies/

Domomguez, G.& P. Rokowski. 2002. Bridging the gap between English for Academic and Occupational Purposes. http://www.esp-world.info/ESP_list.htm

Ellis, R. (1984). *Classroom second language development: A study of classroom interaction and language acquisition.* Oxford: Pergamon.

Ellis, R. (1994). *The study of second language acquisition* . Oxford: Oxford University Press.

Ellis, M., & Johnson, C. (1994). *Teaching business English* . Oxford: Oxford University Press.

Gimenez Moreno, R. and R. Dinapoli. (1999). *"Developing Multiple and Creative Skills in ESP." Studies in English Language and Literature.* Ed. Francisco Fernández, ed. Valencia: Universidad de Valencia

Grant, D., & McLarty, R (2001). *Business basics* . Oxford: Oxford University Press.

Guffey, M.E. (1997). *Business communication: Process and product.* (2nd ed.). Mason, Ohio: International Thomson Publishing.

Guffey, M.E. (1998). *Essentials of business communication* (4th ed.). Cincinnati, Ohio: South-Western College Publishing.

Hammond, J. S. (1980). *"Learning by the Case Method."* Case No. 9-376-241. Boston: Harvard Business School

Hewings, M., & Nickerson, C., ed. (1999). *Business English: Research into practice*. Harlow, Essex: Longman

Krashen, S. (1982). *Principles and practice in second language acquisition.* Oxford: Pergamon.

Lesikar, R., Pettit, J., & Flatley, M. (1999). *Lesikar's basic business communication* . (8th ed.). Boston: McGraw-Hill.

Louhiala-Salminen, L., Charles, M., & Kankaanranta, A. (2005). English as a lingua franca in Nordic corporate mergers: Two case companies. *English for Specific Purposes, 24*, 401-421.

Nickerson, C. (2005). English as a *lingua franca* in international business contexts. *English for Specific Purposes, 24*, 367-380.

Planken, B. (2005). Managing rapport in lingua franca sales negotiations: A comparison of professional and aspiring negotiators. *English for Specific Purposes, 24*, 381-400.

Robinson, P. (2001). Task complexity, cognitive resources, and syllabus design: a triadic framework for examining task influences on SLA. In Robinson, P., ed., *Cognition and Second Language Instruction* (pp. 287-318). Cambridge: Cambridge University

Rogerson-Revell, P. (In press). Using English for International business: A European case study. *English for Specific Purposes.*

Widdowson, H.G. (1983). *Learning purpose and language use* . Oxford: Oxford University Press.

Willis, J. (1996). *A framework f or task-based learning* . Harlow, Essex: Longman.

Viscione, L.A and G.A Aragon, 1978, "*The Case Method in Undergraduate Finance,*" *Journal of Financial Education* 7(No. Fall) 49-52.

Scientific Lexis in Everyday Usage

L. SUSHEELA and B. PRUDHVI LAL

A language is a systematic means of communication by the use of sounds or conventional symbols. It is the code we all use to express ourselves and communicate to others. It is a system for communicating ideas and feelings using sounds, gestures, signs or marks. Any means of communicating ideas, specifically, human speech, the expression of ideas by the voice and sounds articulated by the organs of the throat and mouth is a language. This is a system for communication. A language constitutes written and spoken methods of combining words to create meaning used by a particular group of people.

Language therefore remains potentially a communicative medium capable of expressing ideas and concepts as well as moods, feelings and attitudes.

Nowadays English is considered as the best communicating language. The future of English as a language is very secure. In this era of consolidation and unifying of various aspects of life, it will not be long before English can be made as a single language of the world like the single currency and the union of the various nations.

English for Specific Purpose

ESP refers to the teaching of a specific genre of mostly technical English for students with specific goals, careers or fields of study. ESP (English for Specific Purposes) has been referred to as "applied ELT" as the content and aims of any course are determined by the needs of a specific group of learners. ESP is often divided into EAP (English for Academic Purposes), EST (English for Science and Technology) and EOP (English for Occupational Purposes). Further sub-divisions of EOP are sometimes made into business English, professional English (e.g. English for doctors, lawyers) and vocational English (e.g. English for tourism, nursing, aviation, and bricklaying).

According to Dudley-Evans (2001), the absolute characteristics of ESP are:

- ESP is designed to meet the specific needs of the learners.
- ESP makes use of the underlying methodology and activities of the specialism it serves.
- It is centred not only on the language (grammar, lexis, register), but also the skills, discourses and genres appropriate to those activities.
- ESP is centred on the language appropriate to these activities in terms of grammar, lexis, register, study skills, discourse and genre.
- ESP may be related to or designed for specific disciplines
- ESP may use, in specific teaching situations, a different methodology from that of General English
- ESP is likely to be designed for adult learners, either at a tertiary level institution or in a professional work situation. It could, however, be for learners at secondary school level.

ESP has become increasingly important as:

- There has been an increase in vocational training and learning throughout the world.
- With the spread of globalization has come the increasing use of English as the language of international communication. More and more people are using English in a growing number of occupational contexts.
- Students are starting to learn and therefore master general English at a younger age, and so move on to ESP at an earlier age.

Importance of Science and Technology

The importance of science and technology in national development cannot be over-emphasized. It is a known fact that no nation can develop without science and technology. Science is the study of knowledge which can be made into a system and which depends on seeing and testing facts while technology is the practical application of scientific knowledge. Developed nations of the world like the America, Germany, France etc. boast of several scientific inventions which make them to be rated as the world powers. Science and technology is the pivot of any nation's development.

A nation without science and technology is definitely a backward nation. Such nation will be considered undeveloped. Science and technology is associated with modernity and it is an essential tool for rapid development. Modern gadgets in all aspects of human comfort are inventions of science and technology. Electricity, aircraft, telephone, television, computers and other forms of machinery could not have been invented without science and technology.

Science and technology is also very essential in the production of medicine and treatment of diseases. A nation which lacks the necessary science and technology in this area will have to depend on other developed nations for the existence of its people. Such a nation cannot be said to be independent because it has to depend on the whim and caprices of other nations with the necessary science and technology.

The development of a nation depends solely on the amount of science and technology at the disposal of such nation. A strong and virile nation is a nation with adequate technology to make its people comfortable. A nation without science and technology cannot feed its people because agriculture requires the application of science and technology.

Science deals with "understanding" while technology deals with "doing." Science helps us know how to do something efficiently. Technology is rapidly changing our world. With the worldwide dissemination of science and technology, English for science and technology (EST) has been developed into an important language in the scope of science and technology.

English for Science and Technology (EST)

English for Science and Technology (EST) emerged in the 1950s. It was the outcome of the swift development of science and technology after World War II. Since the 1970s, the EST has aroused worldwide attention and led to much research among different nations. With more and more science papers published in English, the EST, a major variety of English, which is different from the daily English and literary English, has gained importance.

Science and technology is a field that makes innovative dreams a reality. English for Science and Technology (EST) helps undergraduates and graduate students and professionals become more comfortable using English as a common language in the fields of science and technology. Since, technology is rapidly changing our world; It brings us services beyond our grandparents' wildest dreams. It seems that with each year the pace of change quickens, each new process or invention makes still other advances possible.

EST and Scientific Terminology

Each field possesses its own technical terminology that we won't come across elsewhere in other fields. So one should be familiar with those technical words, which in the other way excels them in the chosen field.

The Language of Science

Examples of Some of the scientific terminology which are commonly used are listed below

Acclimatization

Adaptation of an organism to a new environment.

Adjuvant

Insoluble material that increases the formation and persistence of antibodies when injected with an antigen.

Allogenic

Of the same species, but with a different genotype. Also allogenic.

Amplification

The process of increasing the number of copies of a particular gene or chromosomal sequence.

Attenuated

Weakened; with reference to vaccines, made from pathogenic organisms that have been treated so as to render them avirulent.

Bioaugmentation

Increasing the activity of bacteria that break down pollutants by adding more of their kind. A technique used in bioremediation.

Complementarity

The relationship of the nucleotide bases on two different strands of DNA or RNA. When the bases are paired properly (adenine with thymine [DNA] or uracil [RNA]; guanine with cytosine), the strands are complementary.

Differentiation

The process of biochemical and structural changes by which cells become specialized in form and function.

DNA Fingerprinting

The use of restriction enzymes to measure the genetic variation of individuals. This technology is often used as a forensic tool to detect differences or similarities in blood and tissue samples at crime scenes.

Expression

In genetics, manifestation of a characteristic that is specified by a gene. With hereditary disease, for example, a person can carry the gene for the disease but not actually have the disease. In this case, the gene is present but not expressed. In industrial biotechnology, the term is often used to mean the production of a protein by a gene that has been inserted into a new host organism.

Fusion

Joining of the membrane of two cells, thus creating a daughter cell that contains some of the same properties from each parent cells. Used in making hybridomas.

Host

A cell or organism used for growth of a virus, plasmid or other form of foreign DNA, or for the production of cloned substances.

Hybridization

Production of offspring, or hybrids, from genetically dissimilar parents. The process can be used to produce hybrid plants (by crossbreeding two different varieties) or hybridomas (hybrid cells formed by fusing two unlike cells, used in producing monoclonal antibodies). See DNA hybridization of the corresponding repressor.

Library

A set of cloned DNA fragments that taken collectively contain the entire genome of an organism. Also called a DNA library.

Linker

A fragment of DNA with a restriction site that can be used to join DNA strands.

Regeneration

Laboratory technique for forming a new plant from a clump of plant cells.

Single-cell protein

Cells or protein extracts from microorganisms, grown in large quantities for use as protein supplements.

Splicing

The removal of introns and joining of exons to form a continuous coding sequence in RNA.

Translation

Process by which the information on a messenger RNA molecule is used to direct the synthesis of a protein.

Vector

The agent (e.g., plasmid or virus) used to carry new DNA into a cell.

Wild type

The form of an organism that occurs most frequently in nature.

Fields other than Science Where Scientific Terminology is Needed

There is lot of difference between learning English and English learning for specific purposes (ESP). English for Science and technology (EST) makes us to know about those specific words that are extensively used in the field of Science and technology.

The people with scientific background are generally familiar with scientific terminology, but the field of Science provides wide scope for employment to people from non science background with its everlasting new innovations.

For example

- A person with a background of business management (MBA) can enter the field of science as a marketing executive. His function is to sale various scientific kits ad instruments to various laboratories, Universities etc. To do his job perfectly he should be familiar with scientific terminology. For Ex. Polymerase chain reaction, Centrifugation, Sonication etc.
- Similarly a person with a background of computer applications can enter the field of science in the form of the Bio-informatician. His job is to develop Bio soft wares. To do this, he should have enough knowledge about certain scientific terms like—gene, DNA, Nucleotides, protein sequence etc.
- In the same way a public prosecutor (lawyer) if he has to take up the criminal cases like murder, he must be familiar with scientific words like—DNA finger printing etc.
- A PRO who works in a big corporate hospital may be excellent in his communication skills but he will not do justice to his job unless if he not familiar with the medical terminology like MRI, CT scan tests, X-RAYT. .etc

So one must be familiar with the technical terminology to excel in that particular field.

Dominance of English in Science

Concerns about the dominance of the English language in Science are being raised around the world. Researchers in Germany and France, for example, are grumbling about the frustration of working and publishing in English—and, perhaps more surprisingly, so are those in nations that have typically been viewed as consumers of basic science, rather than contributors.

A recent study in South Korea estimated how much an English-dominated setting for science has cost that nation's scientific development. Kumju Hwang of the University of Leeds, UK, interviewed 15 Korean researchers and engineers working in the United Kingdom about their personal experiences in the international arena. All the respondents said that because of language issues they spend a large proportion of their time preparing presentations and papers, and practicing language skills for discussion—and even then, they say, they still miss more than 50% of what they hear. Seven of the interviewees felt that this weakness contributed to Korea's status as a consumer of basic science, rather than a major contributor. Employers prefer to hire researchers who have studied or worked in English-speaking nations, rather than those who did their postdoctoral work in countries such as Japan or France.

Japan, on the other hand, has a history of translating science into and out of Japanese, so linguistic hurdles are accepted. Most Japanese researchers, when asked about such handicaps, will typically say that the language of science is English. Although nearly 75% of the 400 life-science journals published domestically in Japan are written in Japanese, this target applied rather than basic science researchers.

Basic science in Japan is becoming increasingly "English only," as Japanese-language publications dedicated to those subjects disappear. RIKEN, one of Japan's most comprehensive groups of research facilities, has announced that its scientists published just under 2,000 original reports in English in 2005, and only 174 in Japanese. In Japan, a nation where English is the current language of knowledge production, domestic science society meetings are also moving towards English.

Scientific Writing

Scientific writing is writing about science. Scientific writing in English started in the 14th century. The Royal Society established good practice for scientific writing. Founder member, Thomas Sprat, wrote on the importance of plain and accurate description rather than rhetorical flourishes in his *History of the Royal Society of London*.

Robert Boyle emphasized the importance of not boring the reader with a dull, flat style. Because most scientific journals only accept manuscripts in English, an entire industry has developed to help non-native English speaking authors improve their text before submission. It is just now becoming an accepted practice to utilize the benefits of these services. This is making it easier for scientists to focus on their research and still get published in top journals

Different fields have different conventions for writing style, and individual journals within a field usually have their own style guides.

Often, scientific advancement depends upon publishing in high-impact journals, which especially in hard and applied sciences are usually published in English. Consequently, scientists with poor English writing skills are at a disadvantage when trying to publish in these journals, regardless of the quality of the scientific study itself. Yet many international universities require publication in these high-impact journals by both their students and faculty. One way that some international authors are beginning to overcome this problem is by contracting with freelance medical copy editors who are native speakers of English and specialize in ESL (English as a second language) editing to polish their manuscripts' English to a level that high-impact journals will accept.

Journal-Style Scientific Writing

A critical aspect of the scientific process is the reporting of new results in scientific journals in order to disseminate that information to the larger community of scientists. Communication of your results contributes to the pool of knowledge within your discipline (and others!) and very often provides information that helps others interpret their own experimental results. Most journals accept papers for publication only after peer review by a small group of scientists who work in the same field and who recommend the paper be published (usually with some revision).

Peer Review

Though Peer review and the learned journal format are not themselves an essential part of scientific literature, they're both convenient ways of ensuring that the above fundamental criteria are met. They are essentially a means of quality control, a term which also encompasses other means towards the same goal.

The "quality" being referred to here is the scientific one, which consists of transparency and repeatability of the research for independent verification, the validity of the conclusions and interpretations drawn from the reported data, overall importance for advance within a given field of knowledge, novelty, and in certain field's applicability as well. The lack of peer review is what makes most technical reports and World Wide Web publications unacceptable as contributions to the literature. The relatively weak peer review often applied to books and chapters in edited books means that their status is also second-tier, unless an author's personal standing is so high that prior achievement and a continued stake in one's reputation within the scientific community signals a clear expectation of quality.

Importance of English in Scientific Oral Presentations

Communication is a process whereby meaning is defined and shared between living organisms. Communication requires a sender, a message, and an intended recipient, although the receiver need not be present or aware of the sender's intent to communicate at the time of communication; thus communication can occur across vast distances in time and space. Communication requires that the communicating parties share an area of communicative commonality. The communication process is complete once the receiver has understood the sender.

No single accomplishment is more important to success outside the laboratory than the ability to speak excellently in the public.

Scientific knowledge is universal and therefore needs an international language of communication. In our current interconnected world, it is not possible to produce relevant original research without knowing what others have done and are doing in the same field. Communication in the current *lingua franca* of scientific research therefore becomes imperative. English has evolved to fit this role, but as ever-increasing numbers of scientists whose mother tongue is not English undertake research, the strain on the language is beginning to show. The languages of English literature and of scientific communication are diverging. For scientific articles, an array of editors (language editors, author's editors, copy editors, technical editors and manuscript editors) is valiantly bridging the gap by trying to harness the output of scientists, whose mother tongue is often not English, within the syntax and grammar of the English language. They often succeed brilliantly, but the demand is so great and is increasing so quickly for the small and stagnating number of editors, that change needs to occur. While some editors working in this field edit the manuscript to a simplified language that they believe can be widely understood, others take a more literary approach because they believe this makes the manuscript more interesting and readable. There is no international standard for scientific English.

English has many features that favour its international use, in particular its eager and tolerant assimilation of foreign words and expressions and the flexibility and concision with which it can convey ideas. The limited number of verb forms, as well as the general lack of declensions and gender in nouns and adjectives, facilitate its learning. There are, however, sufficient peculiarities in its grammar and spelling to provide plenty of pitfalls for the non-native speaker. A possible solution would be standard scientific English with simplified grammar lacking in irregularities and with phonetic spelling (similar to Esperanto's). It would need to maintain a rich and evolving vocabulary to allow the expression of complex scientific ideas. Such an international auxiliary language for science would facilitate teaching, learning and editing. In this respect it would be different to some of the simple English languages, such as Basic English and Simplified Technical English, which have been proposed. It would be better to give this standard scientific English a neutral name, such as Scientish, both to distinguish it from literary English and from the English of everyday written communication, and to diffuse nationalistic and xenophobic passions. In fact, about half the words in a typical modern scientific article written in English are not of Anglo-Saxon origin. Such a standard language for scientific use would not only reduce ambiguity and improve comprehension, but would also make human translation faster and more cost-efficient. Furthermore, machine and computer-assisted translation would be facilitated. It can become so influenced by English usage that its syntactical characteristics begin to disappear. In addition, the native language could gradually lose its ability to depict new concepts and phenomena alongside their subtle differences. English proficiency, together with research spending by countries, have been shown to be highly correlated with publications in highly-ranked medical journals.

The phenomenon of English as a super language thus has advantages for facilitating scientific communication in certain areas but creates difficulties in other spheres. The problem is multifaceted and has to be tackled in its different aspects. One might, for instance, take steps to help authors with poor English writing skills so that they can be empowered to contribute to the international scientific discourse, or assist readers who have very limited or no knowledge of English. The first task, however, is to acknowledge the existence of the problem and raise awareness within the community of scientific, medical and technical publishing. As Goethe said, "a man who is ignorant of foreign languages is also ignorant of his own."

Publishers could provide more training in English writing and facilitate the polishing of the language of submitted articles by contracting with specialized professionals. In the competitive world of academic publishing, this could be an important advantage to attract authors with a non-native knowledge of English. Publishers could also make their websites machine translation friendly. This would allow non-native readers to quickly understand the gist of the site, even if the translation is sometimes crude. Better still would be to download a device (*widget*) on the website that would allow readers to translate articles into their mother tongues without leaving the webpage. A prototype of such a device has recently been made freely available.

Conclusion

In science, weak English hinders a successful career. Improve your English proficiency, and confidence will follow—or so the people of many non-English-speaking nations believe.

References

Bell, D (2002) 'Help! I've been asked to teach a class on ESP!' in IATEFL Voices, Issue169,Oct/Nov

Dudley-Evans, T (2001) 'English for Specific Purposes,' *The Cambridge Guide to TESO*L, Cambridge University Press

Harding, K (2007) English for Specific Purposes, Oxford University Press

Dudley-Evans, Tony (1998). Developments in English for Specific Purposes: A multi-disciplinary approach. Cambridge University Press. (Forthcoming)

Hutchinson, Tom & Waters, Alan (1987). English for Specific Purposes: A learner-centred approach. Cambridge University Press.

Johns, Ann M. & Dudley-Evans, Tony (1991). English for Specific Purposes: International in Scope, Specific in Purpose. TESOL Quarterly 25:2, 297-314.

Strevens, P. (1988). ESP after twenty years: A re-appraisal. In M. Tickoo, ed., ESP: State of the art (1-13). SEAMEO Regional Language Centre.

Irma Taavitsainen, Päivi Pahta, *Medical and scientific writing in late medieval English*, http://books.google.com/books?id=tIKyquQR1ecC

Joseph E. Harmon, Alan G. Gross, "On Early English Scientific Writing," *The scientific literature*, http://books.google.com/books?id=0Ns56qzBMIUC&pg=PA34

Nature Publishing Group (2010). Writing for a Nature journal "How to write a paper."*Authors&referees*. http://www.nature.com/authors/author_services/how_write.html Writing for a Nature journal. Retrieved 2010-08-05.

International Studies Review (10 March 2010). "Journal house style points". http://www.blackwellpublishing.com/pdf/ FPA_IPS_INSP_ ISQU_MISR_ContentStyleSheet.pdf. Retrieved 2010-08-05.

Nicholas J. Higham, 1998. *Handbook of writing for the mathematical sciences*. Philadelphia: Society for Industrial and Applied Mathematics. p. 56

Talbott, T.; M. Peterson, J. Schwidder, J.D. Myers (2005). "Adapting the electronic laboratory notebook for the semantic era." *International Symposium on Collaborative Technologies and Systems*. 0. Los Alamitos, CA, USA: IEEE ComputerSociety. pp. 136-143. doi:http://doi.ieeecomputersociety.org/10.1109/ISCST.2005.1553305. ISBN 0-7695-2387-0.

Pan, Z; Gao, J (2006). "Crossing the language limitations." *PLos Medicine* 3 (9): E410. doi:10.1371/journal.pmed.0030410. PMID 17002510.

Aristotle. Metaphysics. London: Penguin Classics, 2004 (Reprint).

Ogden CK. Basic English: a general introduction with rules and grammar. Available at: ogden.basic-english.org/be0.html.Accessed June 27, 2009.

ASD simplified technical English [online]. Available at: www.asd-ste100.org/. Accessed June 27, 2009.

The term Globish has also been proposed (although this variety of basic English, which relies on less than 2,000 terms, is too simple for scientific use) [online]. Available at: www.globish.com/.Accessed June 27, 2009.

Rocha e Silva M. Editing by/for non-English speaking writers/readers. Available at: ww.councilscienceeditors.org/events/annualmeeting08/presentations/Silva.pdf. Accessed June 27, 2009.

Gulbrandsen P, Schroeder TV, Milerad J, Nylenna M. Paper or screen, mother tongue or English: which is better? A randomized trial. JAMA 2002; 287:2851-3.

La Madelaine BL. Lost in translation. Nature 2007; 445: 454-5.

Langdon-Neuner E. Let them write English. European Science Editing 2008;34:95-9.

Gallagher R. Speaking your mind. The Scientist 2008; 22:13.

Man JP, Weinkauf JG, Tsang M, Sin DD. Why do some countries publish more than others? An international comparison of research funding, English proficiency and publication output in highly ranked general medical journals. Eur J Epidemiol 2004; 19:811-7.

Vasconcelos SMR, Sorenson MM, Leta J. Scientist-friendly policies for non-native English-speaking authors: timely and welcome. Braz J Med Biol Res 2007; 40:743-7.

Von Goethe JW. Goethe's Opinions on the World, Mankind, Literature, Science, and Art. London: JW Parker, 1853: 112.

Elbes Y. Towards machine translation friendly sites [online]. Available at: www.multilingualism.org/machine-translation/towards-machine-translation-friendly-sites. Accessed June 27, 2009.

Bing Translator Beta [online]. Available at: www.microsofttranslator.com/ Widget/. Accessed June 27, 2009.

The James Lind Library [online]. Available at: www.jameslindlibrary.org/. Accessed June 27, 2009.

SciELO. Scientific Electronic Library Online [online]. Available at: www.scielo.org/php/index.php?lang=en. Accessed June 27, 2009.

Bulletin of the World Health Organization [online]. Available at: www.who.int/bulletin/en/. Accessed June 27, 2009.

The Effect of Task-Oriented Approach on Language Teaching and Learning for Engineering Graduates

CH. RADHIKA and S. KANYA KUMARI

> In the developing world drama, the future is with English and it is an indispensable tool, a cementing force, a key, a bird, and a channel for promoting international contacts. Hence, it is wiser on the whole to foster this bird in hand. (**K.R.S. Iyengar**)

Students of Engineering colleges require an ever increasing range of skills to maintain relevance with the global environment of the new millennium. Communication is the pivot on which the modern globe revolves, recognized by academia and industry alike. Since professional and result oriented companies always seek for the employees who can communicate effectively. Students come with a wide variety of abilities, attitudes, interests, ambitions and levels of motivation that are effective for some students may be relatively ineffective for others. To balance these two categories we suggest task based approach with the help of the Language Lab in acquiring proficiency of the language skills. This approach takes the "pain" out of teaching any language and makes learning to communicate effectively a "pleasure" for the student.

It is a well-known fact that the present generation of students concentrates more on classroom subjects rather than personality development. By the time they get degrees, the students study English for a minimum period of fourteen years. But they are not able to meet the requirements of the new jobs, which demand communication skills. So they rush to Spoken English Centres. If we include Task-Oriented Approach in acquiring language skills then there is no need of the Spoken English Centres. The English learners should have practice in communication skills and should be tested orally in the language lab. This is the only way to prepare the students to meet the industrial needs in the present employment scenario.

The erudition in writing, eloquence of speech and empathy in listening contribute a lot to the conscious evolution of the individual. "The individual who communicates well leads well. The one who leads well succeeds well and those who succeed well will find well motivated followers."

Purpose

The four basic principles for acquiring proficiency in English are Listening, Speaking, Reading and Writing (LSRW). Now, keeping in mind these four important functions of language, the paper suggests few activities to enhance the students' performance in LSRW skills. These skills play a vital role in their campus placements.

Objectives

The objective of this paper is to suggest few task-oriented techniques in order

- To instill interest among the students.
- To better their LSRW skills
- To build up better Vocabulary
- To make them overcome stage fear
- To enhance their creativity
- To make them employable
- To train them to use language effectively to face interviews, group discussions and public speaking

Listening Skills

Unlike hearing, listening demands total concentration. Developing better listening abilities is crucial for anyone in general and students and academics in specific. Most of the students are not very good listeners. The more you use the skills with the right technique, the more adept and effective is the use of language. Poor listening can result in complete breakdown in communication.

Power lies more in listening than in talking. In fact listening is the key skill of a successful person. A good listener alone can become a good speaker or a good writer. Listening effectively and emphatically not only enhances professional advancement but also opens the doors of self-development. Students must know the truth that their minds and hearts will be more receptive for learning new ideas and opinions if they pay more attention to their listening habits.

- Activity on Listening skills:
- Name of the Activity: Shrinking Story

Story:

> Mr. Bejan Daruwalla and his wife Roshini along with his two children Reshma and Rashmi arriving at Bangalore from Mumbai by flight No. IC370 at 7:30am. They are being met at the airport by their estate Manager Rustom Shapunji, who will take them in Mercedes at 10:30 am via Cunningham Road, Longford Town, Trinity Circle and Arugodi to celebrate Rashmi's birthday.

Procedure

Step 1 5 Students are asked to leave the class. The rest of the class is read out a story twice & after the second reading they have to make a summary of the story.

Step 2 The first student is asked to come in & listen to the story once. The 2nd student is called in & listens to the story. The rest of the class notes down the important points mentioned. Student 2 tells the story to student 3, student 3 to student 4, and student 4 to the last one. Student 5 tells the story to the class.

Step 3 Using their notes, the students who were listening and observing report on the changes in the story. Then the original is read once again.

Speaking Skills

We, the English teachers, are struggling to make our students speak effectively in English. Through these kinds of activities, we can initiate the students to speak in the class room which gradually leads to making them communicate confidently and effectively in placements.

In the traditional college set up, the much-neglected area is the skill of speaking, as the teacher alone takes a central role and the learner plays a passive role and does nothing but listening. The art of speaking paves the way for self-development. It is a creative event in which we discover ourselves as we communicate with others. So in educational institutions, an ideal atmosphere has to be created by conducting seminars, symposia and group discussions and students must be motivated to participate in them.

Activity on Speaking skills

Name of the Activity: Consequences

Procedure: The teacher gives each student an action card. Each group should think of the Short term and Long term consequences the action may have. The class discusses the consequences of each action. After the discussion each student has to give a presentation.

For Example:

1). Robots can perform household duties

2). A lorry driver dumps a tank full of poisonous wastes into the river near the town

3). Man also can get maternity leave etc. . . .

Reading Skills

- "Reading maketh a full man, conference ready man and writing an exact man." Francis Bacon

Reading is perhaps the most important tool in all academic advancements. We derive much pleasure from reading novels and poetry. Our vocabulary is broadened as we read newspapers, magazines, journals and other literary works. When we open the books, we open the doors that swing wide to unlimited horizons of knowledge, wisdom and inspiration that will enlarge the dimensions of our life. Reading skills enable the readers to turn writing into meaning and achieve the goals of independence, comprehension and fluency. Through this approach, we can also develop the important skill i.e. reading.

Activity on Reading skills

- Name of the Activity: Reading from the Speeches

- Procedure: Select some celebrities' speeches and give the hard copy of the same. Then ask the students to listen the audio. After that the students are asked to read the speech aloud with all punctuation. The teacher has to check the pronunciation, voice modulation and body language etc. . .

Kalam's Motivational Speech

Excellence is not by accident. It is a process, where an individual, organization or nation, continuously strives to better oneself. The performance standards are set by themselves, they work on their dreams with focus and are prepared to take calculated risks and do not get deterred by failures as they move towards their dreams. Then they step up their dreams as they tend to reach the original targets. They strive to work to their potential, in the process, they increase their performance thereby multiplying further their potential and this is an unending life cycle phenomenon. They are not in competition with anyone else, but themselves. That is the culture of excellence.

Writing Skills

While speech comes to us very naturally and spontaneously, writing comes after serious practice and careful organization of thoughts. In writing, the grammar rules have to be rather strictly followed. While writing, clarity of both thought and expression is essential. Using simple and short words will be more effective than pompous and heavy words.

Activity on Writing skills

- Name of the Activity: Ice breaking situations
- Procedure: Students will be given interesting topics to think innovatively and creatively. Then they are supposed to write a paragraph on the particular topic.

Sample situations

- If you find gold ores in front of your house how will you react?
- If God appears before you and grants you three wishes what would you ask?
- If you were the president of India what are the best things you would do for your nation?

Building a Better Vocabulary

Vocabulary is a treasure to speak with someone. Students need to have a rich vocabulary to attend competitive exams. So Building a Better Vocabulary should be one's goal. Every speaker wants to acquire more words but we know that most of the learners including well-known speakers get frustration at not having the right and suitable word at the time of speaking and writing.

Developing Vocabulary

- Name of the Activity: Reading from the Script
- Procedure: Students are given cuttings of English newspaper articles. One of the students reads out the article, the remaining students note down the words. After the reading is over, they have to write Synonyms and Antonyms for the words.

A Sample Article

A labourer *trapped* in a *collapsed* under-construction tunnel for the past six days finally saw the *light* of the day on Wednesday when rescuers *pulled* him out *safely* in Jhadol tehsil of Udaipur district. 40-year-old Narayan Singh was pulled out of the *debris* at 3:15 a.m. after tireless round-the-clock *rescue* operations in which 30 engineers and 100 labourers were *engaged.*

Recommendations

- Through this Task-Oriented approach, we can make the students overcome their shyness and stage fear. The teacher plays a vital role in motivating the students to participate actively.

- This approach not only improves their LSRW Skills but also brings out their creative and innovative thinking.

Conclusion

To conclude, the Task-Oriented Approach of Language learning skills will help learners to be equipped with LSRW skills. Communication is the pivot on which the modern globe revolves, recognized by academia and industry alike. Since professional and result-oriented companies always seek for the employees who can communicate effectively. For instance, a young employee working in a prestigious private set up got five promotions in five years. When someone asked him the secret of his success, he simply said: 'I could communicate well'.

So, Communication skills were cited as the single most important decisive factor in choosing managers. Lack of sufficient communication skills serves only to be disqualified in the placement interviews. Thus our Task-Oriented Approach enables and enhances learner's proficiency in the use of English language as a means of self-expression in real life situations.

Bibliography

Graham, S. (1997). *Effective Language Learning.* Clevedon, England: Multilingual Matters.

M. Ashraf Rizvi. *Effective Technical Communication*, McGraw-Hill Meenakshi Raman & Sangeeta Sharma. *Technical Communication*, Oxford University Press.

Oxford, R.L. (1990). *Language Learning Strategies: What every teacher should know*. New York: Newbury.

S.C. Sood. *Developing Language Skills*. Foundation Books.

Efficacious English for Engineering Students

P. SIVANJANEYULU

English is the most widely used language in all fields across the world. It is often referred to as a language of opportunities. A person may be technically highly qualified, but he/ she gets good employment only when he/she has English communication skills. Even if he/she gets one without adequate knowledge of English, he/she cannot succeed in his/her career. Good English communication skills greatly enhance one's self-confidence. English is treated as the lingua franca because of its potential presence all over the world. Mahatma Gandhi aptly said, "English is a language of international commerce; it is the language of diplomacy and it contains many a rich treasure; it gives us an introduction to western thought and culture."

Introduction

English has been assigned the status of an associate official language in India. It is also a language of international communication. It gives access to a large wealth of knowledge and technology. India is a vast country with different languages in different parts of the country. These regional languages differ from one another so much that it is not possible to communicate with people of other regions without a common language. This common language can only be English. Thus, it serves as a link language in India. So, English in India is used not only for communicating with the outside world, but also for communication within the states. The importance of English has been growing rapidly because of the global medium of communication through the computer and the internet. India is on its way to becoming a strong and prosperous nation in the world.

In the present time, India is not behind other developed countries in maintaining a good foreign policy. For all this, there is need of a common language i.e., English. Just for the reason of having a common language, all schools and colleges teach English and most of these have it as the medium of instruction.

In today's world, we require to update our knowledge of advanced technologies and all kinds of branches of Science. For this, English is the sole medium through which all knowledge is available. This language is also a rich storehouse of social and political knowledge; therefore, study of English language is of utmost importance for a developing country like India. Without this, our technicians, mechanics and engineers cannot progress.

Today, the USA and other countries have made tremendous development in the field of science and technology. Whether it is space science or neuro-science, we have still a long way to go in this regard. The world is making giant strides in these fields at a terrific pace. To increase and encourage more research work in science and technology, we have to study all these subjects in detail. And for this, the importance of English cannot be denied. Most of books on all such subjects are available in English only. Since, it is not easy to translate all this knowledge in our regional languages, a thorough knowledge of English can prove to be a blessing.

Difficulties of students in learning English

To learn this language requires constant practice and patience. The most common misconception that prevails among students regarding English is that it is a Herculean task to achieve fluency or mastery over English language. This kind of tendency prevents students from learning new languages like English. Since most of the students are first-generation learners of English language, it is obvious that a student grapples with it since he doesn't receive any guidance or counsel from his/her parents. Even though students are studying English, they are not able to speak or write a single sentence without grammatical errors. The reason for this is that they study subjects from the examination point of view only. Our examination system is such that it makes students memorize and mug up lessons rather than testing their analytical and creative skills. In this process, they memorize lessons, reproduce them in exam halls and forget them the next moment. But this method won't help their in matters of language-learning. Ignoring this, students continue to learn basic grammar at school level for the sole purpose of passing the examinations and not to face any real-life situations. Application-oriented advanced grammar is not taught in schools. Furthermore, adequate practice is not given to students to learn a language. This situation needs immediate attention of policy-makers in our country.

Remedial Measures

It is every teacher's responsibility to motivate the students towards active learning. This will remove all the stumbling blocks in their way to achieve quality-learning. Teaching English (or) any other language is not a one-way process. It is a multi-way process. As soon as the formal teaching is completed, students should be made to raise their doubts and questions and seek clarification from their teachers, and then students' communication skills in English will grow. To develop this, sufficient practice must be given to students at the very beginning of learning. For this, continuous practice is the only way to get good command over the English language. This ensures that students learn more and participate more. Above all, a teacher is not only a teacher but also a friend, guide and a philosopher to students. He/she guides students not only to pass in the examination but also to face challenges and take right decisions during times of crisis in life. This is, of course, a real and tough task ahead of a good teacher and language is the most effective tool in their hands.

English for Specific Purposes (ESP)

From the early 1960s, English for Specific Purposes (ESP) has grown to become one of the most prominent areas of EFL teaching today. ESP is defined to meet specific needs of learners. Language-knowledge is very important now-a-days. Today it is the source of technological progress as it enables rapid exchange of information and research on common global problems. The development of language skills (LSRW) aims at active expansion of students' proficiency in English. Language classes at a higher school level should always make use of the texts of specific professional areas (architecture, business, civil engineering, electronics, environment, management, etc.). Such texts should usually be focused on the communicative needs of the students.

The knowledge of English is required in all fields today, even in the non-English speaking countries. Most of the job-sectors in many countries like India, China, Philippines and Singapore require English communication skills as the need for functional English has been increased. Further, English is becoming the sole criterion for selection in corporate sector. The advancement of India in the fields of Space Research, Science, Technology, Business Process Outsourcing (BPO), Call Centres, Hospitality and many other fields is directly proportional to appropriate English communication skills.

ESP advocates the designing of special courses, instead of one multi-purpose course, to suit the needs of various groups of students. The concept of ESP is said to be particularly appropriate for teaching English to students of science and technology (EST). It is impossible to separate activities associated with the development of language skills and acquisition of professional knowledge from educational goals. English for Specific Purposes (ESP) is known as a learner-centred approach to teaching English as a foreign or second language.

ESP meets the needs of adult learners who need to learn a foreign language for use in their specific fields, such as science, technology, medicine; it advocates the designing of special courses instead of one multi-purpose course, to suit the needs of various groups of students. The concepts of ESP are said to be particularly appropriate for teaching English to students of science and technology (EST).

Engineering students of English, as other ESP students, have special needs; they have a general knowledge of the English Language, but require specific training in English, mainly regarding specific vocabulary and functional language for special professional situations they may encounter in their future careers.

Bibliography

Bojarova, M. 1998. *Issues in Practical English. Eltecs*. The British Council. Prague, May.

Johns, Ann M. 1991. "English for Specific Purposes (ESP)," *Teaching English as a Second or a Foreign Language*. Boston, Massachusetts, Heinle and Heinle, 67-77.

Sunita Mishra, C, Muralikrina. *Communication Skills for Engineers*. Pearson, New Delhi. 2006.

Ajay Rai. *Effective English for Engineers & Technologists: Reading, Writing & Speaking*. Indiana Publishing House, New Delhi, 2008.

Andrea J. Rutherford. *Basic Communication Skills for Technology*: Pearson Education, New Delhi, 2001.

Meenakshi Raman, Sangeetha Sarma. *Technical Communication: English Skills for Engineers*. Oxford University Press, New Delhi, 2009.

Cross the Border and Close the Gap through ELT

V. VISHNU VANDANA DEVI

The growing importance of English as a foreign language is recognized all over. It is the only acceptable link language for communication between people living on the planet. Tourism is a major source of income in all the countries and stands as a great support to the growing economies. And so, English has been recognized as lingua franca, a bridge between the people and the foreign tourists. As a part of "tourism industry," it is essential for a country to highlight its cultural and architectural significance to lure the tourists and it is evident that English language would suit the purpose. As a result, it also becomes a major factor to enhance the communication skills required for the job seekers in this industry.

It is the foremost duty of an English teacher to promote integrated language-skills in and among the student community, thereby focusing their attention not only to master the target language but also to help them to take up good careers in Tourism, the evergreen industry in the present scenario. When working with people from different cultures, one needs a solid understanding of the norms of the respective culture and English language helps to cross the barrier. "Tourism can be classified basically into recreational, leisure and business purposes." Whatever it is for, it can be experienced and enjoyed, apart from gaining knowledge about the place.

The paper focuses on relating this leisure-time activity to motivate the learners to enhance their communicative skills. As education has become more learner-centred, the language trainer should make the topic "Tourism," very interesting, by making them active participants in the classroom. The topic certainly, "re-inforces what is taught and increases their motivation," as the zealous and enthusiastic students apply the skills learnt inside the classroom to a bigger world waiting for them outside.

Tourism is gaining prominence day by day due to many reasons. People like to see new places and have new experiences. Some want to have first hand information about the varied cultures of the countries all over the world. Many people are finding ways to get away from their work and their regular lives for more than two weeks a year as an annual holiday, that acts as a real boost-up for tourism industry, Of course, travel now-a-days is not a very difficult thing as everything is got within a click of a button. All we have to do is "google" a place and look for travel sites and blogs that will give us an insight on what to see and where to stay. All this has really increased the employment chances, right from the travel-agents to hoteliers and guides whose essential qualification would be to have excellent communication skills. As the tourists are from all over the globe, the employees involved in the tourism industry should be well versed in the art of communication. Tourism, as the subject by itself is lively, demands the attention of both the learner and the student. I am a language-trainer for the B.Tech students, and we have a chapter 'Travel', in the first year English curriculum. I found the chapter to be interesting and informative, as the teacher finds space for interacting with and among the student community. The same class-room atmosphere can be created even for Tourism students, who would be learning English in the backdrop of tourism.

The college arranged a trip for III B.Tech. Students to Kerala, where they had a great gala time and a grand sense of adventure, which could be just felt and experienced. I wanted to utilize the opportunity and asked one of the members of the trip to narrate the experience, after their return journey. Sindhura, of III B.Tech. shared her experiences with the I.B. Tech students in one of the language lab sessions. She said that they were excited and it was the time when they not only enjoyed themselves, but also learnt the art of communicating very enthusiastically with their peers. It was at this juncture that they made good friendships, helped one another and thus enhanced their interpersonal skills. To put in the words of Sindhura, "I wanted to go to these places in Kerala for the tranquility and the peace they offer to a visitor. The places are nature's beauty at their best," and we can never deny the fact that travelling is utmost fun. The trip also helped them to learn some tips on travel photography all by themselves, which would certainly prove useful to them, as it paves way for those who would like to take careers in free-lance photography and journalism. Thus the youngsters are ever ready to explore new vistas and experience new things outside their mundane lives. "Earn while you learn," seems to be today's trend. The photographs portraying nature, the back-waters of Kerala and the photographs featuring boat-races which they happened to watch incidentally, were published in a local magazine bringing name and fame not only to them but also to the college.

They also learnt the culture, language of the new place while conversing with the residents and the shopkeepers when they were taken out for shopping. As it is given in the first year B.Tech English text book, a chapter on travel helped the students not only to enjoy themselves, but also to gain knowledge about new places in a way they have never thought of. I felt that if given an opportunity, in an environment, where their excitement knew no bounds, the students really make their mark in letting out their emotions of joy and happiness. The students after listening to their friends were very enthusiastic and eager to speak out their impressions when they went on trips. Even the dull students could speak something or the other in a mood of thrill and enjoyment.

> ESP is an approach to language teaching in which all decisions as to content and method are based on the learner's reason for learning. ESP's main goal is to prepare students, in a relatively short period of time, to read, understand and communicate better so they can work properly in a certain activity. The methodology we use should lead students to discover their own needs. (Hutchinson, 1987: 19)

I present here under the travel experience of one of my students M. Ramalakshmi of I B.Tech in her own words:

My family members and I went to Karnataka. And it was a one month trip. Nearly 25 members of our family enjoyed this trip. We started from Vijayawada by train and reached Karnataka in 12 hours. In the journey all our family members played, chit chatted very happily.

We got meals from the railway canteen as we gave an order to them. Throughout the journey, we crossed many beautiful types of scenery. Actually we all went to Karnataka to attend two marriages.

We went to Mysore. There we saw Goddess Chamundi's hill, Mysore Palace and Zoological Park. At Chamundi hill, the Dasara festival is celebrated in a grand way. At night time Mysore palace looks marvellous from the top of Chamundi hill. We went to Brindavan Gardens which was so beautiful, full of greenery. There is a musical water fountain there. From there the next day we went to zoo. It had many kinds of animals, birds, snakes which we have not seen before. From there we went to Chitradurga town which has a big fort. We had to cross seven gates to reach the king's court. Around the hill there were cabins built with stones to have a clear sight of the town. In olden days soldiers used to watch through the cabins, if any enemy entered the town they used to take immediate action. After that we went to Beluru and Halebed. The temples at those two places are star shaped. There are many excellent carvings on that temple. Finally we went to Bangalore. There we saw ISKON temple where there is Lord Krishna's statue. Paintings in the temple reveal the life style of Lord Krishna. From there we went to a water park named wonder Laa. There are many play items there. We have completed our long trip which is really memorable. Again we returned back to Vijayawada by train. Every person has to go to such type of trips to get refreshed from their daily burdens and works. One should have a peaceful brain at least for some hours in this busy life.

Thus this expression is a fine example of how students feel happy in expressing their travel experiences in a subjective manner.

Another activity was designed by me to enhance the principles of grammar and vocabulary among the students. The exercise gave them a scope to make use of the adjectives and adverbs effectively, when they were asked to give a description of an ancient place in India. I would like to list out the experiences of one of the students, where she described the ancient temple town of Rajim, on the confluence of the rivers Mahanadi, Pairi and Sondhul, thus earning it the sobriquet of Prayag of Chhattisgarh. She started off giving a description of how they made an entry into the temple: "The peach-pink rays of the early morning sun gently caressed the ancient temple dome as we climbed down a flight of steps to wash our feet in the sacred waters of the trio - with their distinct colors of green, blue, and pink-red." She also went to denote the different colours of the river waters to the different attributes of human-beings - the Sat, the Rajas and the Tamas to green, blue and red respectively. It was an impressive interpretation put forward in an expressive manner by the learner that it won appreciation of the fellow-students. The same enthusiastic student manifested her expressions stunningly, as she gave an account of Lord Rajiv Lochan in the main sanctum-sanctorum, as she seemed to have gone through an article in *The Hindu*: "The idol of Lord Vishnu is bedecked thrice daily, as a child in the morning, as a youth in the afternoon and as an old man in the evening." This she says symbolizes the three different stages in man's life and that his life would be successful if he performed those actions which would befit his age.

Thus the students, at their entry-level itself, seemed to evolve themselves as they worked on this chapter thoroughly. They learnt communication skills, language, how to work in teams, the essential life-skills that they have to master which would help them to mould their personality and attitude that makes them work with flexibility in their future.

As tourism is gaining importance day by day, especially for students who would like to take careers in this industry, here is an activity lesson designed which focusses on the development of tourism as an industry in their local area. The lesson gives a scope to the learners to use English while developing concepts and discussing socio-economic problems and solutions that come their way.

As a language-trainer, I asked the students to do an activity where they would be discussing the pros and cons of developing local tourism and 'tourism—is there any need to develop it?'

The motive of this activity is that the students get involved in group-activity, where they discuss, explain and reason out their views on the given topic. The students settled in two groups, one group supported the point that tourism should be developed as a local industry and they are actually the representatives of a company who would undertake the project of developing tourism in the town. The other group comprised the residents of the city and they are against this project. Some explanatory notes on the topic were given to the students and their doubts were clarified. The students were given time for 10 minutes to discuss, while I went round and helped them in using their target-language and expression. The students were then asked to take up the actual discussion, where they tried to convince each other of their opinion.

Finally the discussion came to a close when there was a follow-up activity where as a teacher, I checked errors in pronunciation, language and expression. A conclusion, with a comment on the performance of the speakers, was presented by one of them.

The discussion presented the following points

The company representatives, group 1, planned to invest a large amount of money to turn the town into a major tourist-attraction. They have plans to set up a number of hotels and other tourist-infrastructure in the town. Their idea is to make the town a major competitor within the tourist industry in the country, by next five years. They have also come up with some important points that with the promotion of tourism, employment opportunities for the local youth would increase. The money from the tourists adds to the development of the country's economy. The young minds of the city find themselves happy and motivated in involving themselves in this emerging leisure-industry. The progress and development of the city catches the attention of the other states in the country.

Group 2, represented by the city-dwellers, strongly opposed the opinions expressed by the industry people, their argument stated that t tourism industry might lead to pollution and other environmental-issues like climatic-changes and over-crowding of the city. They also dealt with the point that often tourists are trouble-makers as they consume alcohol and drugs and thereby create problems. The prices of essential commodities would go up causing much problem to the local inhabitants. It would also lead to cultural invasions and cause damage to the traditional life-style of the people. So it certainly would not lead to any kind of development.

Thus students found it a good opportunity to express themselves in their target-language as they discussed the positive and negative impacts of tourism. The activity has been designed to improve reading skills, grammar, and vocabulary among the learners. I gave them an article on Tourism and asked them to read it and note down the inference, and contextual meaning of some words. This activity was assigned to them in order to improve their reading skills also. The learners were introduced to various types of reading skills like scanning, skimming, intensive reading and extensive reading. As we find a great need of improving the reading habits among the student fraternity, the special exercise certainly helped to gain the same. Scanning enables the student to go through the material thoroughly; skimming is done on the superficial level, both techniques adopted by good readers, without missing the essential information. Such techniques mastered at this level make a student access himself easily to attend the competitive examinations with more confidence.

I also asked them to choose some of the sentences from the passage which would focus on how to make the city more attractive to the Tourists and rewrite them in present continuous tense and in simple future tense, to denote a future action. The following were the sentences given by the students:

1. I invested a large amount of money to turn my town into a major centre for Tourists.
2. I am improving the city's ancient lakes, temples, mosques, and gardens to give a delightful experience for all the visitors.
3. I have to provide good facilities to the foreign Tourists.
4. I pressurized the government to launch many courses in hotel management and Tourism.
5. The development in Technology and Transport has made many types of Tourism more affordable.
6. Advertising campaigns like "Incredible India" by Tourism Ministry has played a major role in changing the image of India.

7. The Government of India announced a New Tourism Policy to give boost to the tourism sector.
8. A multi-pronged approach has been adopted, which includes new mechanism for speedy implementation of tourism projects.

These are the common mistakes done by students on "Tenses" as they do not know the correct usage of tenses. I checked the work and explained the usage of Present Continuous Tense and Future Tense for actions planned in Future.

Present Continuous Tense also can be used for Future actions thus: Example: My friend is visiting America next week

Be form (is, are) + v1+ ing is the basic rule applied in constructing sentences in Present Continuous. Example: My friend shall visit America next week. The sentence is in future tense as the action is going to happen in future.

The auxiliary verbs will or shall accordingly take the verb in its root form in the construction of sentences in Simple Future Tense. The students then rewrote the sentences correctly understanding the usage and construction of Present Continuous Tense and Future Tense. The sentences given below make it clear:

1. I shall invest a large amount of money to turn my town into a major centre for Tourists.
2. I shall improve the city's ancient lakes, temples, mosques, and gardens to give a delightful experience for all the visitors.
3. I shall provide good facilities to the foreign Tourists.
4. I shall pressurize the government to launch many courses in hotel management and Tourism.
5. The development in Technology and Transport will make many types of Tourism more affordable.
6. Advertising campaigns like "Incredible India" by Tourism Ministry will play a major role in changing the image of India.
7. The Government of India is announcing a New Tourism Policy to give boost to the tourism sector.
8. A multi-pronged approach has been adopted, which will include new mechanism for speedy implementation of tourism projects.

Today, English language has become established as the link language between people all over the world. There is a relation between tourism, tourists and the English language. So students learning about 'Tourism' should enable themselves to become qualified professionals, to be responsible for their work to develop self study strategies. So ESP course should be learner centred.

As a teacher, I also listed out some basic competencies and attitudes to be possessed by students who would like to take careers in this industry. As ESP's main goal is to prepare students in a relatively short period of time to read, understand and communicate better, as put forward by Hutchinson: "ESP is an approach to language teaching in which the content and method are based on the learner's reason for learning."

Thus teaching an ESP course is always learner-centred, a method which attends to all the needs of the learners in a full-fledged manner, because each learner has his or her own specific needs, previous experiences of the places they visited and their journeys to various places. So each student is different in his or her own beliefs, knowledge, and way of thinking, interacting and socializing with others. We should take notice of those differences and take them into class and explore them. It brings cultural variety, critical thinking and self reflection into the class room. Everyone has different skills and talents, it is important to remember that diversity is strength and this holistic approach should be a part of ESP. The students are moulded into personalities with mutual understanding and tolerance.

Thus the class room activity helped the students to learn something new and the class became lively as they showed great interest and enthusiasm in narrating their experiences on journeys to various places.

Therefore with a starting point in analyzing students' needs, ESP develops those aspects to function more confidently in their future professional settings. ESP classes are highly motivated for teachers as well as students. On one hand teachers feel that they are teaching what students will need in the future, it is rewarding to teach according to the perceived needs of one's students, on the other hand it is motivating for the students because they feel that their needs are being fulfilled; the content is designed to fit their needs to improve their abilities, to develop their competencies, to work properly in Tourism one day.

Throughout the world's history there are many examples to illustrate the fact that the inquisitiveness to travel and explore the world has been the reason behind the amazing new discoveries. Education in the backdrop of 'Tourism' is also one such innovative form of education which promises to deliver 'experiential education with a person-centric approach to un-tap creative potential' among the learners. As a part of Tourism classes, educational tours are arranged which are very useful for the students: "Today's young generation has high observation skills and very less innovative skills, and these tours help the students to learn while experiencing something, and not just observe and learn." These tours also enable the students to think and explore for themselves what the world is about, besides enhancing their communicative skills. When the students visit foreign places, they find an opportunity to communicate in their target language. They put to use all that they have learnt in their Communication Skills Lab. The topic 'Functional English' comprises activities which help students to use the right way of expression according to the situations—formal and informal. So they get together, watch, learn and share experiences among themselves. They learn to communicate with the strangers in their outings in the target language, not keeping aside their manners, communicative language, along with their body language and expression. This new kind of learning experience is like a 'breath of fresh air' to them. Such foreign tours enable the students to face challenges and help the betterment of their soft skills as well. The learners also have an opportunity to enhance their oral presentation skills, as and when they are asked to present their experiences in the lab after they come back from the tour. The students find it a rare chance to learn the language, in the true sense of the term, besides having social and cultural experiences. Thus travelling can be educative as it helps the individuals to realize what they want to do as opposed to what they are expected to do. Altogether it becomes a life-changing experience for the students.

The students thus apart from learning the subject, relieve themselves of stress during such tours.

Educating students in the backdrop of Tourism also enhances their employability skills as communication skills have become a major factor in gaining jobs today in the Tourism industry. The teacher also finds an opportunity to train the students not only in enhancing their language skills but also helps them to learn how to face a crowd.

Promotion of effective communication

In today's globalized world, along with communication skills, it is the responsibility of the language-trainer to make the students proficient in life skills also. Life skills include personality development traits like team-work, problem-solving techniques, self-assessment skills, assertiveness, negation, refusal, time-management and stress-management. Mastery of Life-Skills is essential for Tourism students as it increases their employability skills. Good oral communication skills along with these life-skills can make a student not only a better individual but also a talented employee or businessman. So it is the responsibility of the language-trainer to provide the students with necessary techniques and methods, to create opportunities of constructing language, holding practice-sessions after interaction and considering language learning constructively and systematically. It is also the foremost duty of the teacher to make the subject valid, reliable and practical inside the class-room.

Bibliography

Neogy, Jayanth, 2005. *Sure Success in Interviews*, Unicorn.

Rizvi Ashraf, 2005. *Effective Technical Communication,* Tata McGraw-Hill. New Delhi.

The Hindu, Da 29.1.2011, p. 1, *Metro Plus*, 11.4.2011, p. 3, *Metro Plus*, 16.4.2011, p. 3 Eisenberg, E.M., & Goodall, H.L. 2001. *Organizational Communication: Balancing Creativity and Constraint.* New York: Bedford/ St. Martin's.

Vandijk, Teun, 1985: *Handbook of Analysis* Vol. 4, Discourse Analysis in Society. Academic Press, London.

_____, 1997. *Discourse as Social Interaction*: Discourse Studies, a Multi-disciplinary introduction. Volume 2. Sage Publications, London.

www.education planner.org.

Contributors

Sharada Allamneni, Vignan University. sharada.allamneni@gmail.com

Sasidhar Bandu, Res. Sch., Kakatiya University. Sasibandu@gmail.com

Md. John Basha, MBA JNTU-K, Kakinada. Basha2333@gmail.com

Dr. V. Sreenatha Chary, Dept. of English, Palamuru University, Bandameedipally, Mahabubnagar. vschary@gmail.com

Jyothi Hymavathi Devi, English Language Teaching Cell, University of Hyderabad, Hyderabad. hymajyothi@ymail.com

V. Vishnu Vandana Devi, Vijaya Institute of Technology for Women, Vijayawada. vandanamohan1993@yahoo.com

Prof. S.P. Dhanavel, Head, Department of English, Anna University, Chennai 600 025. Dhanavelsp@yahoo.co.in

Dr. A.R.N. Hanuman, Dept of H & S, College of Engg, Andhra University, Visakhapatnam. alapati.dr@gmail.com

M. Jayaranjan, V.R. Siddhartha Engineering College, Vijayawada. jayaranjan_m@yahoo.co.in

Deepak Kumar, Res. Sch. M.Phil (Ele), EFLU, Hyderabad.

K. Kiran Kumar, Assistant Professor, K.L University, Vaddeswaram. shirleykiran@gmail.com

S. Kanya Kumari, Anu College of Engineering and Technology, Acharya Nagarjuna University. kanyakumari.anu@gmail.com

Dr. G. Suvarna Lakshmi, Associate Professor in English, Gudlavalleru Engineering College, Gudlavalleru. suvarna1974@yahoo.com

N. Lakshmi, AITAM, Srikakulam. swatilakshmiabhaya@gmail.com

B. Prudhvi Lal, M.Sc. Biotechnology student, Krishna University.

Dr. A. Madhavi Latha, KVR Govt Degree College for Women, Kurnool. madhu_english@yahoo.co.in

K. Lazarus, Sri Chaitanya College, Vijayawada. lazaras.konumuri@gmail.com

J. Madhavi, Scient Institute of Technology, Ibrahimpatnam, Hyderabad.

Dr. V. Sri Rama Murthy, Associate Professor in English, K.L. University, Vaddeswaram

B. Neelambaram, V.R. Siddhartha Engineering College, Vijayawada. neelambaram_b@yahoo.co.in

A. Padmaja, SRK Institute of Technology, Vijayawada. padmajasun@rediffmail.com

Dr. R. Padmaja, Assistant Professor in Business Management, Krishna University. padmajapeddireddi@rediffmail.com

V.R. Pranuthi, Department of Tourism, Garden City College, Bangalore. pranuthi.mta@gmail.com

Ch. Radhika, Anu College of Engineering and Technology, Acharya Nagarjuna University. radhika.challa@yahoo.co.in.

K. Narasimha Rao, Vikrama Simhapuri University, Nellore. narasimharaokedari@yahoo.co.in

G. Chenna Reddy, Assistant Professor, Department of English, Acharya Nagarjuna University. Crgujju27@gmail.com

Sarmistha Bajpayee Roy, Garden City College, Bangalore. bajpayee1980@gmail.com

Prof. Pingali Sailaja, Director, Centre for English Language Studies, University of Hyderabad. sailajapingali@yahoo.com

Ch. Venkata Sivasai, Associate Professor, Department of Communication and Soft Skills, K.L. University. ncym2030@gmail.com

P. Sivanjaneyulu, Sri Vasavi Engineering College, Tadepalligudem, sivapagolu9@gmail.com

M. Sravani, Assistant Professor in Business Management, Krishna Univ. Sravani_me21@yahoo.co.in.

D. Sridevi, Vignan's Lara Institute of Technology & Science, Vadlamudi, Guntur Dt. sridevi.dasam@gmail.com

G. Sundari, Vijaya Institute of Technology for Women, Enikepadu, Vijayawada. sundari_english@ rediffmail.com

L. Susheela, Department of Biotechnology, Krishna University. susheelalankaku@gmail.com

Ch. Ravi Varma, Doctoral Research Scholar, Andhra University. Varma.Chiruvoori@rediffmail.com

A. Vijay Vishnu, Lecturer, Govt. Junior College, Bhubaneswar.